CW00601492

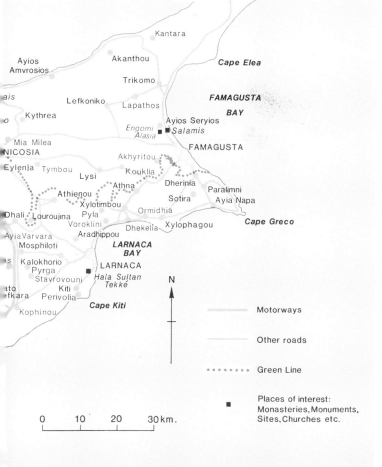

Kantara

Ayios
Amvrosios

Akanthou

Cape Elea

ais

Trikomo

Lefkoniko

Lapathos

*FAMAGUSTA
BAY*

Kythrea

*Engomi
Alasia*

Ayios Seryios
Salamis

Mia Milea

FAMAGUSTA

NICOSIA

Akhyritou

Eylenja   Tymbou

Lysi

Kouklia

Athna

Dherinia

Paralimni

Athienou

Ayia Napa

Xylotimbou

Sotira

Dhali Louroujina

Pyla

Ormidhia

Voroklini

Cape Greco

AyiaVarvara
Mosphiloti

Aradhippou

Dhekelia

Xylophagou

*LARNACA
BAY*

s

Kalokhorio
Pyrga

LARNACA

N

Stavrovouni
ato
fkara

Kiti
Perivolia

*Hala Sultan
Tekké*

Kophinou

Cape Kiti

	Motorways
	Other roads
••••••	Green Line
■	Places of interest: Monasteries, Monuments, Sites, Churches etc.

0   10   20   30 km.

Cyprus

Travellers' Guide

Cyprus

by Derek and Julia Parker

Jonathan Cape London

For George and Anastasia Loizou
with love and thanks

by the same authors:
The Travellers' Guide to Egypt
The Immortals
The Compleat Astrologer
The Compleat Lover
The Story and the Song
How Do you Know Who You Are?
A History of Astrology
Dreaming

First edition by Hazel Thurston, 1967, reprinted 1970, revised edition, 1971, reprinted 1972.
This fully revised and rewritten edition by Derek and Julia Parker, 1989
Text and maps copyright © Helga Greene Ltd, 1967, 1971, 1989
Maps for the 1989 edition drawn by John Hunt
General Editor: Judith Greene

Jonathan Cape Ltd
32 Bedford Square, London WC1B 3SG

A CIP catalogue record for this book is available from the British Library

ISBN 0 224 02524 4

Cover photograph: a view of Lefkara (*International Photobank*)
Cover design by Mon Mohan
© Jonathan Cape 1989

Typeset by Computape (Pickering) Ltd, North Yorkshire
and printed in Great Britain by
Thomson Litho Ltd, East Kilbride, Scotland

CONTENTS

MAPS, PLANS AND CHARTS

CHART OF EXCURSIONS

Centre	Town sights	
	Major	*Minor*
Nicosia (see also **The Occupied North**)	Cyprus Museum (p. 91)	Folk Museum (p. 94)
	Byzantine Museum (p. 93)	Churches and mosques (p. 94)
Larnaca	District Museum (p. 99)	Pierides Collection (p. 100)
	St Lazarus Church (p. 101)	Citium (p. 102)
Limassol	Castle (p. 118)	Medieval Museum (p. 118)
	Limassol Museum (p. 119)	Folk Art Museum (p. 120)
		Municipal Gardens and Zoo (p. 120)
		Winery (p. 120)
Troodos and the Troodos Mountains		
Paphos (Ktima)	The House of Dionysus (mosaics) (p. 153)	Nea Paphos Fortress (p. 156)
	Byzantine Fortress (p. 156)	Roman Theatre (p. 156)
	Tombs of the Kings (p. 154)	Other sites and churches (p. 158)
	Paphos District Museum (p. 159)	

Excursions	
Major	*Minor*
The Tekké of Hala Sultan and Kiti (p. 107) – half-day	Ayia Napa (p. 105) – half-day
	Stavrovouni Monastery (p. 109) – day
	Dhali (Idalion) and Perakhorio (p. 112) – half-day
Colossi Castle, St Nicholas of the Cats and Curium (p. 120) – half-day	Teppes and Bamboula (p. 134) – half-day
Monasteries of Omodhos and Troodhitissa (p. 141) – full day	Amathus, Khirokitia and Pano Lefkara (p. 135) – full day
	Monasteries of Makheras and St Heracleidos (p. 138) – full day
Monasteries of Omodhos and Troodhitissa (p. 141) – half-day	Pitsilia District (p. 150) – full day
Asinou Church and Kakopetria (p. 146) – half-day	
Kykko Monastery (p. 148) – half-day	
Yeroskipos and the Temple of Aphrodite at Palea Paphos (p. 160) – half-day	Ayios Neophytos Monastery (p. 166)
	Polis, the Baths of Aphrodite and the Fontana Amorosa (p. 166) – full day
	Monasteries of Chrysorroyiatissa and Ayia Moni (p. 167) – full day
	Emba, Coral Bay and Peyia Basilica (p. 171) – half-day

The Occupied North

NOTE: At the time of writing it is highly inadvisable to attempt any of the excursions set out below; failure to return to the border within the time permitted, for any reason, may result in not being allowed to re-enter Cyprus proper.

Centre	Town sights		Excursions	
	Major	Minor	Major	Minor
Nicosia	Selimiye Mosque (p. 174)	Beuyuk Khan (p. 174) Other mosques and museums (pp. 174–5)	Morphou, Soli and Vouni (pp. 176–7) – half-day St Hilarion, Kyrenia and Bellapais Abbey (pp. 177–8) – half-day St Chrysostomos Monastery and Buffavento Castle (pp. 181–2) – full-day	Kythrea, Sourp Magar and Antiphonitis Monastery (pp. 183–4) – half-day Lambousa and the Monastery of Akhiropiitos (pp. 184–5) – half-day
Famagusta	Citadel (Othello's Tower) (p. 187) Lala Mustafa Mosque (pp. 187–8)		Salamis and St Barnabas Monastery (pp. 189–92) – half-day	Kantara and the north-east peninsula (pp. 193–4) – half-day

INTRODUCTION

In his splendid book about Alexandria, E. M. Forster advised that 'the best way to see it is to wander aimlessly about'. That is indeed the ideal counsel for any traveller, and one we followed whenever we could.

However, and alas, it is a counsel of perfection, for while in wandering aimlessly about one may find delightful spots unfrequented by other tourists, something may well be missed which would have given pleasure. The visitor to Cyprus will not find every tiny village or its church mentioned here (and it cannot be too strongly emphasised that time spent in wandering aimlessly about the island is unlikely to be wasted); but we have tried to include the major sites and sights, and to give some indication of what really should not be missed.

Anyone who writes about Cyprus at the present time has to face the problem that only a part of the island is open to tourism. The illegally occupied Turkish sector is eager for tourism, but even those who would wish to travel to that part of a country which is occupied against its wish by a foreign power will have difficulty: it is impossible to enter the north of the island except via Turkey, and those Western tourists who do go there now, generally do so as part of a dual-centre holiday embracing Turkey as well – though you may enter the North for one day only, via the Ledra Palace Hotel checkpoint near the Paphos Gate in Nicosia.

We have of course dealt with the history of the country as a whole, and included some description of the most important Northern towns and sites (the great archaeological site of Salamis, the Byzantine castles and monasteries of Buffavento, Kythrea, St Chrysostomos and Bellapais Abbey, for instance); but apart from any view of the morality of the situation, it would be unwise to advise anyone to enter the occupied North except perhaps on a day's excursion through Nicosia – and that only after very careful thought and discussion with the tourist authorities on the island.

To explore the island thoroughly you would be well advised to hire a car; the Cypriots drive on the left, and the roads are in general of reasonable quality. Such exploration will be a great deal easier if your holiday is centred for part of the time in Paphos, in the west, and for part at Larnaca, in the east. Limassol, about equidistant from these two towns, is also in reach of many interesting sites, monasteries and villages.

We have dealt very fully with the archaeological sites, for there are two main reasons for holidaying in Cyprus: one is to seek out the sun, and the other to explore the countryside and the various fascinating sites which illustrate its history. At some sites excavation is still going on, which makes it a little difficult to 'present' the site well; and certainly there are some sites where better guides and maps are badly needed. But the Department of Antiquities seems well aware of this, and the problem is obviously in hand. Some sites – the Sanctuary of Apollo at Curium, for instance – are as well laid-out and explained as any in Europe.

The sun is certainly almost omnipresent, and the way in which – especially during the past decade – Cyprus has set itself to cultivate the area of the tourist trade which emphasises that advantage is quite remarkable. But the advantages such development has brought are balanced by disadvantages, and there is now a danger of a loss of equilibrium: it is fair to say that the island is now within reach of over-kill where the provision of hotels and apartment blocks is concerned, for instance. There are more than enough hotels to supply the demand – yet wherever one looks new buildings are in course of erection, and if the demand is encouraged much more there will be trouble, not only because competition will be fierce (which, after all, is not entirely disadvantageous to the tourist) but because, as it is, the beaches in summer are crowded to a point which threatens discomfort, and the number of quiet, secluded beaches decreases each year.

At the top end of the market this does not, perhaps, matter; the best hotels are wonderfully well equipped, and their private beaches, swimming pools and sunbathing facilities are admirable. The difficulty arises in such areas as Ayia Napa, where hotels and apartments inland pour tourists on to beaches which will soon be too crowded to cope with them. The government has recently made a start on legislation to restrict development; but firmness is badly needed.

There are other areas in which a firm hand should be shown: some restriction on advertisements and the cheap and tasteless souvenir and food shops, for instance, for time and again a charming, secluded village or landscape is ruined by large, bright, superfluous advertisements, while no one can now be found on the island who will not agree that the character of Ayia Napa has been entirely destroyed by every conceivable kind of overdevelopment. And it may be, after all, that holidaymakers who make the long journey to Cyprus are searching for something other than what they can find on the Costa del Sol.

It is by no means too late. The charm of Cyprus is great, its coast is beautiful, its people welcoming, its food and wine beguiling; above all, it is still 'different'. One must hope it can contrive to remain so.

We are extremely grateful to Mr Nikos Kofou, Director of KOT in London, Mr George P. Tsigarides and Mr Panikos Economides of KOT in Nicosia, Mrs Goula Frango, Mrs Noni Christoforou, Mr Peter Machalepis, Mr Michael Frangos, Mr Spyros Neophytou of Cyprus Airways, and Mr Pipis Thrasivoulou and Mr and Mrs Ted Dunne, for their assistance.

The translations from Homer and Virgil on pp. 73 and 113 are by Derek Parker; that from the *Odyssey* on p. 152 by Alexander Pope; that from Ariosto on p. 48 by John Hoole; we are indebted to the estate of Ezra Pound and to Penguin Books for the translation from Anyte on p. 74, reprinted from *Collected Shorter Poems* (1984); and to Ann Arbor Press, the University of Michigan and Mr Guy Davenport for his translation on p. 163, reprinted from *Sappho: Poems and Fragments* (1965). Finally, the Librarian and staff of the London Library have as usual been generous with time and advice.

GETTING TO CYPRUS

AIR

First it must be emphasised that you may enter Cyprus legally only through Larnaca international airport, Paphos airport, or the ports of Larnaca, Limassol and Paphos. Nicosia airport is now on UN territory and no longer used for commercial flights, and you may *not* enter the country through Tymbou (Ercan) or Lefkoniko airports, nor through Famagusta, Kyrenia or Karavostasi, which have been declared prohibited ports of entry.

Cyprus has been on an international air route since at least 1930, when Imperial Airways flying-boats en route to the Lake of Galilee used to land on the Akrokiti salt-water lake. There are now regular flights to Cyprus from London, Manchester and Birmingham, with economy, business and first-class fares, as well as the usual excursion flights valid for between seven and ninety days; at least one of these carries a reduction for night travel. The flights are run by Cyprus Airways (Euston Centre, 29 Hampstead Road, London NW1, in conjunction with British Airways (75 Regent Street, London W1). The Nicosia office of Cyprus Airways is at 21 Alkeou Street, Enkomi, Nicosia (tel. 445201); British Airways is at 52a Makarios Avenue (tel. 442188). Cyprus Airways hopes, within a few years, to be operating a fleet entirely composed of A329 airbuses. You can also travel by Olympic Airlines and Yemen Airways, via Athens.

Tour operators offer a great range of packages inclusive of air travel from a variety of airports, transfers and accommodation, with or without meals, and some deals include reduced car-hire contracts. Prices vary between the height of the season in late September and the low season at the end of April. As usual, the contracts should be carefully read, for extra supplements often apply. There are also, of course, considerable bargains to be secured; shop around.

Firms which currently offer excellent package facilities include Grecian Best Travel (31 Topsfield Parade, Crouch End, London N8, Delta (University Precinct, Oxford Road, Manchester 13, and also in Liverpool and Birmingham), Cyprair (23 Hampstead Road, London NW1), and Nicholas Bros (7 Bovay Place, London N7). Timsway Holidays (Nightingales Corner, Little Chalfont, Bucks) have an interesting (if perhaps slightly arduous) seven-day fly-drive package under which overnight accommodation is booked in Larnaca, Protarus, Nicosia, Platres, Polis, Paphos and Limassol. This can of course be linked to a further stay in one particular centre.

Larnaca airport is 6 km. from the centre of the town, and 48 km. from Nicosia. It has the usual facilities: duty-free shop, restaurant and snack-bar, currency-exchange counter and car-hire desks. You should allow ninety minutes for check-in on leaving the country, and – especially if you are travelling independently – remember to confirm your return flight at least two days before your departure date. There have, here as elsewhere, been cases of overbooking. Taxis are available, and so are scheduled airport buses for three or more passengers; there are a few larger buses to and from Larnaca and Limassol.

Paphos airport is approximately 12 km. from that town, and handles mostly charter flights, though there are a few scheduled flights as well. There are currency exchange facilities and a duty-free shop.

RAIL, ROAD AND SEA

It is, of course, possible to travel by rail or car down through Europe to Piraeus and take the ferry to Limassol. The fastest train journey will last about sixty hours; by car, journey time depends on your driving skills, but will certainly be eight or ten days, and more probably the latter.

Ships voyage to Limassol from various European ports, among them Marseilles, Ancona, Venice and Naples – ask at the French and Italian national tourist offices. Some of these have limited space for cars. The AA or RAC will advise, and you will have no trouble in taking your car provided you have the necessary documents. Via Mare Travel of Linburn House, Kilburn High Road, London NW6 and Xenia Travel of 166 Bishopsgate, London EC2 are among the specialised travel agents which may also be able to help you to arrange such a journey; and the Cyprus Tourist Office (see p. 31) may have other interesting suggestions in this respect – including, currently, a Black Sea shipping line that calls at London en route.

PASSPORTS AND CUSTOMS

The normal international Customs rules apply, and Customs officers at airports and seaports are no more and no less courteous than elsewhere.

You will of course need your passport, but no visa is required if you are a British or American citizen. At present, if you wish to visit the Turkish-occupied sector, it is possible to do so for twenty-four hours via the checkpoint at the Ledra Palace Hotel near the Paphos Gate in Nicosia, and a day's excursion may not be too much of a problem; but there is always the outside chance that difficulties may occur, and it is wise to think twice before venturing across the border. If for some reason you are delayed, you may experience considerable frustration re-entering Cyprus.

Political situations are always volatile and the current situation may change, so check with the Tourist Information Office at the Cyprus High Commission (tel. 01 734 2593) before you leave. If relations between Greece and Turkey over Cyprus, the oil in the Aegean, etc., improve, the present restrictions may be eased. If they deteriorate, even more stringent ones may be imposed.

TRAVEL IN CYPRUS

CAR HIRE AND DRIVING

Cars may be booked in advance, from England, through one of the international services, or may be hired on arrival either at one of the airports or in the larger towns. The Cyprus Tourist Organisation (KOT – see p. 30) will have a list of car-hire firms. You will need of course a driving licence, though a Green Card is not necessary. Charges vary considerably according to the size of the car and whether it is high or low season. Read contracts carefully, and enquire what insurance is included and whether extra insurance may be advisable.

Although driving is on the left, and the main roads are well maintained, there is only one motorway on the island, running between Nicosia and Limassol. The speed limit on this is 100 k.p.h. Elsewhere, the limits are 80 k.p.h., slowing to 50 k.p.h. in built-up areas. The police can be very strict in maintaining traffic law, and there are radar and other speed traps. Parking is cheap, when you can find it, both at meters and car parks; there is an on-the-spot £Cy5 fine for improper parking (see p. 31 for currency equivalents). Road signs are international; those showing distances will probably be in kilometres.

Anyone writing a guide to a country where the old, English measures of mile and foot are being or have been turned into kilometres immediately faces a problem. The solution we have reluctantly come to is to opt for kilometres for all distances; but we have provided a conversion chart on page 196.

You will be hard put to it (and ill-advised) to attempt to drive at speed on many roads, particularly those in mountain areas, which are unsurfaced and thus treacherous in both wet and dry weather. Often a glance to left or right will reveal a precipice steep enough to persuade you to be extremely careful, especially on the 'hard shoulder', which is usually composed of loose stones. Beware too of stones which have fallen on to the road, especially after rain. Cypriot drivers have no specially strong devotion to traffic lanes, and where the road is narrow it is usually a case of *sauve qui peut*. Road works are rarely accompanied by temporary traffic lights; again, be careful. Allow plenty of time for your journey, especially in the mountains, and if you are at all uncertain about driving on strange roads at night, remember that darkness falls very suddenly in Cyprus.

Signposting is on the whole good (in Greek and Roman characters); major monasteries and archaeological sites are indicated, though often the signs are insufficiently repeated, so that it is possible to take wrong, minor roads.

Petrol stations are reasonably plentiful, except in the more remote areas (especially of the Troodos region). They are open from early morning but tend to close at six o'clock or even earlier, and many are closed on Sundays. Those which are open are listed in the Cyprus Sunday newspapers.

Motor-cycles, mopeds and pedal-cycles may be hired (enquire, again, of the KOT). It is particularly important to check the insurance provision in your contract.

Car-hire charges vary according to season, and there are many different firms available. Hertz's daily charges range from about £Cy11 for a Subaru 700 and £Cy15 for an Opel Cadet in low season to £Cy15 and £Cy18.50 in high season. Collision damage waiver and personal accident insurance are extra; you pay your own traffic fines, and rental charges are payable in advance. Usually a substantial deposit will also be required.

MAPS

Most maps of Cyprus are to some extent unreliable – for the best of reasons: much work has been done on the roads over the past decade, and map-makers have not caught up. None currently, for instance, shows the Nicosia-Limassol motorway as an established fact. If you are going to leave your map-buying until you get to Cyprus, the Tourist Map published by the Efstathiades Group (Athens) is as reliable as any, and available almost everywhere, though it is as well to expect some differences on the ground: roads will often be better than the map suggests; sometimes they will be worse. Hildebrand's 1:3500 touring map of Cyprus (No. 16 in their series) is an excellent one which is readily available in Britain; but, again, remember that many changes are taking place currently. Really detailed maps for walkers are not easily obtainable, because of the military situation.

Your map should show the 'Green Line' or border between Cyprus and the Turkish-occupied zone. You will be extremely ill-advised to stray over this line, however innocently and accidentally. For insurance reasons, you are not allowed to drive a Cypriot hire-car in the Occupied North.

Finally, in Nicosia and Limassol in particular, take careful note of landmarks: many streets are not marked on local maps, and even when marked on the maps, are not accurately signposted.

FOR WALKERS

There is excellent walking to be had in Cyprus; we mention a few of the more spectacular walks throughout this book. Hitchhiking is a sort of national pastime, and is easier and probably safer than in most of Europe. There is always a danger of fire – avoid starting one, being specially careful, for instance, in disposing of cigarette-ends. Remember also that many parts of the island are isolated; try not to get lost. No one may find you!

TAXIS

There has been no rail service on the island since 1952, and the most common way of travelling around Cyprus, if you have no private transport, is by a splendid invention known as the 'service taxi'. These taxis, seating seven or eight people, connect the major towns, and currently run every half-hour between 6 a.m. and 7 p.m. You can book seats (single or multiple) by telephone, and the taxi will call for you at your hotel, or any other address.

There are conventional taxis, too, which ply for hire in the usual way.

SERVICE TAXI CHARGES

NOTE: No service taxis operate between Larnaca and Paphos and their respective airports. Charges from the main towns should be approximately:

NICOSIA to *Larnaca*, £Cy1.15 per seat (telephone numbers: 472525, 444141, 466201). To *Limassol*, £Cy1.50 (462269, 464811, 464114). There is no direct service to Paphos, Polis, Ayia Napa, Platres, Kakopetria or the Troodos hill resorts.

LIMASSOL to *Nicosia*, £Cy1.50 (62061, 63979, 64114). To *Larnaca*, £Cy1.40 (65550, 66766). To *Paphos*, £Cy1.40 (62061, 63979, 64114). For *Polis*, travel to Paphos and change; for *Ayia Napa*, change at Larnaca. There is no service between Limassol and the Troodos hill resorts.

LARNACA to *Nicosia*, £Cy1.15 (55555, 52929, 55100). To *Limassol*, £Cy1.40 (55555, 52929). For *Paphos*, travel to Limassol and change. There is no service between Larnaca and Ayia Napa, Paralimni or the Troodos hill resorts.

PAPHOS to *Limassol*, £Cy1.40 (32459, 32376). To *Polis*, £Cy1.15 There is no service between Paphos and Nicosia, Larnaca or Ayia Napa: travel via Limassol.

CONVENTIONAL TAXI CHARGES

For travel to areas not covered by service taxis, conventional taxis may of course be hired. There is an initial charge of 35c and a minimum charge of 60c; charges for a one-way trip are 17c per kilometre (or about 27c per mile); for a return journey, 13c (20c). There is an additional charge of 15 per cent for journeys taken between 11 p.m. and 6 a.m., a minimum night-time charge of £Cy1, and an extra charge of 2c for every piece of luggage after the first. Approximate charges for the airports and from the main towns are:

NICOSIA to *Ayia Napa*, £Cy18; to *Platres*, £Cy17; to the *Troodos hill resorts*, £Cy16; to *Kakopetria*, £Cy12; to *Kykko*, £Cy18.

LIMASSOL to *Polis*, £Cy17; to *Ayia Napa*, £Cy18.30; to *Platres*, £Cy11; to *Prodhromos* and *Pedhoulas*, £Cy11–16.

LARNACA to *Paphos*, £Cy22; to *Polis*, £Cy28; to *Ayia Napa*, £Cy7; to *Paralimni*, £Cy8; to the *Troodos hill resorts*, £Cy24.

PAPHOS to *Polis*, £Cy6; to *Limassol*, £Cy11; to *Nicosia*, £Cy24; to *Larnaca*, £Cy22; to *Ayia Napa*, £Cy29.

AIRPORTS *Larnaca* to its airport and vice versa, £Cy1.50; *Paphos* to or from its airport, £Cy3–£Cy4.

BUS SERVICES

There are bus services between the major towns, running several times a day. Local bus services between villages tend to run only twice a day – morning and evening. Central bus stations and major stopping places: *Nicosia* – Solomos Square; *Larnaca* – along Hermes St; *Limassol* – between the market and Anexartisias St; *Paphos* – in Thermopyles St.

WEEKEND EXCURSIONS

It is worth remembering that the Holy Land is only a bare twenty-minute flight from Larnaca, and that a weekend excursion to Jerusalem and Bethlehem is practicable and relatively inexpensive. Egypt, too, can be visited cheaply over a weekend. Do not attempt to visit Turkey, however, as you may not then be able to return to Cyprus proper without considerable difficulty and expense.

THE DISABLED

Most major new hotels have been careful to provide ramps and other easy means of access and movement. Most museums, however, have flights of steps, and wheelchair access to beaches and archaeological sites varies from the very difficult to the impossible.

ACCOMMODATION

HOTELS AND APARTMENTS

Most people, however interested in archaeology or exploring the villages of the island, will also be interested in comfortable hotels and comfortable, roomy, and if possible reasonably secluded, beaches on which to lie and from which to swim. Seclusion is difficult to find; during the high season, the best beaches are carpeted with shoulder-to-shoulder tourists and Cypriots. But drive around the coast and you will find many beaches on which to sunbathe and from which there is safe bathing. Though many coastal areas have been developed, if not overdeveloped, there are places – the horn of western Cyprus in particular – which remain among the least spoiled parts of the Mediterranean, with wonderful isolated bays. The Cypriot government has now enacted laws governing property development, in order to maintain the character and beauty of the unspoiled areas of the country.

The main towns, like other Mediterranean resorts, have carefully managed beaches, often with restaurants and bars, and the vast number of hotels are as good as any to be found in Greece, Italy or Spain. The four best hotels on the island are probably the Amathus Beach in Limassol, the Annabelle in Paphos, the Palm Beach in Larnaca, and the Cyprus Hilton in Nicosia. All these have beautifully designed public rooms and recreation spaces, excellent and often individual public service, and a tolerable 'international cuisine'; their Cypriot food can be excellent. Daily rates range from about £Cy34–38 per person per double room, with a 20 per cent low season discount, at the Palm Beach, and £Cy36–45 with a 10 per cent or 20 per cent low-season discount at the Annabelle, to £Cy53–73 (20 per cent discount) at the Amathus Beach and £Cy50–72 at the Hilton. Low season runs from November to March, inclusive.

The lowest rates to be found at KOT-recommended hotels are about £Cy8.50 per person per day, bed and breakfast, in a double room without private bath or shower (Nicosia). At the beach resorts, rooms with bath or shower can also be found for as little as £Cy8.50; but the average minimum charge is probably around £Cy12 (though this can be discounted by as much as 40 per cent in the low season).

A comprehensive list of hotels and apartments with current prices is published annually in a brochure which any good travel agent should have, or be able to acquire. In this book a selective list of hotels and apartments in each major resort is given under the main heading of that resort.

As with tourist hotels in almost every country, it is worth making quite sure where your hotel is before you book: a hotel whose address is Limassol may in fact be some way from the centre of the town. This may be what you want; on the other hand, it may not be. Hotels which claim to be near or on the beach are almost certainly so.

If you elect to rent a self-service apartment, ignore the super-markets and search out the ordinary town market (it will be shown on the KOT tourist map of each major town). Here you will find excellent meat and fish at the most competitive prices, fresh fruit and vegetables (the fruit, especially, will seem ridiculously cheap), as well as wild mushrooms and asparagus, nuts of all kinds, delicious *sutzuko* (a sweet made from grape juice), Turkish Delight (*lokoumi*), fresh bread, strings of garlic, excellent wine for all palates . . .

Away from those hotels and apartments built for – and admirably suited to the needs of – tourists, it is usually possible to find somewhere to stay on a more informal basis, though the small family hotel has sadly almost vanished. However, a coffee or glass of wine at the local taverna will usually put the visitor on the track of a house where a room may be available.

CAMPING AND PICNIC SITES

There are official camping sites at Forest Beach, near Larnaca (tel. 22414), Polis (48 km. from Paphos, 063–21526), Troodos (21634) and Ayia Napa (21946). These are excellent, with electricity supplies, lavatories, showers, washing facilities and food stores. Daily charges vary from £Cy1.25 to £Cy2 per tent or caravan per day, plus 25c per person. It is possible to camp on some beaches – enquire locally; most farmers will be happy to respond to a courteous request. It is not advisable just to pitch camp wherever you fancy. Caravans may be hired in Nicosia and Limassol.

There are now over twenty official picnic sites on the island, with piped water, toilets, and barbecue facilities at which your own food can be cooked. KOT will provide a list.

YOUTH HOSTELS

There are four good youth hostels in the island – at Troodos, Paphos, Limassol and Nicosia. Book accommodation well in advance through Cyprus YHA, PO Box 1328, 18 Solon Street, Nicosia.

MONASTERIES

It used to be the case that most monasteries would put visitors up for a night, though not all would accept women. Alas, over the course of the past decade or so tourists began to take the monasteries for granted as free doss-houses, and most of them no longer offer accommodation except in real emergency. If they do so, it will be in a very bare room with only the absolute necessities.

Understandably so: they are not hotels, and should be treated rather as places which will help out in emergency – or, as in England, places where you can make retreat. Food is not usually provided; no charge is made, but of course a donation should be made to church funds.

WHERE TO STAY

Though Cyprus is a relatively large island, it is not difficult to explore it fairly thoroughly in, say, three weeks, using two or three town centres. Paphos, Limassol and Larnaca are perhaps the three centres offering the most convenient starting-points from which to cover the western, central and eastern areas. Protarus and Ayia Napa are two notable beach resorts, and of course there are also the hill resorts in the Troodos mountains.

PAPHOS (KTIMA)

Paphos is perhaps the most up-market of Cyprus resorts. The new town lies alongside the old, and is perhaps the best resort for those who wish to spend half their time on the beach and the other half exploring some of the remains of ancient Cyprus. It has now the advantage of its own airport. There are indifferent beaches along the waterfront of Paphos itself; some hotels have their own private beaches. Wind-surfing and scuba-diving are specially popular.

There are more beaches east of the town, within twenty minutes' or half an hour's walk, and those north-west of Paphos are among the best in Cyprus. Coral Bay with its coral-pink sands is especially famous. There are public buses or taxis for those who wish to ride, but a walk will give enormous pleasure, especially around King's Area, a 5 km. stretch of coast with innumerable coves to explore, and the occasional banana plantation. If you should chance upon one of the increasingly rare breeding grounds for the turtle you are especially asked to leave these creatures in peace and on no account disturb their eggs.

Tala: At this small, quiet village in the hills 8 km. from Paphos are spectacular views and more self-catering apartments.

LIMASSOL

Limassol is a ninety-minute drive from either of Cyprus's airports, and has traditionally been popular with British tourists. The Troodos mountains are only an hour away, and there are many small villages near the city, offering little oases of quiet individuality. *Curium* and *Amathus*, two important archaeological sites, are within easy reach, and the town and this part of the coast are particularly sheltered: winter temperatures are moderate and welcoming to visitors escaping the European ice and snow. Near Limassol is the island's main wine-producing country. Though sherry is Cyprus's best-known wine, and while few connoisseurs would claim that Cyprus produces great wine, the wine it does produce is eminently potable (see p. 80).

Limassol is said to be the best Cyprus shopping centre, and apart from its hotels offers a splendid range of restaurants and tavernas with barbecue and bouzoukia nights as well as the ubiquitous discotheques: for these, head for the **Potamos Yermasoyias** district – though the five-star hotels have their own bands.

The beaches of Potamos Yermasoyias are excellently organised, the best (but also most popular) being Dassoudi Beach (run by the Cyprus Tourist Organisation), with its backcloth of mimosa and pine trees. The **Amathus** beaches are sandy with occasional pebbly patches, and are especially beautiful, laid out around a natural amphitheatre and with marvellous vistas; the main beach runs for miles, with the ruins of ancient *Amathus* near by. Swimming and water sports are popular everywhere. Those hotels not within easy reach of the beaches almost invariably have their own swimming pools.

LARNACA

Cyprus's main airport is at Larnaca, but the town manages to preserve an atmosphere as redolent of the past as the present: its palm-fringed promenade is mustily sedate. Souvenir shops of varying quality are scattered through the town, but so are excellent boutiques.

To the east is a long, sandy beach which stretches all the way to the British base at **Dhekelia**, and it is along this coast that the major new hotels have been built, many of them within the past decade. There are tavernas, restaurants and bars – and many more in the town centre. There is an excellent marina (see p. 97).

PROTARUS

If some of the Cyprus resorts are now so cosmopolitan that it is difficult to catch the individual flavour of the country, this is certainly not so at Protarus, on the east coast of Cape Greco. The ruggedness of the landscape, the fine sand of the beaches and the deep blue of the sea – said to be the clearest water in the Mediterranean – make it a notable exception. The beaches are claimed by some Cypriots to be the best on the island, and certainly could be the best place for water sports: Flamingo Beach and near by Fig Tree Bay Beach are perfectly sheltered and almost always calm enough for water-skiing. Indeed, the conditions make it an ideal place to learn the art. Near by are other small coves where often you can find a completely secluded corner: try Ayii Anargyri Cove or Pernera Beach, for instance.

AYIA NAPA

Centuries ago, Ayia Napa was a small fishing-village tucked around the pink-stone church with its pencil-slim campanile and its beautiful little fountain. Now it is one of Cyprus's most popular resorts, mimosa and oleander framing lovely small coves and beaches near by, and all within an hour's drive from Larnaca airport. You can bicycle, drive or take a boat around the coast to explore local beaches and their caves, in some of which you will find resident sheep. Nearer your hotel apartment will be the usual tavernas and restaurants, discos and nightclubs. The main beach is perfectly adequate; three miles away is a usually less crowded one, Makronissos Beach. Nissi Beach, west of Ayia Napa, attracts mostly young people, some naturists. There are beach-bars, you can hire recliners and umbrellas, shower and changing cubicles. The sand is fine and clean, the bathing excellent; but be warned – at the height of the season the beach gets very crowded and very noisy. The usual water sports are available.

THE TROODOS HILL RESORTS

In the hottest months of the summer, you may find it cooler and pleasanter to stay in one of the Troodos hill resorts.

Troodos itself is also the ski centre of Cyprus and the sport can be enjoyed on the slopes of Mount Olympus between the beginning of January and the end of March (in March 1987, there were still over 2 metres of snow in Troodos Square, though this was somewhat exceptional). Troodos is 5 km. from **Platres** and its hotels, and an hour's drive from both Limassol and Nicosia.

Cyprus Ski Club operates from PO Box 2185, Nicosia (tel. 441933). It organises the four ski-lifts at Troodos, has a ski-shop in Troodos where skis, ski-boots and sticks can be hired, and employs qualified instructors. There are three cafeterias at the main ski slopes – Sun Valley 1, Sun Valley 2 and North Face. Temporary membership of the club costs about £Cy15 (family membership), £Cy10 (adults) and £Cy7 (children under eighteen). The lifts cost from £Cy3.50 (members) and £Cy7 (non-members) per day; there are similar discounts for members on the hire of equipment and instructors. Finally, it is indeed true that one may swim on the coast at 11 a.m. and by 3 p.m. be on the ski slopes.

PRACTICAL INFORMATION

THE CLIMATE

For practical climatic purposes, Cyprus is the most eastern of the Greek islands, and except in the mountains, when a certain amount of rain may be expected, there are clear, blue, sunny skies during most months of the year, and low humidity. So it is an island where you can find alpine flowers, but also banana trees. There can be rain almost anywhere between October and February, but along the coast there is an average of 340 days of sunshine a year – the sun shines for 90 per cent of the time in July, and for 62 per cent of the time even in March. Though Cypriots tend not to swim in winter, Northern Europeans usually find the sea warm enough at almost any time: the sea temperature at its lowest, in January, is 16° Centigrade (61° Fahrenheit), and in July 26° Centigrade (79° Fahrenheit).

Ideal holiday times are perhaps between the end of March and mid-June, and again between September and November, though visitors from countries with a colder climate will find the low season very attractive too, with cool sunny days ideal for walking and sightseeing. A low-season holiday also has the advantage that the hotels – many of which are now open for twelve months of the year – offer discounts, sometimes as high as 50 per cent.

It can be fiercely hot during July and August (43° Centigrade, 110° Fahrenheit has been registered in Nicosia), but along the coast there is usually a cooling sea breeze, and relief from burning heat can always be found in the mountains. Snow falls there in January and February, but there is also sun – and more rain than anywhere else in the country: as much as 127 cm. in a year, most of it falling between October and May. Certainly, in winter, you may experience a Cypriot storm, but this will probably only last a day, and rain falling like stair-rods and being carried along horizontally by a wind that sends slate-grey Mediterranean rollers crashing over the promenade at Limassol while sheets of violet lightning illuminate the sky – all this is really little more than a dramatic contrast to the bright blue skies of yesterday and, no doubt, tomorrow.

TEMPERATURE TABLE FOR NICOSIA

Month	Average	Maximum	Minimum	Hours of Sunshine
January	10.6	14.4	5.5	5.5
February	11.1	15.0	5.5	7.0
March	12.5	18.3	6.5	7.5
April	16.7	23.3	10.0	9.1
May	21.1	28.3	15.5	11.4
June	25.5	32.7	18.3	12.5
July	25.5	36.1	20.5	12.8
August	28.5	36.1	20.5	12.0
September	25.4	32.7	18.3	10.8
October	21.2	27.2	14.4	9.0
November	16.0	22.2	10.5	7.0
December	12.0	16.6	7.2	5.4

0C = 32F, 4 = 40, 10 = 50, 16 = 60, 21 = 70, 27 = 80, 32 = 90, 38 = 100

WHAT TO WEAR

At the hottest time of year, dress as for the Tropics, though if you intend to ski or spend time in the mountains a sweater or two will be useful. In fact even in summer you may be glad of a light woolly for evenings. In winter, take clothes you would wear during an English spring, including a light raincoat.

Though topless sunbathing is now accepted, nudity on the whole is not; there are no approved nudist beaches, and naturists run the same risk of trouble that they would run in Britain. For what it is worth, however, they have been sighted at Nissi Beach, near Ayia Napa, and are not unknown on more secluded beaches.

Off the beach, dress is pleasantly informal; at the smartest hotels fashionable clothes can be seen and suits are worn at dinner, though ties – even jackets – are not now invariably demanded. When visiting Orthodox monasteries and churches shorts should not be worn either by men or by women, and women should wear reasonably long skirts and take a shawl to cover bare shoulders (though not necessarily their heads).

HEALTH

Wise travellers do not now leave Britain without taking out health insurance: travel agents, your own insurance company or some credit-card companies will arrange this, and it is particularly important when, as in Cyprus, the local authorities do not offer free medical treatment. Doctors are entirely professional and capable, and almost always speak English. All hotels should be aware of the nearest surgery and hospital.

Standards of cleanliness in hotels, restaurants and tavernas are excellent, but it should be remembered that Greek-influenced cooks use a great deal of oil, and those not used to this may find their stomachs somewhat slow to adjust. Though no mandatory inoculations are required, a shot of gamma globulin before you leave home (your doctor will arrange this for a very moderate fee) will be a good prophylactic against an upset stomach, though your favourite remedy will surely be found in local chemists' shops.

You are holidaying in the sunny Mediterranean, and should take the precautions you would take anywhere else in the area against sunburn: go slow, and use the sun with care; take a good sun-shield (total blockage for nose and other prominent and sensitive areas).

Tap-water is safe to drink, and indeed in country areas is particularly fresh and inviting. A range of bottled waters is usually available. Mosquitoes are extremely prevalent during the summer months, and it is advisable to bring your favourite repellant (though many brands can be bought on the island).

TOURIST INFORMATION

The Cyprus Tourist Organisation – Kypriakis Organismos Tourismou (KOT, sometimes known as COT) – is excellent, and you should not hesitate to enlist its help either before you leave for your holiday, or when you are actually on the island. In the UK it is based at the Cyprus Tourist Office, 213 Regent Street, London W1R 8DA. In Cyprus there is an office at Larnaca airport, which should be open at whatever hour you arrive (tel. 36833). The Organisation's offices elsewhere on the island are at:

Nicosia: 18 Theof. Theodotou St (tel. 444264) and 35 Aristokyproy St, Laiki Yitonia (443374).
Larnaca: Zenon Street, Democratias Square (54322).
Limassol: 15 Spyrou Araouzou St (62756).
Paphos: 3 Gladstone St (32833).

KOT provides excellent maps, not only of the island but also of the major towns.

SHOPPING

The larger shops should operate exactly like those in European towns: bargaining is definitely out. Shopping hours are usually from 7.30 a.m. until 1 p.m., and again between 2.30 p.m. and 5.50 p.m.; Wednesdays or Saturdays are early closing days, when most of the bigger shops open only in the morning.

Smaller town shops and village shops open and close at the whim of their owners, and here too there is not a great deal of bargaining, though you can (and should) query any prices which seem inordinately high. You will have no difficulty in finding shops and stalls which sell souvenirs, the more worthwhile of them silver- or copperware, lace and embroidery, and pottery. Good small silver bracelets and necklaces can be had for as little as £Cy5, and embroidery from £Cy2 – though of course the elaborate work is much more expensive.

It is worth visiting the Cyprus Handicraft shops, where there is quality work at reasonable prices. They can be found at Laiki Yitonia, Nicosia, and Kosma Lyssioti, Larnaca.

CURRENCY

The Cypriot pound is divided into 100 cents; there are 1, 2, 5, 10 and 20c coins, and notes for 50c, £Cy1, £Cy5 and £Cy10.

All prices in this guide are quoted in Cyprus pounds: £Cy1 started out as the equivalent of £1 sterling; in fact, the exchange rate is now considerably weighted against the visitor: as we go to press the official exchange rate is around 81p. To convert, multiply the £Cy by a factor of 1.22.

You can change travellers' cheques or money at your hotel, though as usual the rate given will be poor. Banks will give the official rate. Most credit cards are accepted by shops, restaurants, hotels and car-hire firms, though not at most petrol stations. Banks are normally open between 8.30 or 9.a.m. and midday on weekdays (Saturdays, 11.30); many banks in the larger towns open for a couple of hours in the afternoon, specifically for tourists wishing to change money.

NOTE: Prices are, of course, liable to fluctuation, but the Cypriot inflation rate is low and the difference within a year or two should only be a few cents.

TIPPING

Where no service charge is made (and check your bill at restaurants and tavernas), tipping is on a standard European basis: moderate tips would be, say, 10 per cent to a barman, taxi-driver, hairdresser; 20c per bag to a porter, perhaps 50c per day to a maid. It is not necessary to tip a service taxi-driver unless he handles your luggage.

ENTERTAINMENT AND SPORT

If you are on a package holiday your agent's representative at your hotel will provide you with information about whatever kind of entertainment you favour. The hotel information desk or porter will, as usual, be a fund of information.

Along the coast, all the usual water sports are common; swimming, scuba-diving, water-skiing, and so on. The local tourist offices will know where to send you if you want to hire water sports equipment or arrange cruises, will know where the best tennis courts are, have lists of the films being shown in town (many in English – with Greek subtitles – and often at outdoor cinemas (a list of local cinemas will be found under each town in this guide) and will have details of special events – including open-air performances of plays or music, some (between June and September) in the ancient amphitheatre at Curium, where ancient Greek plays can often be seen, and where there are concerts by moonlight.

Formal sport on the island includes football, golf, horse-racing; you can hire horses for riding in the Troodos mountains, shoot partridge (Oct.–Jan.) and wood-pigeon (June–Sept.), or (in Nicosia) clay-pigeon, and there are squash and tennis courts. Walkers will find many fine routes in the Troodos mountains, and winter sports are also held there – the Tourist Board and the Cyprus Ski Club in Nicosia will help with details.

HOLIDAYS AND FESTIVALS

Though local folk festivals and feast days are perhaps not quite what they were, there are usually enjoyable jollifications of some kind, perhaps including a market, a fair, decoration of the streets, drinking and dancing. Public holidays comprise not only local Cypriot festivals, but some Greek ones as well. They include the following (only those marked with an asterisk* are bank holidays):

January 6	Epiphany*
January 19	President Makarios's name-day*
January 24	Ayios Neophytos at Ayios Neophytos Monastery
February	the Famagusta Orange Festival, celebrating the orange harvest: free oranges and folk-dancing.
50 days before Easter	Limassol carnival
40 days before Easter	Green Monday (a reminiscence of the ancient Dionysian Feast)
February 2	Panayia (Purification of the Blessed Virgin) at Chrysorroyiatissa Monastery
March 25	Greek Independence Day*
April 1	the day of Cyprus's Struggle*
April 23	Ayios Yeoryios celebrated in many villages
Fifty days after Easter	Cataclysmos, originally the Paphian Feast of Anadyomene; sea games and dancing, particularly at Larnaca
May Day	A Flower Festival which (whatever anyone may say) is directly associated with the ancient Feast of Aphrodite; it is no coincidence that revels are most enthusiastic at Paphos
May 1	Labour Day*
May 21	Ayios Constantinos and Ayia Helena at Tokhni, near Larnaca
June 28	St Paul at Kato Paphos

Early July	Folk-dancing Festival at Limassol
August 3	Anniversary of President Makarios's death*
August 15	Panayia (The Assumption) at Kykko Monastery, Makheras Monastery and Apostolos Andreas Monastery*
Late August	Peach Festival at Kato Mylos, Village Fair at Prodhromos
August/September	Folk festival at Platres, in the Troodos mountains
Early September	Lace Festival at Pano Lefkara
September	Limassol's wine festival, to celebrate the harvest: folk-dancing, singing and wine-tasting
Late September	Fig Festival at Zakaki
October 1	Cyprus Independence Day*
October 28	OχI Day (anniversary of the Italian invasion of 1940)*
December 24	Christmas Eve*
December 25	Christmas Day*
December 26	St Stephen*

On the Greek Orthodox Church's Holy Days there are special church services, some of which are still faintly associated with pre-Christian festivals. They include:

January 1	New Year's Day*
January 6	Epiphany
January 30	SS Chrysostomos, Vassilios and Gregory
February 10	St Charalambos
March 25	The Annunciation
Movable	Green Monday*, Good Friday*, Easter Saturday*, Easter Monday*
April 23	St George
May 21	SS Constantine and Helena
Movable	Ascension Day and Whit Sunday
June 11	St Barnabas*
June 29	SS Peter and Paul
August 6	The Transfiguration
August 15	The Dormition of the Virgin Mary*

August 29	The beheading of St John the Baptist and the Nativity of the Blessed Virgin
September 14	Exaltation of the Holy Cross
October 18	St Luke
November 30	St Andreas
December 12	St Spyridon
December 25	Christmas Day*
December 26	St Stephen*

WEIGHTS AND MEASURES

Perhaps sadly, European measures are used in Cyprus, and the old Cypriot measures are no longer in use. These were pleasantly confusing. The Cyprus mile, for instance, was the distance which could be comfortably travelled by a heavily laden donkey in one stage: about three English miles. You are not likely to need the land measures: the *evlek* (400 square yards) and the *donum* or *scala* (1,600 yards or about one-third of an acre). Measures of weight were:

1 *dram* = 0.112 oz	44 *okes* = 1 Cypriot *kantar*
100 *drams* = 1 *onje* or *onka*	180 *okes* = 1 Aleppo *kantar* of carobs
400 *drams* = 1 *oke*	200 *okes* = 1 *kantar* of fuel or onions

The Cyprus litre, used only occasionally, is 2.8 quarts. Rarely, an *oke* or *okka* of liquid may be ordered in the smaller villages: this represents just over two and a half quarts. The *kouza* and the *gomari* are now even more rarely used: they represent a jar (2.25 gallons) or a donkey-load (36 gallons) of liquid.

For travellers with more practical needs, the metric equivalents for inches, yards, miles and gallons are shown on p. 196. As a kilo is roughly twice as much as a pound (2.2 lbs) and the metric tonne only fractionally less than the imperial ton (0.984 ton), the modern everyday dry weights can be very quickly approximated.

ELECTRICITY

Standard current is 220/240 volts, 50 cycles AC, and the power sockets usually take 13-amp, square three-pin plugs, as common in England. If you should need an adaptor, your hotel will usually have one. There are usually 110-volt sockets for electric razors.

TIME

Cyprus time is two hours in advance of GMT. Daylight Saving Time or Summer Time operates during the summer months, usually coming in on the same dates as in Britain.

TELECOMMUNICATIONS

Post offices are usually open between 7.30 a.m. and 1.30 or 2 p.m., and again from 3.30 on weekdays; on Saturdays they normally open between 8 a.m. and 1 p.m., and 4 and 5 p.m. Only the larger offices handle telexes and telegrams.

There are direct-dialling telephone facilities for all calls. To call the UK from Cyprus, dial 00 44 first, then the number you want – omitting the 0 at the start of its UK dialling code. To call Cyprus from the UK dial 010 357 first. The current direct-dialling codes for the main tourist centres in Cyprus are:

Ayia Napa	037	Nicosia	02
Larnaca	041	Paphos	061
Limassol	051	Troodos	054

When dialling from the UK, omit the 0 at the start of these internal dialling codes also.

You can usually 'borrow' the telephone at cafés, newspaper kiosks and food-shops, for local calls.

IN EMERGENCY dial 199 for fire, police or ambulance.

CHEMISTS

The familiar red cross identifies chemists or pharmacies. Local newspapers have lists of those with an all-night service. There are good stocks of proprietary medicines, but prescriptions are required more often than in the UK. However, the chemist will advise on straightforward treatment for sunburn, upset stomach and so on.

TOILETS

There are public toilets in larger towns, but these are not very common and not always impeccably clean. Museums usually have reasonable facilities, as have good cafés, restaurants and hotels; if you use those, it is a courtesy to buy at least a cup of coffee as an acknowledgment. The toilets on the tourist beaches are usually very clean. Signs are in English, with silhouettes clearly indicating which are for men and which for women.

NB: It is very important to follow the instruction, when it is given, not to put toilet paper into the lavatory basin; the diameter of the pipes is sometimes insufficient to accept it. A sanitary bin is provided where this is necessary.

THE LANGUAGE

English is spoken almost everywhere – even in remote villages there is almost always someone who speaks it. But the Cypriots react with pleasure to the slight effort involved in learning a few words of greeting in Greek: *parácolo* for please, *epharistó* for thank-you, *kaliméra* for good morning, and so on. Buy a simple phrase-book – but in the confidence that you will probably never have to use it to make yourself understood. The Greek spoken on the island, incidentally, will often sound entirely dissimilar to the Greek you may have heard in mainland Greece: there is a very pungent local accent.

THE COURTESIES

Natural courtesy is recognised everywhere, and all it is necessary to remember is that, especially where the older generation is concerned and away from the main tourist areas, behaviour is still rather more formal than one might expect. There will always be friendliness, and you will often find yourself offered little gifts of friendship – simply an orange or a drink; to refuse is to offend.

Cyprus is in many ways still an appallingly chauvinistic country, and visiting male tourists offering even the most cursory courtesy to Cypriot women will be rewarded by surprise and approval – at least by the women.

PHOTOGRAPHY

Remember the strength of the light, and buy slow-speed film. Be tactful when near anything which looks like a military installation, and refrain particularly from taking photographs anywhere near the border with occupied Cyprus. You will see signs prohibiting photography in certain areas. When in museums, ask whether photography is permitted; usually it is not, though special permission can sometimes be obtained from the Directorate of Antiquities. It is tactful to refrain from using your flash in churches, especially if there are worshippers present, and in some churches you are asked not to take photographs at all.

NEWS

European newspapers and magazines are freely available at a price. The *Cyprus Mail* and the *Cyprus Weekly* are English-language newspapers; Cyprus has its own *Time Out*, invaluable for its listings of cinemas, live performances, discos and so on; it is, however, irregularly published and not always easy to find.

CBC (the Cyprus Broadcasting Corporation) periodically broadcasts radio news in English. The BBC World Service can be received loud and clear, as can BFBS – the British Forces Broadcasting Service. Currently, there is a special broadcast for tourists at 8.30 a.m. every day, and in the summer it is repeated at 6 p.m. There is one TV network, which besides brief newscasts in Greek, Turkish and English shows foreign films and serials, often BBC repeats.

THE SIESTA

The siesta is not just a strange Mediterranean excuse for avoiding work. In the height of summer, it is well to observe it by retiring to the cool of your room and resting; sunstroke and heat-exhaustion are both unpleasant and time-wasting. In any case you will find no one very willing to serve you, or to do anything else, between the hours of 2 and 4 p.m. In the cooler months the siesta is observed perhaps a shade less obsessively, but is never entirely ignored.

MUSEUMS, SITES AND CHURCHES

KOT will have a certain amount of information about museums and archaeological sites, but if these are among your main interests it would be as well to apply to the Department of Antiquities at the Cyprus Museum in Nicosia, where you will get all the information you require. It is to the Department, too, that students or professional archaeologists should apply for free passes. Otherwise, the entrance fee to the sites is usually 25c per person, and information sheets are usually available, describing the antiquities and often providing a map. The Bank of Cyprus Cultural Foundation is sponsoring an excellent series of short illustrated guides to the principal sites, produced in collaboration with the Cypriot Department of Antiquities. These are good value at £Cy1.50, though they are not yet available at every site. It must be admitted that there is a certain Mediterranean vagueness about site opening times, but in general they open at 7.30 or 8.30 a.m., and remain open until dusk.

Churches, at least those outside the main towns, will more often than not be locked; but the local priest will almost certainly be somewhere about, and will usually be extremely pleased to show you round in exchange for a modest contribution to church funds. The local taverna or coffee shop will help you find him. Do not expect the rural churches to be as well cared for as the most run-down English country church; and do not be surprised at horrifying vandalism which has deprived many of them of their treasures, often replacing beautiful icons and other furnishings with cheap modern substitutes of astonishing vulgarity. Old paintings have been plastered over or ruined by over-painting, delicate acanthus carvings have been given coats of emulsion or gloss paint. The Department of Antiquities has now, however, embarked on an excellent and far-reaching scheme of repair and restoration, expertly and tactfully done. There is no comparison with the fate of churches in the North, where invading Turkish troops have done great damage: looting has been comprehensive and destruction widespread, icons have been stolen, fabric wrecked, murals and mosaics completely removed from some churches by the invaders, to be illegally sold. Some antiquities have been subsequently discovered, offered for sale in Europe, and the Cypriot government has succeeded in purchasing them and returning them to the island, where they can be seen in the national collections.

Be even more discreet in your approach to Greek Orthodox churches than you would to a church at Cheltenham or Tunbridge Wells: remember that women are still not allowed into the sanctuary, and men must enter by the side doors in the screen leading to it, and not the central Holy Door. In fact you will often find the sanctuary altogether closed; visitors have too often stolen icons and other items.

It is worth pointing out that while one iconostasis – the screen which divides the sanctuary from the nave – may look exactly like another, all the many icons which decorate the screens are individual works of art, some of them authentic masterpieces. It is useful to carry a torch to examine them, for they are often poorly lit.

ICONS AND FRESCOES

Cyprus is one of the great centres of Byzantine art: in the whole island, before partition, there were something like 5000 churches and chapels, 500 of which retained their original frescoes, and hundreds of which contained icons. Some of the anonymous painters fully merited the title of master; many of them came from Constantinople itself.

Frescoes, wall-paintings on plaster, at their best (as developed in Italy between the thirteenth and sixteenth centuries) are extremely permanent. The wall is first rough-plastered, then a cartoon of the work to be done is traced on to it. An area sufficient for one day's work is covered with smooth plaster, the cartoon is redrawn on to it, and the artist paints on the damp plaster using pigments mixed with plain water. As the plaster dries, a chemical reaction makes the painting part of the wall itself. At the time of writing, this work can be seen going on in the church of the Monastery of Stavrovouni (see p. 111).

An icon was originally a picture of Christ or the saints painted on a panel, as distinct from a wall. The oldest icon known dates from the sixth century – the oldest on Cyprus from the tenth century (see p. 94). Earlier examples were no doubt destroyed by Arab raiders between the seventh and tenth centuries. Despite the influence of Western art, the Byzantine tradition was maintained here – and is to this day; good modern examples can be seen (see p. 111). The icons and frescoes, naïve but often infinitely moving, are among the best reasons for visiting Cyprus.

ECCLESIASTICAL TERMS

In the text we occasionally use ecclesiastical terms, some of which are peculiar to the Greek Orthodox Church or Muslims. Among them are:

ayia/ayios (*ayii/ayias*) – the Greek for 'saint', female or male, singular or plural

iconostasis – the screen separating the sanctuary of a church from the *naos* (nave); women may not usually go beyond it

narthex – the porch at the west end of a church

panayia – literally, 'All Holy'; in the Orthodox Church this is almost always a reference to the Virgin Mary

pantokrator – Almighty God, often used to describe a portrait of Christ set in the dome of a church
petra – a stone
prodhromos – St John the Baptist
stavros – the cross
stoa – a portico or colonnade
mihrab – a niche in a mosque, facing Mecca
tikké – a Muslim monastery

THE NORTHERN ARCHAEOLOGICAL SITES

These have sometimes been severely damaged – the necropolis at Vounos, for instance, a Bronze Age site where splendid clay bowls were found marvellously decorated with horses and riders, has been ploughed over and the tombs wrecked. Archaeological exploration and maintenance work in the Occupied North has come to a complete halt, and it is impossible to check how many sites survive, or what damage has been done to them, partly because any archaeologist working in the Turkish sector is at present effectively banned from ever working again in a Greek-speaking country; this is understandable but extremely unfortunate, for it will almost certainly mean not only time lost in the exploration of sites, but very possibly considerable deterioration of those already excavated.

GEOLOGY AND ECOLOGY

Cyprus was originally formed by one of the bursts of molten rock which erupted through the floor of the Mediterranean during the period when the Alps, Carpathians, Himalayas and other mountain ranges were elsewhere being formed. The island was originally two separate land masses, with a sea dividing what is now the Troodos mountains from the Kyrenia range. That sea is now the Mesaoria plain. The Troodos are substantially composed of exposed igneous rock within which there are rich caches of copper, asbestos, pyrites and other ores. The northern Kyrenia range was less exposed, so the original limestone cladding remains, carved by time into spectacular peaks and crags.

DEMOGRAPHY AND THE ECONOMY

Cyprus has an overall area of 9,251 sq. km. and a population estimated at 719,000, including the Turks who have occupied the northern third of the island since 1974. It is estimated that Greek Cypriots total about 79 per cent of the population, and Turkish 18 per cent (one of the reasons why Greek Cypriots are so bitter that the Turks have seized 30 per cent of the total land available). In 1987 it was estimated that the population of the Turkish sector was 165,000, but there has reportedly been a considerable influx of Turks since then, and some emigration of Greek Cypriots, which cannot be taken properly into account. About 23,000 Turkish troops are stationed in the occupied sector of the island. The density of population in Cyprus proper (i.e. excluding the Occupied North) is 73 persons per sq. km.

The Cypriot economy remains on a sound basis, with inflation stable at 5.5 per cent and unemployment at about 3 per cent. The major crops, in descending order of metric tonnage, are: grapes, potatoes, oranges, barley, grapefruit, lemons and wheat. The island also produces sheep, goats, pigs and cattle. Asbestos, cement, mosaic tiles, wine, beer, footwear and cigarettes are all important features of the economy, as is tourism.

FLORA AND FAUNA

BIRDS

Hundreds of different species of European migratory birds pause at Cyprus on their journey to and from the south, for the island lies almost due north of the Nile delta, and between December and April the salt lake near Larnaca is covered with flamingos, egrets, ibises and herons. The migrating swallows arrive on their way to northern Europe on about 19 February, and in early August storks and cranes arrive in a great mass to spend just one night on the island before passing on to Egypt. The Siberian starling and the Palestine bulbul visit, as do the dotterel, the pintailed sand-grouse and the smew. The golden oriole can be seen and the cuckoo heard and nightingales nest south of the Troodos range and at Lapithus near Kyrenia. But wild duck and blackcaps must beware, for they are hunted down as luxury food.

The Cyprus Ornithological Society, which was formed in 1957, has recorded over 300 species of birds as being reliably observed on the island, and the following are among those worth watching for:

Cetti's Warbler   This is the only bird peculiar to Cyprus: about 13 cm. long, it is brown with whitish underparts and a prominent rounded tail. It is best recognised by its song, which begins with a sudden *pwit*, then there is a pause, and then, in a nutty, fluty voice, a series of what sound like expletives – *pitchewitchewit*! It is generally to be seen in the Troodos mountains.

The hoopoe   About 26 cm. from tip to tail, this bird is named after its peculiar call – *hoo-poo-poo* – though it also mews like a cat. It is easily recognised by its long, curved beak, cinnamon head and body, its large crest (erect when it is excited), and its broad rounded wings with bold bars. It can be seen walking about the Troodos mountains, looking for insect larvae.

The Griffon vulture   There is no mistaking the look of a vulture: this one, which again can be seen in the mountains, has a short, squat tail and a small head, a sandy plumage with blackish flight- and tail-feathers, white down over the head and neck; when it is on the ground, you can see a white ruff about its neck. It usually holds its peace, but occasionally grunts and hisses in a grumpy sort of way. It soars to great heights on the look-out for food, and when one griffon spots a carcase – maybe a dead donkey, maybe something rather more succulent – others will not be far behind. Incidentally, it lays only one egg in a nest about 40 cm. across, built of dry grass and palmetto.

Bonelli's eagle   Dark brown, with perhaps a pale patch on its back, this smallish eagle (only 61 cm. or so long) has a grey tail with a black band and a white lower body with a broad black band under its wing. It whistles, and calls *klu-klu-klu* in a pleasingly mellow voice. It can be seen usually on the lower slopes of the Troodos range, and anyone attempting to approach its nest should be warned that it has been known to attack predatory humans. It may be small, but it can take hare and game birds, falling on them from a great height.

Eleanora's falcon   This is a rare bird, but it has been seen on the cliffs of Akrotiri, not far from Limassol. It is about 37 cm. and dark-sooty in colour, streaked with black with yellow cere and legs, a white throat and cheeks and a black moustache. Slender, it has a long tail and narrow wings. Its call is determinedly unpleasant – a sort of grating screech – but it flies like a little spitfire, capturing small birds and insects on the wing.

ANIMALS

It would be an unselfconscious tourist who would be prepared to boast, on his return from Cyprus, that he had been savaged by a sheep; but this is not as altogether unlikely as it seems. The sheep in question would certainly be a moufflon. Happily (or perhaps unhappily) you are unlikely to meet one in the wild, though once this breed was the chief prey of Lusignan or Crusader hunters working with dogs or tamed leopards. Its flesh was said to be especially sweet. In fact, the moufflon sheep were hunted so single-mindedly that by the turn of the present century the breed was virtually extinct. It is now easiest to see the moufflon in the special enclosure at Stavros tis Psokas Forest Station in the Troodos mountains – the headquarters of the Paphos Forest District. And it is worth seeing a moufflon: the males have splendidly impressive, noble curled horns. If you walk the mountains you may possibly meet one or two in the wild; they like peace and quiet and extreme seclusion, and react somewhat irritably when approached by strangers – or, for that matter, friends.

There is no other animal on the island which should be particularly sought out for its rarity: there are fox and hare in the mountains, and some very pretty snakes and lizards. There are only two poisonous snakes: the *coupli*, which is seen only occasionally – most usually at Salamis (now occupied by the Turks) – and for the record, about three feet long, with a green skin and dark spots; and the light grey *saittaros*, which is extremely shy and generally hides at an oncoming footstep.

Maybe because of the English influence, Cypriot cats and dogs are inordinately friendly, and cats seem more or less to run the monasteries at Ayia Varvara, near Stavrovouni, and at Akrotiri (the latter called, indeed, St Nicholas of the Cats). They are good at hunting snakes. You will see plenty of donkeys at work, and perhaps a bullock cart or two. There may be some camels still working in the occupied sector.

One of the trials unlikely to be undergone by a modern visitor to Cyprus is a plague of locusts. Until only about a century ago, these were not uncommon – the creatures would arrive in great clouds or drifts, their mass even obscuring the sun; in 1668 a plague is recorded which lasted for a whole month, until the locusts, having devoured everything in sight, died of hunger and left their corpses to stink in the summer heat.

FLOWERS AND PLANTS

In Cyprus, the seasons are in a sense reversed: drought lays the countryside waste in the dead of summer, and spring comes in autumn – after the first rains. Scilla, grape hyacinth and dwarf narcissi are the first to be seen, then crocus and autumn-flowering cyclamen before the whole island is coloured by thyme and vetch, ranunculus and lupins, gladioli and peony. Small blue irises, crocuses and wild tulips can be seen all over the island, with poppies and yellow oxalis, while huge wild fennel glare yellow.

There is a Cypriot orchid (*Kotschyi*) which you may be lucky enough to find in the woods near Paphos, and all over the island is the flower perhaps most significant to Cyprus – the asphodel which Persephone picked before she was carried off to the Underworld. Pedhoulas, in the mountains, has wonderful cherry-blossom, while in blossom-time one should also visit Trikoukkia in the Troodos (apple trees) and Phassouri, near Limassol (for all kinds of trees, including bananas). In late autumn, as a sort of bonus, a reddish-orange carpet spreads over the hills as the vines mark the end of another grape harvest.

There are cedars (a protected tree), and the Aleppo pine appears as high as 1,370 m. up in the mountains – the Troodos pine with its distinctive flat top grows even higher. The dwarf golden oak is particularly striking – more a bush than a tree, with very decorative foliage, dark green on one side, light yellow on the other. Cypresses are used as windbreaks for fruit plantations; there are groves of bamboo and eucalyptus, olive and carob trees. Sadly, no one seems to have given a great deal of attention to the nurture of the olive on the island, and neither the fruit nor the oil are specially good.

The Forestry Department of Cyprus has done excellent work in the past twenty years, not only planting for timber but watching for fires, which in the past have scorched many acres.

HISTORY

THE ISLAND'S EARLY HISTORY

The limestone rocks of Cyprus first thrust from the great European sea sometime in the Cainozoic Age, about 100 million years ago; but the sandstone deposits above them indicate that they had another period of submersion before the island became permanently dry – though not yet as an island, but as part of an Asian promontory over which roamed mammals during the Ice Age. At the end of the glacial period, some 50,000 years ago, the Mediterranean sea formed, and Cyprus became the island we recognise.

No traces of Palaeolithic man have yet been found on Cyprus, but many Neolithic sites have been excavated – traces of circular huts dating from about 8,000 years ago, together with the usual flint and stone tools. At the Stone Age site at Khirokitia fifty huts have been comprehensively excavated, little circular homes where the living existed happily with their dead ancestors buried beneath the floor. A popular architectural form here was the beehive hut, a design which reached its apogee in the magnificence of Agamemnon's great tomb at Mycenae, 4,000 years later.

Man began to use copper tools in Cyprus fairly early – in about 3000 BC – and the copper mines of the island supported a useful export trade. By now, flint and stone tools were much improved, and handmade pottery appeared, of good, red clay with basic decorative patterns – made before the invention of the potter's wheel, but none the less extremely decorative and handsome. There are signs of a sophisticated religious movement, too, from this period, when bull-sacrifices took place, and perhaps the sacrifice of children; there seems also to have been a snake-goddess cult. During the second half of the Third Millennium bronze was invented, and many tools and weapons have survived from this period.

By now, we begin to find imported artefacts – weapons, pottery and jewellery made of gold, ivory, glass and enamel from Egypt and Syria, Crete and Mycenae. And in about 1500 BC came an enhanced Egyptian influence when Cyprus was conquered by the Pharaoh Tuthmosis III in the course of his campaign against Syria and Phoenicia. The impression is that the invaders were not particularly interested in trade with the island, or in settling it; they simply kept the islanders in their place, and out of the Egyptians' hair. Apart from establishing olive trees, they left little trace of their 100-year stay.

A much greater influence was to be exerted by Phoenicia. The Phoenicians controlled several Mediterranean cities and, since they depended on maritime trade, eagerly established one on the island – Citium, most of whose ruins lie beneath the modern town of Larnaca. Amathus, Tamassos, Idalion and Lapithos were other Phoenician cities, each governed by a local 'king' (who was carefully prevented from exerting more than local power). The Phoenicians brought their own gods, notably Astarte and Melkarth.

The ancient script of Cyprus has a clear relationship with the writing found among the ruins of the palace of Knossos, on the island of Crete. The Assyrians cast their eyes, and their hands, on the island: Sargon II, who led the children of Israel into captivity, received the homage of seven Cypriot kings, and in 668 BC ten kings fought for Assurbanipal against the Egyptians. The Egyptians fought back – at first unsuccessfully, but then in 588–69 BC there was a great sea battle in which the Cypriot fleet was defeated, and the Pharaoh Amasis seized the island and demanded tribute, mostly in wood for shipbuilding; the King of Salamis, Evelthon, who ruled most of the island's minor kingdoms, was subservient to Egypt. Nevertheless, this was a time of prosperity, and a time of fine art – as can be seen from the terracotta figures discovered at Ayia Irini in 1929 by a Swedish expedition, and now to be seen in the Cyprus Museum in Nicosia.

EARLY GREEK COLONIES

The Greek colonisation of Cyprus was a simple process; the Greeks who went there had left home not to conquer, but just to make a new life in what seemed fairly easy circumstances – and they brought with them the art and culture of their country. The various Greek colonies within Cyprus – Salamis, Soli, Marion-Arsinoe, Paphos and Curium and the others – were independent, each with its own ideas about politics and trade.

The Greek cities formed the skeleton of the Cyprus of modern history. Salamis was the chief city among them, said to have been founded after the fall of Troy by Teucer, king of the island of Salamis near Athens. Behind its splendid harbour it stood on the east coast, north of the Pedias River. From that harbour corn, wine, salt and oil went out to Phoenicia, Egypt and Cilicia, and the city's kings became famous in battle against the Persians. The ruins of this Salamis lie under those of the later, Roman, city, for it was destroyed by an earthquake and completely rebuilt.

Soli stood on the north coast, near the more modern port of Karavostasi, and was one of the island's most famous cities, the capital of one of its nine kingdoms. Men of Attica are said to have founded it, again after the Trojan war, under the name of Oepea; it was renamed as a tribute to Solon, who devised the laws of Athens. As with so many ancient sites, not only in Cyprus, local people took the stones of Soli to build their modern houses, and little of the city remains to be seen – though near by, at Vouni, there are vestiges of what was evidently a handsome palace, probably belonging to one of the fifth-century kings who was fond of the creature comforts of hot baths, central heating and good drainage.

The city of Marion stood on the site of the modern town of Polis, and was reputedly founded by Acamanthus, an Athenian. A centre of the copper trade, it was destroyed in 312 BC by Ptolemy I because of the support of its king, Stasieikes, for the Syrian King Antigonus in his campaign to subdue the island. Rebuilt, it was renamed Arsinoe by Ptolemy Philadelphus (285–247 BC), and prospered under Roman and Byzantine rule.

Palea Paphos, at the western end of the island, was originally a Mycenean settlement, and there are various theories about its origin. Ovid attributes its foundation to the son of Pygmalion and Galatea, whose name was Paphos – and there is certainly a strong tradition that Pygmalion ruled here. On the other hand, an even stronger tradition says that Paphos was founded by Cinyras, a high priest of Aphrodite's temple (the remains of which may be seen at the near-by village of Kouklia). He was rash enough to challenge Adonis to a musical duel, and paid for it with his life. However, the first real clue to the existence of Palea Paphos is in an Assyrian tablet in the British Museum, which mentions a certain King Ithuander, who ruled the city in 672 BC. Its fame rested, of course, on the famous temple to Aphrodite, and the enthusiastic sexual rites practised there. The island, and Paphos especially, was evidently a popular stop-over for the fleet. As Ariosto put it:

The sailors issue on the flow'ry shore,
For traffic some, and some the land to view,
Where Love resides, with pleasures ever new.

Curium was probably founded by men from Argos, in the Peloponnese; a huge Temple of Apollo stood here, but of it, and the acropolis which crowned the almost inaccessible hilltop site with palaces and temples, only parts have so far been uncovered. The city and its rulers shared a fascinating history: one, King Stasanor, defected to Xerxes at the battle of Salamis in 498; another, King Pasicrates, fought for Alexander the Great at the siege of Tyre. There has been much archaeological work here since a first expedition in 1873, and among the revelations are the handsome villa on the hill, the theatre, the equally handsome baths with their mosaic floors and admirable plumbing, and, most recently, the Forum and Nymphaeum.

THE PERSIANS

Cyprus was part of the great Persian Empire, but when war broke out between Greeks and Persians, the Cypriot cities – apart from Amathus, which was a Phoenician settlement – took the Greek part, led by Onesilos of Salamis, who had usurped the throne of his pro-Persian brother Gorgos. In 499 BC a great Persian army sailed for the island and deployed itself on the plain outside Salamis, where the Cypriot princes faced it, Onesilos placing himself directly opposite the Persian general Artybius. The battle was fought on sea and on land; on sea, the Greeks and their Cypriot allies conclusively defeated the Persian fleet; on land, the battle went the other way, swayed by the desertion of Stasanor, the king of Curium, and his forces. The Cypriot army was scattered, Onesilos and Aristocyprus, king of Soli, were killed, and the Greek fleet, seeing that the cause was lost, sailed for home, leaving the victorious Persian army to conquer the remaining cities, and to install quisling princelings to rule for them.

Greece's power was failing, and since it was unable to support its patriotic Cypriot dependants, a Cypriot hero was almost inevitable: King Evagoras I proved to be the man for his time. A handsome, intelligent and highly political young man, he ingratiated himself with the people of Salamis at a period when a Tyrian named Abdemon was ruling the city. Abdemon was conscious of the challenge posed by Evagoras, who claimed to be (and no doubt possibly was) a descendant of the city's ancient kings. Before Abdemon could have him killed, Evagoras escaped to Cilicia, whence he and a band of fifty friends came, in darkness, to Salamis, contrived to enter the city, and seized the citadel. Disposing of Abdemon, Evagoras made Salamis into the most flourishing city of Cyprus, and ended up as virtual ruler of most of the island. He engaged the help of Artaxerxes II of Persia in Greece's war against Sparta – though Artaxerxes eventually turned against him – and for ten years waged war alone against the Persians until despicably murdered by a eunuch.

This was a period – continued under the reign of Evagoras's son, Nicocles – when Greek culture exerted a strong influence; but a final attempt in 350 BC to throw off Persian rule completely was doomed to failure – despite the fact that no less than nine Cypriot kings joined the revolt against Artaxerxes Ochus, the then king. Failure probably stemmed from a simple lack of coherent planning, the result of continual squabbling between the Cypriot city-states. They were only to be united as the result of a train of events set in motion by King Philip of Macedon, who had ambitions to seize the leadership of Greece and then conquer Persia. He formed a magnificent army but was assassinated before he could put it to full use.

His son, who succeeded him, was the twenty-year-old Alexander, a pupil of Aristotle who spent two years consolidating his position in Macedon and Greece before crossing the Hellespont into Asia with a 30,000-strong army. The kings of Cyprus hitched their wagon to the brightening star, and sent 220 warships to Alexander's siege of Tyre. Alexander's success in defeating the Persians opened a new epoch in Cypriot history. Its Persian period was over; its Greek period began.

THE GREEKS

One of the motives of Alexander the Great was his belief in Greek culture and his desire to spread it abroad. When he died, and civil wars were sparked throughout his empire, they were at least wars between civilised cities and states rather than barbarians. In Cyprus, the wars were substantially between three men – Antigonus (governor of Phrygia), Seleucus (one of Alexander's most trusted generals) and Ptolemy (governor of Egypt). The latter set out in 318 BC to conquer Cyprus and subdue the four cities which favoured Antigonus. He did so, not without carnage: King Pygmalion of Citium was put to death, and the whole population of Marion was despatched to Paphos and the city razed. The other hostile kings were deported to Egypt, and King Nicocrean of Salamis was made overall ruler under the guidance of Ptolemy's brother Menelaus.

Only one king continued to oppose Ptolemy's rule – Nicocles of Paphos. Menelaus's troops surrounded his palace, and delivered a sentence of death. Nicocles fell upon his sword, and his wife, Axiothea, having killed her young daughters, slew herself at his side. The palace was fired, and the ancient line of its kings ended.

In 306 BC, Antigonus attempted an invasion with an army of 15,000 men led by his son Demetrius, who succeeded in destroying half of Menelaus's army and besieged the ruler at Salamis, assaulting the city walls with a great nine-storeyed tower 150 feet high containing 200 men. He was repulsed, and when Ptolemy came to his brother's rescue he himself was defeated. For a decade Demetrius ruled as king in Salamis, only to be defeated in 295 BC – though Ptolemy treated his defeated enemy with great honour, allowing him his life. Paphos became the capital of the island.

The Ptolemies reigned in Cyprus, through viceroys, for the next 300 years, particularly valuable to Egypt for the timber supplied for Egyptian shipbuilding. The Egyptian court at Alexandria was in essence a Grecian court, and its cultural influence – through its great library and its philosophers and teachers – was felt in Cyprus.

In c. 336 BC, Zeno, perhaps the most famous of all Cypriots, was born at Citium, the son of a Phoenician merchant. He studied at Athens, and impatient of both Platonic and Epicurean philosophy founded the Stoic school, which took its name from the *stoa* or painted corridor in the Athens market-place, where he taught. He was devoted to the idea of a universe ruled by divine reason, of man's life governed by rationality, and put forward a concept of the brotherhood of man which remains deeply sympathetic. Whether by coincidence or not, after his death in 264 BC there is no further record of dissension between the cities of Cyprus, nor of any distinction between Greek and Phoenician Cypriots.

The decline of the Ptolemaic kingdom began under the degenerate (and illegitimate) Ptolemy IV, and the rumour that the last 'true' Ptolemy had bequeathed the island to Rome was welcomed by the Empire as an excuse to annexe Cyprus in 58 BC.

THE ROMANS

The historian Strabo describes how the last Ptolemy, an uncle of Cleopatra, was deposed and offered the high priesthood of Paphos. He preferred death, and after a time (during which the island was given, briefly, by Antony to Cleopatra, as a present) Cyprus became in 52 BC a part of the Roman province of Cilicia, with M. Tullius Cicero as governor. The island made an instant contribution to the empire in the shape of the royal treasure of Salamis (worth, at today's rates, perhaps £2½ million), which was seized by Marcus Cato from the last Ptolemy's estate when the latter committed suicide, and taken to Rome. Under Augustus, in 27 BC, the island was separated from Cilicia and became an imperial province under a military governor; by then it had settled into peaceful acquiescence to Roman rule, and Augustus's tax reforms commended themselves to the Cypriots, who had for too long been paying through the nose to acquisitive tax-collectors who had bought the taxation rights at auction. The emperor also set in train ambitious plans for new harbours, roads, bridges and public buildings. Strabo reports that new harbours were constructed at Carpasia, Salamis, Arsinoe, Leucolla, Curium, Paphos and Soli, and docks at Lapithos; splendid new metalled roads connected them, with excellent, firm bridges. Water supplies were brought in by aqueduct; the great temple at Palea Paphos was rebuilt.

Salamis now became the chief commercial centre (the administrative capital was still Paphos), and it was at this time that the great Forum was built there, with its shops and houses, its reservoir and its temple to Jupiter. Trade with the whole Mediterranean was now excellent, for the Romans had suppressed piracy; and there was a ready market in Rome for Cypriot wine, oil, wheat, iron, copper and silver.

The Christian era now dawned, and a native of Salamis was closely connected with its earliest years. Joseph, a Jew of the tribe of Levi, was born in Cyprus during Augustus's reign, and while visiting Jerusalem heard of the birth of Jesus. Having sold his property and donated the proceeds to the Apostles, he was given the name of Barnabas, worked for a while at Antioch, and eventually returned to Cyprus with Paul, landing at Salamis and going on to Paphos, where the two men converted the Roman pro-consul, Sergius Paulus – the first ruler to become a Christian. Ten years later, Barnabas was martyred at Salamis at the hands of the Jews. His body is said to have been hidden by his then companion, St Mark, but was to reappear under dramatic circumstances in the year 477.

After the expulsion of the Jews from Cyprus under the Emperor Trajan in AD 117, Christianity flourished, though the island at that time was said to be notorious for the sloth and luxury of its inhabitants and their ox-like stupidity. The heat, nineteenth-century historians believed, was responsible for the sexual immorality for which Cyprus was also a byword (of course the reputation was clearly connected with the rites practised centuries earlier at Paphos).

The prosperity of the Roman Mediterranean began to decline after the death of Marcus Aurelius in 180; a great famine in 324 decimated the island's inhabitants – despite free corn distributed at the Emperor Constantine's behest. Constantine's mother, Helena, offered the islanders free land and exemption from certain taxes when she visited Cyprus on her way back from her quest for the True Cross at Jerusalem. While she was there she founded the monastery at Stavrovouni and presented it with certain holy relics she had about her (including pieces of the True Cross and the cross of the Penitent Thief).

Helena succeeded in mitigating Cyprus's troubles, and there was for a time renewed prosperity, though the islanders' enthusiasm for Christianity was tested in 334 and 345 by two fearful earthquakes which largely destroyed Salamis. Constantine II rebuilt the city in 350, renaming it Constantia. On his death, when the Roman Empire was divided into East and West, Cyprus fell under the control of the Emperor Valens, whose capital was at Constantinople. The island was to remain under the domination of the East for the next 800 years – the centuries of the Byzantine period.

BYZANTIUM

Early Christianity showed its most sympathetic face in Cyprus, where we are told the bishops put their hands to the plough like the poorest of their flock, lived lives of poverty and submission, and exercised their ecclesiastical power with discretion and wisdom. Paphos was regarded as the metropolis, though the Bishop of Salamis ruled the Cypriot Church as direct successor to Barnabas. There seems to have been some quite mild dissension among the many bishops – there were at least fourteen on the island – and Archbishop Epiphanios I was forced to ask the Emperor Theodosius I to uphold the Orthodox Church by banishing the dissentients. This seems to have been achieved with surprising lack of bitterness – though the patriarchs of Antioch insisted for a while on exercising ecclesiastical jurisdiction over Cyprus, and after some argument the general council of the Church at Ephesus granted the island the right to consecrate its own archbishop. This judgment held until the reign of the Emperor Zeno (474–91), who supported the claim of Archbishop Peter of Antioch to supremacy over Cyprus. Providentially, just as Archbishop Anthemios of Cyprus was pointing out that his Church, having been founded by Barnabas, was apostolic in the truest sense of the word, and should be left to itself, what should turn up to support his view (it is said that the evidence came by way of divine revelation) but the body of Barnabas himself, found in a cave near Salamis together with a copy of St Matthew's Gospel in the saint's own handwriting. Anthemios took the relics to the Emperor in person, and the latter was so impressed that he immediately granted the archbishop the right to wear a purple cloak, to carry a sceptre rather than a staff, and to sign all documents in red ink.

The rise of Islam as a world power had considerable consequences in the history of Cyprus, which soon became a battlefield between East and West. The island was invaded in 647, but stubbornly resisted the Muslim attack, which had one remarkable result: attending the invading army was one Ummul Haram, an aunt of the Prophet Mohammed's secretary, serving with the armed forces. Two miles from Larnaca she accidentally fell from her mule and broke her neck: the shrine of Hala Sultan (her Turkish name) marks the spot: after Mecca and the Shrine of Mohammed at Medina, it is the third most holy site in the Muslim world – for it was believed for centuries that the lady was the aunt of the Prophet himself.

Though that first invasion was repulsed, a second, in 654, was successful, and the Arabs held Cyprus for some years through an uneasy truce during which Christians, who had been exiled, had fled, or had emigrated under the instructions of the Emperor Justinian II, were repatriated. The Arab garrison withdrew again in 680.

For the next 300 years Cyprus was continually raided by Muslim fleets from Syria and Egypt, unprotected by the ineffective Byzantine navy, and thousands of Christians were massacred or taken as slaves. In 743, for instance, during the reign of Constantine V, the Caliph Yezid III attacked the island and carried off large numbers of prisoners; in 790 Admiral Theophilus, trying to defend the island against another invasion, was captured and martyred for his faith. In 902 three successive invasions devastated much of the island, destroying churches and monasteries and forcing the inhabitants of the coastal towns – Paphos, Carpasia, Lapithos, Aphrodisium and others – to flee inland. In the tenth century the Muslims captured all Cyprus, though it was recovered in 964 by the forces of the Emperor Nicephoros Phocas in a conclusive victory after which there were no further invasions for two centuries.

THE CRUSADES

Cyprus was right on the route taken by the Crusaders in their pilgrimages to and from the Holy Land between 1096 (when the feudal kingdom of Jerusalem was founded) and 1291 (when that kingdom finally perished).

In 1054 there was an open breach between the Eastern and Western Churches – the culmination of friction between the popes of Rome and the patriarchs of Constantinople. The Orthodox Church founded by the Apostles refused to contemplate the amendments of the Creed formulated by the Council of Nicaea, and rejected Roman doctrinal legislation. As disagreement reached its height, Christendom was treated to the spectacle of the Patriarch of Constantinople issuing an encyclical letter rebuking the errors of Rome, and the Pope replying by excommunicating him. A thousand years have not sufficed to heal the breach between the two Churches.

The schism came appositely for the Muslims, for it greatly weakened the Christian Church in its conflict with their forces; the Crusades, as the conflict – or series of conflicts – was known, thus began with a natural disadvantage to the Christians. The Crusades centred of course on Jerusalem, which had been occupied by Muslims since 637 – though the Christian Church there had not been molested, and pilgrims were allowed to visit the city (the Emperor Charlemagne, indeed, had been acknowledged by the Caliph Harun-al-Rashid as Protector of Jerusalem, and held the keys of the Church of the Holy Sepulchre). In 1071, when Jerusalem was captured by the Seljuk Turks, the Roman Emperor Alexius Comnenus (founder of the Comneni dynasty) mounted the First Crusade, with the support of Pope Urban II, to reconquer the city. There was much support from rich Roman merchants on the lookout for new markets in the East.

The First Crusade resulted in the slow and painful capture of Antioch, and eventually (after a forty-day siege) of Jerusalem, where the victors knelt in praise at Jesus's tomb while the streets around ran with the blood of 70,000 Muslims. The Christian kingdom of Jerusalem was established. In 1145, the capture of Edessa by a resurgent Muslim army led to the disastrous Second Crusade, which collapsed almost before it began.

In 1187, Saladin, the supreme ruler of Islam, mounted his holy war for the recapture of Jerusalem, and succeeded in defeating the army of Guy de Lusignan and taking the city. The European Christian kings were appalled, and instantly prepared for the Third Crusade. In 1191 the army of the Holy Roman Empire marched overland towards Acre, which had been under siege for two years; the English and French forces under Richard the Lion Heart and Philip of France went by sea to Sicily, and then made across the Mediterranean to join the army outside Acre.

Cyprus had not, so far, been involved, and had troubles of its own: Isaac Comnenus, a great-nephew of the Byzantine emperor, had commandeered the island as his private kingdom (with the backing of the Norman King of Sicily, his brother-in-law) and was ruling with the greatest cruelty and avarice. Fortuitously, a storm scattered Richard's ships, and three of them were wrecked off the Cypriot coast. Some of the crew reached shore near Limassol, but were immediately taken prisoner by Isaac, who also set his eyes on a fourth English ship which took refuge in Limassol harbour. On board were Richard's sister, Queen Joanna of Sicily, and his fiancée, Princess Berengaria of Navarre. Just as Isaac was about to attack the ship by force and carry off the two ladies, the remainder of Richard's fleet sailed into the harbour. Furious at the insults offered his ladies and his shipwrecked men, he landed and reduced Isaac's inefficient army to a flying rabble. Delighted, most of the Cypriot nobility came down to Richard's camp and offered him their support. Three days later Guy de Lusignan, King of Jerusalem, arrived with many of his men and swore fealty; whereupon Isaac, who knew a bad thing when he saw it, appeared before Richard, handed over 20,000 marks in gold and 500 men-at-arms to help in the Crusade, and made off swearing to be revenged.

On 12 May 1191, King Richard of England and Princess Berengaria were married at Amathus, and Bishop John of Evreux crowned the bride Queen of England. Isaac chose that moment to appear at the Abbey of Apostolos Andreas at Cape Andreas, in the east of the island; he was bound with silver fetters and sent off to imprisonment and eventual death in Syria. Few Cypriots mourned.

Before leaving for Acre with the King of Jerusalem, the Prince of

Antioch and their forces, Richard garrisoned Cyprus, and the island was to remain under Western domination for four centuries. The Cypriots, pleased though they were to have been released from Isaac's rule, now realised that they had jumped from the Greek frying-pan into the Norman fire, and resolved to regain their independence. A small revolt was squashed without much trouble, but when he heard of it Richard decided that the last thing he needed was an island populated by insurgents who would distract his attention from his main course. So he sold Cyprus to the Templars for 100,000 bezants.

The Order of the Knights Templar was founded in the twelfth century specifically to protect the pilgrims journeying to Jerusalem after the First Crusade. In 1291 the Order was to be ruled from Cyprus; but a century earlier the news that the Order owned their island was not particularly welcome to the clergy of Cyprus, for among its special privileges were exemption from the payment of tithes and allegiance to the Pope alone – so Templars could safely ignore the edicts of local bishops and clergy. It was already an enormously wealthy order, and there were rumours of moral laxity (especially a predilection for homosexuality).

The worst fears of the Cypriots were swiftly realised, for the Templars were cruel rulers; indeed, so hated were they that on Easter Day 1192 the islanders planned bloody insurrection. The Templars, who were relatively few, got wind of the plot and took refuge in their castles, sending out a message promising to leave Cyprus if their lives were spared. The islanders, in turn, were in no mood for mercy, and refused the bargain. The Templars, taking a gamble, left their strongholds before dawn and slaughtered a large number of Cypriots – men, women and children – terrifying the island into submission. However, they took the hint, and hastily returned the island to King Richard. Slightly embarrassed, he took advantage of the deposition of Guy de Lusignan as King of Jerusalem, and presented Cyprus to him as a gift.

THE LUSIGNAN DYNASTY

Between 1192, when Guy became Lord of Cyprus, and the abdication of Caterina Cornaro in 1489, the island was ruled by the Lusignan dynasty, whose influence on the history of the island was arguably greater and the intrigues of whose dynasty were certainly more interesting than those of any other ruling faction. The Lusignans were used to power: the family had its root in the French town of that name, in the department of Vienne on the Yonne not far from Poitiers, and various branches exerted a wide influence throughout Europe. In Cyprus, they became absolute rulers who indelibly marked their presence on the island's fabric and history.

Guy found the island in an almost ruined state: the reigns of Isaac and the Templars had resulted in social chaos. One of the first things the new ruler did was to restore their lands to any Cypriots driven abroad who returned during a fixed period. His knights and barons (granted estates on the island) and some Cypriot gentry formed a new aristocracy on the island – 300 nobles and knights and 200 squires. Below them were the bourgeoisie, with the Parici at the bottom, who had almost the condition of slaves; then the Perpiriarii, who were granted their freedom on condition that they made annual donations to their lord; the Lefteri, who had purchased their freedom outright; the Albanians, who had intermarried with Cypriots; and the Venetians, descendants of the Crusaders of 1123 who had settled on the island.

Guy, the uncrowned head of a limited monarchy, was titular Lord of Cyprus, and defended a constitution modelled on that of Jerusalem. He presided at a High Court which ratified laws and defended customs; a lower Court of Burgesses had no legislative powers, and concerned itself with administration. When Guy died in 1194 he left a settled State to his brother Amaury, who had himself crowned first King of Cyprus in 1197. Shortly afterwards Pope Celestine III set up a Latin archbishop at Nicosia who used Orthodox Church funds to establish bishops at Limassol, Paphos and Famagusta. The Orthodox Church was not best pleased, and while King Amaury was abroad receiving the crown of Jerusalem, rebelled; the leader of the rebellion, one Kanakes, kidnapped the queen and her family – who were rescued only by the intervention of King Leo of Armenia.

Meanwhile, the usurper King of Constantinople, Alexios III, was plotting to recover Cyprus for the Eastern empire, and was foiled only by the forces of the Fourth Crusade, who captured Constantinople, routed Alexios, and divided the Eastern empire among themselves. Cyprus henceforth depended for protection on the Western navies, and was for that reason strategically tied for three centuries to Western powers.

Cyprus now settled into a period of considerable and steady

comfort, perhaps because its kings tended to be ambitious for military glory and were often absent on foreign quarrels, leaving the throne to young princes under the thumbs of their womenfolk. There were tourneys and sports meetings, hunting and other peaceful pursuits. The merchandise of the East flooded through Cypriot ports – silk, wool, leather, furs, spices, carpets, jewellery . . .

The ruling class took precautions to protect its interests, and the island was in fact under a sort of benevolent martial law: the castle of Kyrenia, on the northern coast, was built (by Jean d'Ibelin) to guard the harbour, and became the stronghold of the Lusignan kings, buttressed by its attendant castles of St Hilarion and Buffavento. But there was more peaceful building: of the great Abbey of Peace, Bella-pais, near Kyrenia (in 1206), and of the Cathedral of St Sophia in Nicosia (in 1209–28).

The feud between the Orthodox and Latin Churches continued, but at the 1222 Council of Famagusta the Orthodox Church was brought firmly under the control of the Latin Church: the Orthodox bishops had to surrender most of their functions and were deprived of most of their income, though Queen Alix (wife of King Henri I, son of Hugues I) ensured that they were protected at least during her lifetime. The Lusignans, indeed, were great protectors of the Orthodox Church against the harshness of papal edicts.

Real persecution, however, took place: Orthodox monks were imprisoned for allegedly speaking disrespectfully of Roman rites, and when they declined to submit were tied by the feet to mules and dragged out to be burned at the stake. When the Orthodox Patriarch appealed to the Pope, he was told that the sufferings of his Church were entirely due to its separation from the true Church of Rome, and the breach widened.

It was in 1228 that the Holy Roman Emperor, Frederick II, looked in at Cyprus on his way to Palestine, stepping into the middle of an argument between Queen Alix and her relative Jean d'Ibelin, most powerful of the Cypriot barons. Jean wanted to succeed his brother Philippe as regent of Cyprus during the minority of King Henri I. The Queen wanted to appoint her own man, Sir Amalric Barlais. Amalric succeeded in persuading Frederick to support his candidature, and when Jean d'Ibelin greeted the emperor with the seven-year-old King Henri I at his side, Frederick instantly demanded that he forfeit all claims to the regency. D'Ibelin refused, but the emperor, rather than risk open conflict and a split in the forces he hoped to take with him on Crusade, patched an uneasy peace and took d'Ibelin with him to Palestine, leaving Cyprus in Barlais's charge. He immediately imposed heavy taxes on d'Ibelin's supporters.

When he heard of this oppression, d'Ibelin returned to Cyprus, defeated Barlais in battle, and forced him to relinquish his claims. King Henri keenly supported d'Ibelin, but when the latter made the mistake of leaving Cyprus to fight in Syria, Barlais took control of the island, with the exception of the castles of Buffavento and St Hilarion, where the king's sisters took refuge. D'Ibelin finally returned to Cyprus in 1232, and drove the imperialist forces into the castle of Kyrenia, where they were besieged for over a year before surrendering.

The Emperor Frederick had now completely lost control of Cyprus; neither did things go well for him in Palestine, where his determined opponents, the d'Ibelin family, held Jerusalem against him – until the Holy City was taken, not by the Holy Roman Emperor but by the Muslims, who were to hold it until General Allenby re-took it for Christendom almost seven centuries later.

Meanwhile, in Cyprus, the long struggle between the Orthodox and Roman Churches was re-ignited. Hugo di Fagiano, a peasant-born Augustine Roman canon, was elected Archbishop of Cyprus – but in his temporary absence, the Orthodox bishops elected Germanos Pesimandros Archbishop, which the Pope, Innocent IV, technically enabled them to do. Fagiano, furious, immediately exiled himself. In 1260 a new Pope, Alexander IV, less conciliatory than his predecessor, issued a *Bulla Cypria* which restricted the Orthodox sees and placed Orthodox bishops under the supervision of the Roman archbishop, who had the right to veto the appointment of any new Orthodox bishop. Under this Bull, the Orthodox Church fell entirely under the control of the Church of Rome.

The ruling family of Cyprus had by this time firmly established itself – in particular, after the death of the last Lusignan of the male line, by the marriage of Isabelle d'Ibelin to the regent, who called himself King Hugues III. Hugues the Great was a splendid ruler, a soldier and man of action but also a learned student of history and literature and a founder of monasteries – he was buried in his monastery of the Abbey of Bellapais. It was to him that St Thomas Aquinas dedicated his *De Regimine Principum* ('For the Guidance of Princes') which was to be valuable throughout Europe in defining the relationship between Church and State. During his sixteen-year reign

Hugues also showed great pity and humanity in relieving the suffering of the island after plague and famine.

At the end of the century the Templars returned to Cyprus, having been granted the town of Limassol as a reward for loyalty to King Henri II. They showed their gratitude by conspiring with his brother Amaury, Prince of Tyre, and forcing Henri to abdicate in his favour. Henri was sent abroad, a prisoner. Happily (it might be thought) the Pope heard of this, and of some of the Templars' more peculiar practices; he summoned the Grand Master, Jacques de Molay, to Rome to answer charges of heresy and the practice of profane rites, and eventually burned him as a heretic and ordered the Order to be disbanded. All the property the Templars had acquired in Cyprus was confiscated and handed over to the Knights Hospitaller, who like the Templars had originally been formed to protect pilgrims but were now a successful military organisation. They built a stout castle at Colossi, and set up other command posts at Paphos and Kyrenia. They were at least considerably less obnoxious than the Templars.

It was under the rule of Hugues IV (1324–59) that the dynasty of Lusignan reached its high point. Cyprus was an important staging-point on the trade route between Europe and the East and, since the Christian ports of Syria were no longer available, the richest merchants of Genoa, Pisa, Marseilles and Barcelona now established themselves at Famagusta, which became one of the greatest Mediterranean ports. Its merchants were celebrated for their wealth: one was said to have given his daughter, at her marriage, jewels more valuable than all the regalia of the Queen of France. As a visiting Westphalian priest, Ludolf, put it (*Excerpta Cypria*, p. 20):

Cyprus is the furthest of Christian lands, so that all ships and all wares, be they what they may, and come they from what part of the sea they will, must needs come first to Cyprus, and in no wise can they pass it by, and pilgrims from every country journeying to lands over the sea must touch at Cyprus.

Unsurprisingly, the merchants of Venice and Genoa were extremely jealous of the island – and particularly irritated that Cypriot galleys interfered with their smuggling of military supplies to Alexandra and Damietta in exchange for merchandise – in direct contravention of the instructions of the Pope, who had forbidden trade with Egypt.

Hugues IV was not specially interested in all this; he much

preferred the quiet life, home rule, and literature (Boccaccio dedicated a book to him). His one trouble, at the end of his life, was the dreadful toll taken in Cyprus by the Black Death, which in 1349 compelled the cessation of trade and killed so many nobles that Hugues was forced to promote many merchants to the ranks of the aristocracy.

His son Pierre, handsome and audacious, immediately upon his succession set out for Asia Minor, a naked sword at his side to symbolise his determination to recover Jerusalem. He had some brilliant successes, which he related at the courts of England, France and Flanders, and was welcomed by the Pope at Avignon. Then, in 1365, he succeeded in capturing Alexandria – though the cowardice of the knights of Europe, who deserted him, forced him to retire from the city after three days. When even the Pope declined to support him in his ambition to take Jerusalem, he reluctantly arranged a truce, and returned home to find that his queen, Eleanor of Aragon, had been unfaithful to him. His understandable reaction against her alienated the court, and in 1369 he was assassinated; his thirteen-year-old son succeeded as Pierre II, under the regency of his two uncles.

King Pierre II was crowned in the Cathedral of St Nicholas at Famagusta, in 1372. As the vivid coronation procession made its way through the city streets towards the celebratory banquet, a dispute broke out between the Genoese and Venetian representatives: the latter insisted it was their privilege to hold the right-hand rein of the young King's horse, while the left-hand rein (the inferior one) was for the Genoese. The Genoese took exception to the suggestion, and at the banquet fighting broke out and many of them were killed. Hearing the news, Admiral Pietro di Campo Fregoso set sail from Genoa, landed troops on Cyprus, and took not only the cities of Nicosia and Famagusta, but the King as a prisoner. He then laid siege to the castle of Kyrenia, in which Queen Eleanor had taken refuge with Prince Jacques of Antioch, Constable of Cyprus. The defenders succeeded in defying the great catapult the invaders deployed against them, and successfully fought off attacks by sea; the Genoese were forced to make a treaty in 1374 under which the King was restored to his throne, though Jacques was taken hostage to Genoa; and, more important, Famagusta, the greatest city and port of the island, was ceded to the Genoese.

When Pierre II died, in 1382, Jacques was released to succeed him, and became a friend of the English kings Richard II and Henry IV (who, as Bolingbroke, visited him on his way home from pilgrimage). Jacques I, understandably, was continually in conflict with the Genoese, and built Larnaca up as a trading port to replace Famagusta. His son Janus attempted to regain Famagusta, but failed; and after plague had weakened the island's defenders, the Egyptian fleet fell on Larnaca and Limassol in 1425 and sacked them. The following year the Mamelukes defeated Janus's forces at Khirokitia, captured the king, slew most of his army, and went on to sack and plunder Nicosia and massacre its inhabitants. The city was almost completely destroyed. King Janus was released after ten months, but his spirit was broken.

After his death in 1432 his son Jean II married (as his second wife) Helena Palaeologus, a determined Orthodox Christian who immediately began intriguing to return the Orthodox Church to ecclesiastical command in Cyprus. When the Roman Archbishop of Cyprus died, Queen Helena nominated an Orthodox churchman to replace him; the Pope declined to approve the appointment, and the King, under his wife's thumb, declined to accept the Pope's nominee. However, the Grand Master of the Hospitallers managed to gain the King's ear, and in the Queen's absence persuaded him to receive the Pope's man; and, moreover, to select John, Duke of Coimbra – a Catholic prince – as husband for his only daughter, Charlotte, heir to the throne.

John proved an excellent man, and advised the King well; but his advocacy of the Catholic cause did not commend him to the Queen, who very possibly had him poisoned. At all events, he died. The King, perhaps by this time irritated by the Queen, unexpectedly appointed his bastard son Jacques as Archbishop of Nicosia. The Pope refused to approve the appointment (Jacques was only sixteen), but Jacques was an ambitious lad, and held on to his seat. He got on well with his half-sister Charlotte, and when she suggested that the royal chamberlain had been implicated in John's death, the young archbishop broke into his house and murdered him. Deprived, for this, of his archbishopric, he removed himself to Rhodes for a time, only to return in 1457 with a small army and murder one of the King's friends, who had spoken unkindly of him. The King made only a slight gesture of annoyance before granting Jacques a full pardon and restoring him to the archbishopric, which he enjoyed for the rest of his life (though there is no evidence of his taking much interest in religion). Perhaps providentially, though it seemed he might succeed his father, before this could be confirmed the King died and his daughter Charlotte automatically succeeded.

Jacques, who had been dissuaded from taking any part in her coronation, made off immediately to Egypt, where he proclaimed himself the rightful male heir. In 1460, supported by a Muslim army, he landed at Larnaca, was greeted enthusiastically by the mass of the people (who approved of him because his mother had been Greek), and chased Queen Charlotte and her husband, Count Louis of Savoy, off to the castle of Kyrenia. When the castle was surrendered by its traitorous commander, the royal couple fled abroad.

Jacques was now King, though the Pope would not recognise him. He at least recaptured Famagusta from the Genoese, but then, thinking to form an alliance with Venice against Savoy, he decided to ask for the hand of the daughter of a prominent Venetian family. The Cornaro family was delighted, and Caterina was immediately married to Jacques II by proxy, given a dowry of 100,000 ducats, and packed off to Famagusta. The following year Jacques died – under suspicious circumstances – and Queen Caterina succeeded. By default, Venice had achieved her centuries-old ambition, and now virtually owned Cyprus. In 1489 the Venetians strengthened their hold by gently deporting the Queen to Venice, where she remained in exile until her death. On 26 February 1489, the banner of St Mark was seen flying over the cities of Cyprus.

THE RULE OF VENICE

The Venetian lion came in like a lamb. Venice needed Cyprus as much as a trading centre as a base for her fleet, and decided on conciliation. All nobility and clergy were confirmed in their privileges and their estates were secured. The Latin archbishop remained, but the Pope sent a message that the Orthodox Church was not to be oppressed. Peasants who could afford it were allowed to buy their freedom, and taxation was restricted. The Turks were furious that the island had fallen into the hands of their enemies, and also (with reason) feared for their pilgrim ships making for Mecca.

The Venetians began quietly to make Cyprus a modern stronghold, modernising some Cypriot castles by installing the best cannon and strengthening them to withstand attack by gunpowder, and dismantling those (St Hilarion, Buffavento and Kantara, for instance) which might be used against them in case of a popular rising. They reinforced the castle of Kyrenia and built a great wall around Nicosia, and in 1550 the military engineer Giovanni Girolamo Sanmichele fortified Famagusta by building the magnificent and effective Martinegro bastion.

The inevitable attack came on 1 July 1570, when a Turkish fleet was seen off Larnaca. The Cypriots stood by and watched the Turks landing men and guns, and even supplied them with provisions: the Venetians had not succeeded in winning their loyalty. Lala Mustapha Pasha, the Turkish commander, assembled an army of 50,000 infantry, 2,500 cavalry, 30 heavy guns, and 50 lesser artillery, and besieged Nicosia for six weeks before he succeeded in breaching the walls on 9 September. The massacre was complete: 20,000 people were killed, including the governor and the bishop, the city was looted, and the able-bodied young men taken as slaves. The commander of Kyrenia immediately surrendered, and was emulated by the rest of the island – except for Famagusta, defended by the Venetian Marcantonio Bragadino, which held out until 1 August, when terms of surrender were agreed. After the garrison had been allowed safe conduct and left the city, Lala Mustapha agreed to meet General Bragadino for a discussion of the future of the citizens. A dispute arose, and Mustapha massacred Bragadino's companions, tortured the general for a fortnight, then after forcing him to kiss the ground under his feet had him flayed alive in the main square of Famagusta. His skin was stuffed with straw and exposed to the ridicule of the Turkish troops. (It was later recovered, at great expense, from Constantinople, and buried honourably in the Church of SS Giovanni and Paolo in Venice).

The news of the fall of Famagusta and of the Turks' treachery finally roused the European powers to action, and a fleet of over 300 ships – Genoese, Spanish, Venetian – sailed for Cyprus under the command of Don John of Austria. At the Battle of Lepanto – the last great naval battle fought by oared vessels – the Turkish fleet was destroyed, and 15,000 Christian galley slaves released from captivity.

THE TURKISH CENTURIES

Despite the cruelty with which the Turkish rule began, the Cypriots tended to welcome it: not only because they had cordially disliked their Venetian masters, but because the Turks re-established the

Orthodox Church and its archbishopric and abolished feudal serfdom, so that for the first time for centuries the Cypriots actually owned their land. It was now the turn of the Latin Church to suffer: many places of Christian worship became mosques, others warehouses or stables.

Undisturbed by the prospect of invasion (the European powers were not particularly interested in reconquering Cyprus), the Turks settled down to make money from the island, and did so in particular by heavy taxation: the Cypriots might now own their land, but they made precious little profit from it. In 1572 severe famine struck; there was no seed to plant crops. Within two years the population was reduced by five-sixths, from 150,000 to 25,000. The Turkish civil service was inefficient in the extreme, and gradually the bishops began to take over the administration of the island, a task they continued to fulfil for many years.

In addition to the neglect of the Turkish civil service, the eighteenth century brought earthquake, a locust-inflicted famine, drought and finally a plague which killed a further one-third of the population. When the bishops appealed for help, the Turkish authorities, headed by one Chil Osman, simply demanded additional taxes. The bishops met Osman to protest, and secured a document from the government denying him the right to levy additional taxes. When they went to his palace to present the document, the floor of the meeting-room gave way, and the crowd outside, hearing the clamour and believing their bishops were being murdered, broke into the palace, killed Osman, and retired with all the valuables they could find, leaving the building in flames.

By the end of the eighteenth century the bishops were so powerful and their influence so manifest that even the sleepy, lazy and inefficient Turks became envious. They were also worried at news of the Greek rebellion against the Ottomans in Morea. The Grand Vizier, fearing a similar revolution in Cyprus, summoned the Cypriot archbishop, Kyprionos, and the bishops of Paphos, Citium and Kyrenia, with other senior clergy, to the palace in Nicosia, murdered them, and threw their bodies into the street. When Christians gathered to mourn them, they too were massacred. Between 1818 and 1821 terror reigned throughout the island.

But the Turks had pushed too hard and too far. When Greece itself became independent, many Cypriots travelled there to achieve Greek nationality, and the Greek Cypriots began to be ambitious for freedom from Turkish domination. Despite the rather kindly and civilised rulership of Abdul Mejid I (1839–61), when the governance of the island was much reformed, pressure from the outside world supported the movement away from Ottoman rule. Britain, in particular, was aware of the continual muddle and maladministration of the island, and, when it became clear during and after the Crimean War (1854–6) that Cyprus would be extremely useful as a British outpost from which Russian movements in Asia Minor could be monitored, a treaty was negotiated with the Turks which allowed a British occupation of the island.

THE BRITISH OCCUPATION

The British came to Cyprus prepared to like it and its people. After all, had they not received a positive if patronising report on the islanders from their vice-consul, Mr H. P. White, in 1862?

> The Cypriots are of a quiet and inoffensive disposition; they are social and hospitable, and remarkably fond of pleasure. But they are naturally lazy and given to idleness; they waste much of their time in their cafés, and are great frequenters of the fairs which are held at short intervals in different parts of the island; they are frugal and temperate in their living, coarse bread, cheese, olives and vegetables forming the ordinary food of the peasantry – yet owing to the abundance and cheapness of wine drunkenness is not uncommon among them.
>
> Brigandage, burglaries and assassinations are so rare as to be almost unknown in Cyprus; political agitation or opposition on the part of the people to the constituted authority is equally unknown. The Christians . . . have a reputation in the Levant for cunning and keenness in business which is perhaps not altogether undeserved. The Moslems have little of the fanatical spirit and bigotry which characterises the Arab Moslem; they live in harmony with their Christian neighbours in town and country, but at Nicosia, where they form the majority of the population, they are more inclined to assert their superiority.

The British were to govern Cyprus for sixty years, under a High Commissioner and a Legislative Council consisting of six British government officials and three Muslim and nine non-Muslim Cypriots. A High Court was established under British judges, and the police force was reconstituted along British lines. Taxation, too, was reformed, and the Turkish tithe system abolished.

The British soon discovered the difficulty of devising a governmental system agreeable to all Cypriots. From the first, the Greek Cypriots approved of the Legislative Council, while the Turkish Cypriots violently disliked it; racial tension was actually exacerbated by the mere existence of the Council. Then there was the problem of Enosis – the movement for union with Greece, which Winston Churchill praised as 'an example of the patriotic devotion which so nobly characterises the Greek nation'.

Even had the British government as a whole shared his view, the truth was that under the convention of 1878 by which Cyprus was assigned to Britain, the island remained part of the Ottoman Empire, and Britain had no power to consent to any movement towards Greece. And when, in 1914, Turkey entered the war against Britain, and Cyprus was offered to Greece on condition that she also entered the war – but on the British side – the offer was actually refused.

In 1925, Cyprus became a Crown Colony, under a governor, and Christian and Muslim Cypriots accepted British nationality. The pressure for Enosis continued, however, and in 1931 there were a number of riots, during one of which Government House was burned to the ground. The movement was suppressed and its leaders deported. During the Second World War the subject was in abeyance, and when, in 1947, Archbishop Leontios met leaders of the British Labour Government, it was made clear to him that there was to be no question of Britain relinquishing control of the island: the Colonial Secretary dismissed the Archbishop's pleading with the tactless statement that 'people in the grip of nationalism are impervious to rational argument'.

The Cypriot Orthodox Church then threw itself wholeheartedly into the Enosis movement, and in 1948 its bishops formed the Ethnarch Council to lead the fight for union with Greece; two years later, when the Ethnarch died, Bishop Makarios of Citium was elected to leadership of the Church. Suspected of collaboration in violence, he was deported, but from the Seychelles stepped up pressure on the British government through appeals to the United Nations and the formation in Athens of a Panhellenic Committee for Cyprus which in 1954 claimed self-determination and supported a campaign of violence organised by EOKA – Ethniki Organosis Kyprion Agoniston, or the National Organisation of Cypriot Fighters

– led by General Grivas, who took the name of the Byzantine hero Dighenis Akritas (see p. 77). A shadowy, mysterious figure, Grivas became a leader of almost mythic proportions.

At a tripartite conference in Switzerland in February 1959, the Prime Ministers of Greece and Turkey met the British Foreign Secretary and agreed a solution to 'the Cyprus problem'; and later that month Harold Macmillan, Mr Karamanlis and Mr Menderes signed an agreement which made possible the birth, on 16 August 1960, of the Republic of Cyprus, with Archbishop Makarios III as its first President.

THE REPUBLIC OF CYPRUS

The constitution of the new republic (which was a member of the British Commonwealth) officially shared administrative power between the Greek and Turkish Cypriots in a 70 per cent/30 per cent proportion. The President was to be a Greek, the Vice-President a Turk, and the House of Representatives composed of members in the proportion agreed. The same rule applied to the civil service and the police force; the army of 2,000 men was to be 60 per cent Greek and 40 per cent Turkish. Tribunals were to try civil disputes, and an article of the constitution specifically forbade land to be taken from a member of one community and given to a member of the other. A treaty concluded between the UK, Turkey, Greece and Cyprus guaranteed the constitution, and a military alliance between Cyprus, Greece and Turkey supported that treaty. The most active supporters of Enosis agreed to pay the price of abandoning their ambitions for union with Greece in order that the island should achieve its independence – for Cyprus was now, for the first time, entirely independent (apart from certain small areas maintained as British bases).

Given the long history of conflict between the Turkish and Greek Cypriots, it now seems naïve to have expected the constitution to work. And indeed, after only three years there was serious trouble. Arguments between Greek and Turkish citizens spilled over into violence, and when British armed force was used to control rioting, Turkey and Greece showed signs of openly intervening, and the United Nations – fearing for the peace not only of the island but of the whole Mediterranean – sent a peace-keeping force which on the whole succeeded in minimising violence. But the heated debate continued, and the UN's suggestions for a permanent *rapproche-*

ment were scornfully spurned. In 1964, Turkish representatives withdrew from the Cypriot government, claiming that they were being forcibly prevented from participating in decision-making, and asserting that their walk-out made the whole system of government unconstitutional. The Greeks, however, argued that the Turkish withdrawal was voluntary – they could participate in government if they wished – and continued to rule, alone.

Perhaps only Turkey would argue that the government of the island was not immensely more efficient under the sole control of the Greek Cypriots; and it may be that the seizure of power in Greece by the colonels, in 1967, contributed towards stability in the island – for few Greek Cypriots felt inclined to consider Enosis with that offensive junta. But despite the rising standard of living and the increased prosperity of Cyprus – based not only on its traditional trading, but on an enormously enhanced tourist trade – conflict between Greek and Turkish citizens continued, and sometimes broke out into open violence, as in the first attempted assassination of Archbishop Makarios in 1970.

The Greeks had for some time been offering the Turkish Cypriots local autonomy in communal affairs and representation in the government; while the Turks, fearing union with Greece, had been demanding administrative control over their local government bodies, which in the Greek view would lead inevitably to the creation of a State within a State, and eventual union with Turkey.

The principal Greek opponents of President Makarios doubted his enthusiasm for Enosis, and attempted to assassinate him in October 1973, murdering two of his supporters in the following January. Makarios found it impossible to act against his attackers because of their strong links with Greece and the colonels. After the death of General Grivas, in January 1974, he pardoned Grivas's followers, but was forced by anti-government factions to proclaim EOKA an illegal organisation. Relations between President Makarios and the National Guard worsened, and Makarios protested at its Greek officers' attempts to intervene in government, insisting on the dismissal of 650 of them. On 15 July 1974, they staged a coup, and he was forced to flee the country.

A former EOKA terrorist, Nikos Sampson, was appointed President by the National Guard. Reacting to this, the Turks took it as an excuse to invade the island. Just before his own removal by the Guard, President Sampson dismissed his Cabinet and called on the exiled Konstantinos Karamanlis to form a government. A ceasefire was proclaimed, but it failed to hold, and in August the Turkish army advanced to occupy one-third of the island.

Cyprus was now in chaos: prisoners-of-war were exchanged, but as winter approached one-third of the island's population was living in tents, and the economy was in ruins. The country faced a deficit of £350 million and the Turks now occupied land which had previously produced 70 per cent of the country's wealth. President Makarios returned to the island to acclamation, but faced an enormous task of reconstruction.

Cyprus now settled into an uneasy peace: none of the 200,000 Greek Cypriots driven from their property in the North of the island was able to return, but they gradually began to build a new life in the South – where nothing short of an economic miracle was to be achieved within the decade that followed. Discussions with Rauf Denktash, installed as president of the illegally occupied Turkish zone, were conducted in a suspicious atmosphere in which nothing was achieved, and when Makarios died in 1977 and Spyros Kyprianou succeeded, the relationship between the two communities did not improve.

The Greek Cypriots made enormous economic strides: the tourist trade was increasing, and production of raw materials was already running at four-fifths of the pre-invasion level. In the North, on the other hand, few tourists were to be seen and the economy was depressed, virtually the only trade being with the Turkish mainland. Rapid inflation led to open demonstrations by the Turkish Cypriots. In 1979 Denktash imposed severe restrictions on shopkeepers and banned the importation of many goods except from Turkey.

Talks on reunification, or some kind of regularisation of the situation, continued to be unproductive, and in 1983, condemned by the entire world community, Denktash made a unilateral declaration of independence, recognised only by Turkey. There was now no contact between the legal government of Cyprus and the illegal self-styled 'Turkish Republic of Northern Cyprus'. The continued presence of the UN peace-keeping force was even more necessary.

Since 1983, there have been spasmodic attempts at a resolution, but these have foundered due to intransigence on both sides. In 1985, for instance, Presidents Kyprianou and Denktash met in New York to discuss a draft agreement for a solution worked out by the UN Secretary-General, Javier Perez de Cuellar; but nothing came of the meeting, Kyprianou in particular simply declining to sign anything. Denktash, who had been prepared to sign, appeared to have won the psychological battle, for he went home to win 70 per cent approval of a new constitution, while Kyprianou had to face censure by the Cyprus House of Representatives – though later in the year he succeeded in winning an election.

At present, the tragic division of the country continues. In the North the economy remains shaky, production low and tourism virtually non-existent; in the South agriculture, tourism and service industries are booming, inflation and unemployment are stable.

RELIGION AND MAGIC

THE PAGAN GODS

Cyprus played an important part in the development of Greek religion, and particularly in the strength of the cult of Aphrodite. There was worship of various gods on the island as early as the twelfth century BC: in Enkomi there was a sanctuary of the Horned God and of the God of the Copper Ingot, and in Citium one of the Smith God, while at Paphos the sanctuary which later became Aphrodite's was in existence long before she was worshipped there.

Aphrodite

Aphrodite's origin is obscure, though there is good reason to believe that she originated at Paphos, and that her ancestor was the ancient Semitic goddess of love, Ishtar, divine prostitute and consort of kings. She was worshipped with incense altars and dove sacrifices and was connected with the sea and with gardens.

Some Greek legends say that Aphrodite was the daughter of Zeus and Dione, daughter of Air and Earth; others that she was engendered from the foam which gathered around the genitals of Uranus, thrown into the sea after he had been castrated by his sons, the Titans. At all events, as the Homeric hymn tells it, she rose naked from the waves, riding on a scallop-shell (as shown of course by Botticelli in his famous painting), and first set foot on land on the island of Cythera, off the Peloponnese. Finding its rocky barrenness unpleasing, she mounted her shell once more and travelled on to Cyprus, where she made her home at Paphos, at the western end of the island (the modern town is called Ktima).

There, the Horai, or four Seasons, daughters of Themis, were distressed by her nakedness – one of their duties was to regulate the relationship between the sexes, and they evidently thought an unclothed Aphrodite might offer an insupportable temptation to Cypriot youth. They therefore clothed and adorned her, and she was then considered ready to take her place on earth. The story is told in a fragment of a poem by Homer:

> The balmy breath of the west wind brought her
> Over the heave of the muttering sea
> In a froth of foam; the gold-crowned Horai
> Welcomed her joyfully, wrapped her in robes,
> God-like, balanced on her immortal brows
> A crown of marvellously crafted gold,
> And in her pierced ears set rings
> Made of a glowing copper from the hills.
> Bands of pure gold embraced her slender neck,
> Lifted her silver breasts . . .
>
> . . . and all the gods
> Welcomed her gladly, held out their hands towards her,
> Shocked by her beauty, Kythera amid the violets,
> Each one of them ambitious to possess her.

The ground turned green wherever Aphrodite stepped, and beneath the soles of her feet flowers sprang. Her subsequent amorous adventures are legion, but she returned to Paphos from time to time to renew her virginity in the sea (it sounds a dubious proposition). On Cyprus her surname was Eleemon, 'the merciful', and she was worshipped at shrines at Old Paphos, Idalion, Amathus, Tamassos, Soli, Kythera, Curium, Golgi and on the topmost peak of Mount Olympus.

The happy consummation of sexuality was Aphrodite's prerogative: *aphrodisia* denotes quite simply the act of love, and the old abstract noun for sexual desire, *eros*, became the name of the God Eros, Aphrodite's son. She was usually depicted as classically beautiful, and was far from unapproachable – there is a charming picture of her in an early hymn telling how she set out to find the herdsman Anchises, whom she had chosen to be the father of Aeneas, moving over the wooded hills followed by fawning grey wolves, bright-eyed lions, bears, and swift panthers (whom she so enchanted that they paused to couple in shady glades, putting aside their savage natures to follow her call to love).

A notable temple to Aphrodite – one of her oldest and most powerful shrines – was set up near the beach at Petra tou Romiou where she is supposed to have come ashore, and at the spring festival the young people of Cyprus gathered there during three days of worship and feasting to watch for the vision of the goddess, which would make them as beautiful as she. Elsewhere in the Mediterranean she was often known as Kypris – 'the Cyprian' – and always had a strong connection with the sea. The third-century BC Arcadian woman poet Anyte wrote of Cyprus:

> This place is the Cyprian's, for she has ever
>   the fancy
> To be looking out across the bright sea,
> Therefore the sailors are cheered, and the
>   waves
> Keep small with reverence, beholding her
>   image.

Her sanctuary was sacred to sex, which (as Sir James Frazer put it in *The Golden Bough*) was 'regarded not as an orgy of lust, but as a solemn religious duty performed in the service of that great Mother Goddess of Western Asia'. Benedetto Bordone, a Paduan, wrote drily in 1528 that Cyprus was famous as the home of 'the first woman who made a habit of selling her body for money'. The funds received at Paphos for services rendered were initially dedicated to Astarte, for the sanctuary was first established for the worship of Astarte and Tammuz, who later became associated with Aphrodite and Adonis; Aphrodite was worshipped here in the form of a conical stone, but interestingly was also sometimes worshipped elsewhere on the island as Aphroditos, a bearded man – particularly at Amathus (the capital of one of Cyprus's city-kingdoms). This symbolised the union of married couples as *androgyno* or man/woman. Virgil said that in his day there were over 100 altars to Aphrodite on Cyprus, and a busy priesthood whose year revolved around the two major festivals of Aphrodisia (in spring) and Adonia (in summer).

Adonis

The death of Adonis is sometimes said to have taken place in the Cypriot hills, and his myth seems to have originated on the island, though his very name (from the Semitic *adon*, Lord) is one of the hints that he came from further east. His story began with the beautiful Myrrha, daughter of King Kinyras of Cyprus, who sadly fell desperately in love with her father, made him drunk, and came anonymously to his bed. When, one night, he saw her face in the lamplight, he was appalled, and chased her away with a naked sword. But she was already pregnant, and the gods, seeing her shame, turned her into a myrrh-tree, whose trunk split open to give birth to Adonis. The child was so beautiful that Persephone and Aphrodite came to blows over possession of him.

When, years later, he was gored to death by a boar (Shakespeare's poem *Venus and Adonis* gives the most famous interpretation of the story) his blood ran into the ground, and red anemones sprang from it. At annual festivals in the month of Tammuz, in June/July, his death was remembered in a mock funeral procession during which a statuette was laid on a bier and borne amid clouds of incense to a grave, after which it and a little garland of herbs were thrown into the sea. Priestesses at Adonis's temple are said to have offered themselves to strangers in commemoration of Aphrodite's love and mourning – or, if this seemed excessive, to have sacrificed their hair in his honour.

Pygmalion

The third most famous legend associated with Cyprus is that of King Pygmalion (incidentally, his name may really have been Pygmaion, derived from *pygmaios*, a dwarf). The early Christian writer Arnobius in his *Adversus Nationes* tells us that the king fell desperately in love with an ivory figure of the naked Aphrodite – and it is certainly true that such objects did exist in the early years of her cult. He so idolised the little statue that he wanted to marry it, and laid it in his bed. That is as far as Arnobius, rather disapprovingly, goes; but Ovid in his racy *Metamorphoses* relates that Pygmalion was himself a sculptor who fell in love with his own life-sized ivory statue, and prayed to Aphrodite to resolve his dilemma. The goddess obligingly turned the statue into flesh and blood, and Pygmalion married his living doll (surely a sort of incest?). They had a child, Paphos, whose son Kinyras founded the city of Paphos – near which is Aphrodite's shrine.

CHRISTIANITY AND ISLAM

The Greek Cypriots are Christian, and mostly belong to the Cypriot Orthodox Church, though there are a very few Anglicans, Roman Catholics and Noncomformists. There are even fewer Jews. The Orthodox Church, frequently spoken of as the Greek Church, is part of the Holy Orthodox Catholic Apostolic Eastern Church. By a right granted in 478 elects its own archbishop.

The history of the Orthodox Eastern Church is lengthy and complex; it consists of those churches which accepted all the decrees of the first seven general councils and have remained in full communion with one another, and such churches as derived their origin from these by missionary activity or separation without loss of Communion. It has no creed in the Western meaning of the word, and while its ancient liturgies were numerous, that of Jerusalem or of St James generally prevailed, in the short form revised by Chrysostom and the longer called the liturgy of St Basil, generally recited in Old Greek.

Turkish Cypriots are Muslims – followers of Mohammed, who was born in Mecca in AD 570 or 580, married a rich widow when he was twenty-five, and later was convinced by visions that he was the special messenger of God to the Arabians. Rejected by his own people, he left Mecca in 622 and went to Medina, where he resorted to force to gather a following, and establishing an army returned to Mecca in 630 and conquered it, dying two years later.

Mohammedan doctrine includes worshipping one God, with Mohammed as His earthly representative and the greatest of the prophets – not divine, but simply an interpreter of the law – and believing in a final Day of Judgment. Muslims also have a divine book, the Koran, written not like the New Testament by disciples, but by Mohammed himself.

For a short glossary of the ecclesiastical terms used in Orthodox churches and mosques, see p. 40.

GODS AND HEROES

As in Greece and elsewhere in the Mediterranean countries, one can still see remnants of pre-Christian customs in Christian worship. One of Cyprus's festivals, *Cataclysmos*, has nothing at all to do with Christianity – it is simply the old feast of Aphrodite, appropriated by the Church, inserted in its calendar (on the fiftieth day after Easter) and renamed Cataclysmos in an attempt to identify it with Noah's Flood.

In place of the ivory or wax models of Aphrodite, wax models of people who are ill, or of their afflicted limbs, dedicated to the saints who have cured, or who it is hoped will cure them, can still occasionally be seen, especially in country churches; while near sacred wells or other shrines with magical properties, rags or handkerchiefs deck the bushes or trees. Christ's bread, *sesamotá*, is baked and eaten at Christmas; so is cooked wheat, *kolliva*, blessed and consumed in memory of the dead. Real belief in evil spirits was more particular a couple of generations ago, but stories of the *kalikandjaros* who roam the air between All Saint's Day and Epiphany, and are only to be dismissed by an offering of *xerotiana*, a kind of doughnut, can still be heard.

Distant echoes of the festivals of Adonis survived until recently in the *chattismata* – towards the end of the day, sitting in the sun with a drink or three, arguments would be held in often fairly rude doggerel. The real skill seems almost to have died out, alas, but the practice holds on doggedly, especially at Cataclysmos, when seawater is sprinkled generously over tourists and locals alike in a sort of pastiche of the Venetian practice of blessing the sea. Larnaca in particular is a pleasant place to be at this time, for it is there that the carnival spirit survives at its freshest, in an annual fair at which it would be extremely difficult to swear whether most people were honouring the Virgin Mary or Aphrodite, so closely have the two personalities been associated.

Another personality inseparable from the island is simply known as Regina, who was originally the mistress of the Greek Byzantine hero Dighenis Akritas, a doughty fighter much given to hurling rocks at his Arab enemies from mountain peaks, which he did as a matter of course for at least three centuries, round about the seventh to tenth centuries BC. Dighenis has been strongly associated with Cyprus since General Grivas linked his name with EOKA and its struggle for Cypriot independence.

FOOD AND DRINK

EATING IN CYPRUS

Cyprus has its own cuisine, which it would be the greatest pity not to sample. As one might expect, the preparation of food in Cyprus is

Greek-influenced – but with additional flavours from the Near East, and Turkey and the Levant in particular. It is now perfectly possible to find restaurants, both in and outside the hotels, in which 'international cuisine', as the travel brochures call it, caters for those whose taste is for bland pap and instant coffee, and there are the usual pizzas and hamburgers; but some of the best hotels occasionally present local dishes, and local restaurants and tavernas are well worth exploring. Their menus almost invariably carry English translations.

The best meats are lamb and pork; chicken is also good. Meals frequently start – and often go on! – with *mezs*, a mixture of small portions of many of the island's specialities, with which you can if you wish drink that peculiarly Greek appetiser, *ouzo*. A *mez* can turn into the largest and longest meal of your life. It may include: *taramasalata* (smoked roe with garlic and olive oil), *ktapothi vrasto* (boiled octopus), or *mithia tiqhanita* (fried mussels), *dzadziki* (yoghourt with cucumber and garlic), *keftethakia* (meat-balls) or *kalamarakia tiqhanita* (fried squid), with *houmous* (a chick-pea dip with spices) and almost certainly *melidzanosalata* (a puree of aubergine) and *ktapothi me saltsa* (octopus in sauce), together with various smoked meats and sausages, and of course *dolmathakia* (stuffed vine leaves).

Soups may include *revithia* (made of chick-peas) and the delicious *kotosoupa avqholemono*, a chicken soup with vegetables and an egg and lemon sauce; there will certainly be some ambitious fish soups. The pasta is good, too: *kypriakes ravioles* is the local ravioli, stuffed with ewe's-milk cheese, eggs and mint.

Rather surprisingly, fishing is not good around the Cypriot coast, so seafood is not a speciality of the island; even squid is likely to be frozen. However, there may well be swordfish steak (that meatiest of fish: ask for it with delicious black butter), and there are red mullet and red snapper, and the small Mediterranean fish, *psirika*.

The most typical Greek dish, *moussaka*, is readily available: a casserole of aubergine and minced meat, with tomatoes, parsley, white wine and a topping layer of bechamel sauce with egg yolks and cheese. Cypriot, as opposed to Greek, cooks also use potato in this dish. *Stifado* is a beef or veal stew with wine, onions and herbs; *arni kapama* is a splendid lamb stew with lemons, tomatoes and possibly a piece of cinnamon. *Patcha*, sheep's head stewed with lemon and garlic, is possibly an acquired taste, but chicken is everyone's dish, and here can be served in almost every conceivable way: *kotopoulo lemonato*, or sautéd chicken with lemon, is delicious and tender, while *kotopoulo me hilopites*, chicken stew with onions and tomatoes, is served with noodles. And of course, there is *aphelia*, Cyprus's own delicious speciality, pork marinated in red wine and crushed coriander seeds then slowly roasted. The charcoal grill is widely used, and so are traditional domed outside ovens.

Vegetables include the usual beans and peas, with black-eyed beans (*louvia*) and courgettes also popular. The Cypriot potatoes are excellent. You will find Greek-style salads, garnished with olives (though the local ones are not as good as those from the Greek mainland), peppers, onions, and *fetta* cheese – perhaps a little stronger than the mainland kind. The local 'cottage cheese' is excellent, and very different from anything you will have tasted elsewhere, and exclusively Cypriot hard cheeses include *kefalotiri* and *halloumi*, both made from ewe's milk.

Cyprus sweets are very sweet indeed. There is, for instance, *baklava*, consisting of pastry sheets with layers of almonds, sugar, cinnamon and cloves in a syrup of sugar and lemon juice. *Loukoumades* are small 'doughnuts' of batter dipped in syrup; *halva*, a sweetmeat made of pounded sesame seeds and honey. The villages of Yeroskipos and Lefkara specialise in Turkish Delight. Unless you have a very sweet tooth you may prefer fruit, which at its best is marvellous: honeydew or cantaloupe melon, watermelon, cherries, tangerines, peaches, figs, grapes, pomegranates, oranges (all in season). You will be surprised at the quality of the simple fare to be found at small and apparently rough roadside cafés; at the very least you will usually find good bread and an excellent omelette, flavoured with lemon juice and local herbs and made from eggs still warm from the hens clucking about your feet and contesting with the ubiquitous cats for scraps from the table.

Tea-bags are now freely available for those who do not drink coffee; for those who do, they will find that outside the tourist hotels and restaurants, where instant powders are as available as in Europe, Cypriots take their coffee seriously, as the Greeks do. Since the invasion, it is tactful to ask for 'Cypriot' or 'Greek' rather than 'Turkish' coffee: but they are really the same – coffee ground to the finest powder, placed in a small copper vessel with cold water, and barely brought (classically, three times) to the boil. Tea-drinkers tend to compare this liquid to mud: all one can say is that many people find it ambrosial mud, though when sampling it for the first time you should certainly prepare your taste-buds for a frontal assault. Do not ask for milk or cream: it is never taken with Turkish coffee. It is difficult, too, to persuade waiters that you want it without sugar. A glass of iced water will be brought with it. If you want very sweet coffee, ask for *gliko*; sweetish, *metrio*; without sugar, *sketo*.

CYPRIOT WINES

The Cypriots were wine-producers and wine-drinkers in ancient times; then the rule of Islam resulted in a period of drought, before under British rule the vineyards flourished again – and now Cyprus, though no producer of fine wines, can offer a number of robust vintages with which to bring added drowsiness to a hot afternoon.

The Cypriot wine best-known in England is still probably sherry; originally, Cypriot sherries tended to be rather sweet, but within the past decade or so the producers have studied Spanish methods, and the range is now very considerable. *Cyprus Flor*, extra dry, is as light and fresh as any Spanish sherry.

The Cypriot vineyards are high in the Troodos mountains, and the wines are shipped through Limassol, mainly by three dealers – Keo, Sodap and Haggipavlu. The most typical and individual Cypriot wine is the famous *Commandaria*, made chiefly in the villages of Kalokhorio, Zoopiyi and Yerasof. This is a very ancient type of wine, made from dried grapes, and it has been drunk since antiquity – much before the time of the Knights Templar, who are sometimes said to have originated it. It is intensely sweet (it can have four times as much sugar as port), and the ancients diluted it with water. It is now drunk as a dessert wine, often with an added liqueur. It is almost impossible to find a century-old, thick, almost treacly Commandaria of the original type. This offers a strange but superb experience – an almost caramel flavour from an almost black liquor – to be treasured even by those who do not normally like sweet wines.

The table wines are mostly red: *Othello* is perhaps the best-known dry red, but *Mavron* can be equally dark and rich. *Rosella* is a strong medium-sweet rosé, and *Kokkineli* another. *Aphrodite* is a medium-dry wine, *Arsinoe* a drier white, and *Bellapais* rather fizzy and sweet.

LOCAL DRINKS

The island has a domestic cocktail, though of what ancestry it is impossible to discover. This is the Brandy Sour: a generous measure of brandy, three drops of Angostura bitters, the juice of three lemons, one teaspoon of sugar. Add ice, top up with soda, and stir.

Sadly, this drink is now almost always made with lemon squash – but it is nevertheless refreshing in the heat of the day.

Other alcoholic specialities include *filfar*, a fragrant orange liqueur, *sourmada*, flavoured with almonds, and of course the local brandy, *zivania*, which is very strong, quite difficult to find and should be drunk with open eyes.

RECOMMENDED RESTAURANTS

We give under the town headings a few recommendations of local restaurants serving, mainly, Cypriot food. But it must be stressed that here in particular the situation is very volatile, and a restaurant which is excellent this year may be execrable next. Do not be put off by the fact that the restaurants and tavernas, even in central Nicosia, will rarely be as well-appointed as European restaurants. They may even look faintly grubby. But they are seldom anything but scrupulously clean, and the food is remarkably cheap. At a restaurant in the tourist quarter of Nicosia you can lunch off moussaka, Greek salad with fetta, good fresh bread, a glass of wine and a Greek coffee for about £Cy5 – and only the very greedy will not be entirely satisfied.

TOURIST ROUTES

Since most tourists will be staying on the coast rather than at Nicosia, the routes we suggest for an exploration of the island start from either Larnaca, Limassol or Paphos instead, and follow the accounts of those three towns. A series of excursions based on Troodos is also described (see p. 149f.). The only area which is somewhat troublesome to reach from these four centres is that between the occupied north and the Troodos mountains; this may specially be true during the winter months, when some of the mountain roads are likely to be snowy or icy, and consequently treacherous.

There is now a motorway from Limassol to Nicosia (see the endpaper map). Joining this from Larnaca, one can strike off to the east at Dhali, or even go almost into Nicosia and then drive on through Akaki and Peristerona before turning south towards the Troodos. It takes about an hour to drive from Larnaca to Nicosia, but beware – the first half of the journey, until you meet the motorway, is extremely dangerous, with continual examples of lunatic overtaking on blind bends by lorries, coaches and every other form of vehicle. Be careful.

Diagram of Routes

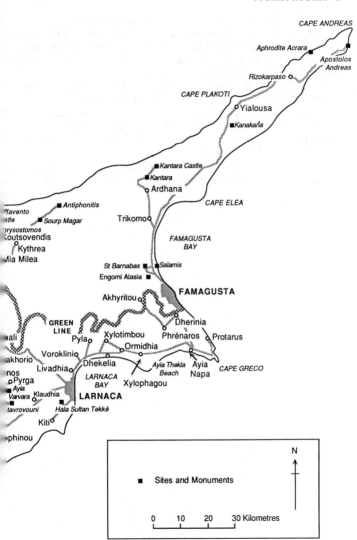

CAPE ANDREAS

Aphrodite Acrara

Apostolos
Andreas

Rizokarpaso

CAPE PLAKOTI

Yialousa

Kanakaria

Kantara Castle

Kantara

Ardhana

CAPE ELEA

Antiphonitis

ffavento
stle   Sourp Magar

Trikomo

FAMAGUSTA
BAY

rysostomos
Koutsovendis

Kythrea

Mia Milea

St Barnabas   Salamis

Engomi Alasia

FAMAGUSTA

Akhyritou

GREEN
LINE

Dherinia

ali   Pyla   Xylotimbou   Phrénaros   Protarus

Voroklinio   Ormidhia

akhorio

Livadhia   Dhekelia   Ayia Thekla   Ayia
                              Beach   Napa   CAPE GRECO

nos
Pyrga   LARNACA
Ayia   BAY   Xylophagou
Varvara   Klaudhia

tavrovouni   LARNACA

Hala Sultan Tekké

Kiti

phinou

N

■   Sites and Monuments

0   10   20   30 Kilometres

Whether one takes this option or braves the mountain roads, the journey is likely to be somewhat confusing; the only really useful advice is to consult the local tourist office about any route of which you are not entirely confident, and to make sure you have the most detailed and up-to-date maps you can find.

Venturing into the Occupied North is inadvisable in the current political climate, as we have already suggested. But since day trips from Nicosia are permitted and some travellers to Cyprus may wish to visit the North in spite of our warnings, excursions to Salamis and the other principal places of interest there appear as a separate section at the end of the book.

The routes and excursions described are shown in the Diagram of Routes above and summarised in the Chart of Excursions on pp. 10–12.

NICOSIA

NOTE: In 1964 a 'Green Line' was drawn to separate the Turkish and Greek sectors of Nicosia, and since July 1974, when the invading Turkish army entered the city, the northern and southern parts have been totally separated. The boundary runs roughly from the Paphos Gate along Paphos St, then up most of Hermes St, swinging north to a point between the Flatro and Loredano bastions. At present, the only crossing point between the Republic and the occupied sector is through the checkpoint at the Paphos Gate, near the Ledra Palace Hotel. Outside the old city, the line continues as the Green Line which separates the illegal northern sector from Cyprus proper. We deal below with the history of the city, and with those points of interest in the unoccupied, southern part of it; descriptions of the buildings of the Turkish-occupied sector are to be found in the part of the guide dealing with the Occupied North (p. 173ff.).

Hotels

Five-star: the Cyprus Hilton (tel. 464040) is a few minutes from the city centre, and has the facilities one would expect, including four restaurants, a health club and beauty salon, squash courts and a jogging track.

Four-star: the Ledra Hotel (441086) is ten minutes' drive from the city centre, stands in its own gardens, and has several suites as well as conventional rooms. The Churchill (448858) is a smaller hotel in the centre of Nicosia, as is the Philoxenia (499700).

There are half-a-dozen *three-star* hotels, including the Asty (473021), the Cleopatra (445254) and the Europa (454537).

Some restaurants

Athineon, Makarios III Avenue; Corner, Demosthenis Severis Avenue; Corona, Orfeos St; Cosmopolitan (music), Prodromou St; Tembelodendron, Kefalinias St; Tsalamatis, Laiki Yitonia.

Some tavernas

Astakos (fish), Menelao St; Cellari (music), Korai St; Mikis Tavern (music), International Fair Highway; Kalimnos Tavern, Kallipolis St; Plaka, Makarios Square, Engomi.

Some nightclubs

Crazy Horse (cabaret), Florines St; Elysee (bouzoukia), Pantheon Building, Evagoras Avenue; Fraktis (bouzoukia), Nicosia-Limassol road; Maxim (cabaret), Zenas de Tyras St; Casanova, Makarios III Avenue.

Cinemas

Alamo, Constantinou Polis St; Athineum, Evagoras I Avenue; Diana, Stassicrates St; Messokeleus, Kitium St; Metropol, Theodotou St; Mimoza, Alkeus St; Pallas, Arsinoe St; Pantheon, Diagores St; Regina, Regaena St; Varnakkides, Athena St; Zena Palace, Theodotou St.

Tourist Information Bureau

At the east end of Aristokyproy St (443374).

Perhaps because the division of Cyprus is more obviously signalled in Nicosia than elsewhere on the island, the city attracts fewer tourists than formerly: its hotels seem now to be occupied mainly by those who have business there. Nevertheless, it remains a fascinating city, and it is arguable that anyone coming to the island and not visiting the

Nicosia Outside the Walls

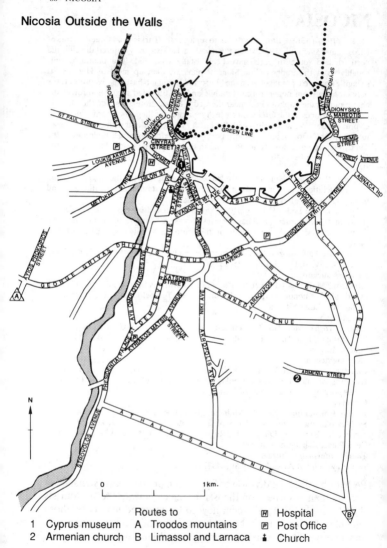

Routes to

1 Cyprus museum   A Troodos mountains
2 Armenian church   B Limassol and Larnaca

Ⓗ Hospital
Ⓟ Post Office
⛪ Church

Cyprus Museum (Outside the Walls, *Map* 1) can have no real idea of the island's history or heritage. Nicosia can be very warm at the height of summer: a temperature of over 43°C has been recorded. However, there are many narrow, shady streets, and more green open spaces than are obvious in any map – notably the Municipal Gardens near the museum.

Nicosia as one could explore it before the occupation was a perfect example of a sixteenth-century walled city, embraced by five kilometres of walls, defended by a moat and eleven protective bastions. Had it been possible to stop time at the end of the last century, to prevent motor traffic from entering the town, the result would have been a Medieval city preserved in aspic, attracting tourists from all over the globe as, say, Carcassonne does. But of course that is a counsel of perfection, and new roads have burst through the walls, though most modern buildings – hotels, administrative offices, factories, supermarkets, and so on – are outside the old city, and new building within the walls has been mercifully sparse, so it is still possible to lose yourself in a tangle of narrow lanes. Even Ledra Street, originally the main shopping street, is nothing like a modern thoroughfare, and the Laiki Yitonia (Within the Walls, *Map* 6), near Eleftheria Square at the south end of Ledra Street, is a tactfully conceived pedestrian precinct which offers small shops and restaurants with a quiet and intimate air, mostly housed in beautifully reconstructed old houses.

HISTORY

Though Nicosia did not become really important until the Lusignan period, the discovery of Bronze Age tombs shows that the area has been occupied since very early in the history of the island, and people clearly lived here right through the Roman occupation. It seems almost certain that Nicosia stands on the site of the city-state known as Ledra, founded in 280 BC by Lefcon, the son of Ptolemy Soter, the founder of the Ptolemy dynasty of Macedonian kings (Ledra Street, of course, commemorates the theory). It is not until 1192, when two or three hundred Templars fled from a mob and took refuge in a castle here, that we have evidence of the site of Nicosia being fortified. A traveller of the period says that in 1211 a castle existed which housed the rulers of the kingdom. The denizens of the houses that clustered around the castle and beneath the towers of 250 churches were, he writes, wealthy, and lived in luxury comparable only to that of the then famous city of Antioch. During the next century, Pierre II set up the ramparts of Nicosia; but in 1426 the Egyptian Mamelukes nevertheless succeeded in defeating King Janus and taking the city, which they sacked, burning the castle to the ground.

The area was by then established as a major city site, however, and when the Venetians invaded in 1489, they found Nicosia once more a large and prosperous place. They decided upon a new scheme of fortification, and under a Venetian engineer, Francesco Barbaro, new walls were built – the ones that still exist, constructed of stone above great earthworks and with eleven bastions named after prominent Italian families. The work was ruthlessly done: many fine Lusignan buildings vanished to make way for the walls, among them the great Abbey of St Domenico, where for centuries the rulers and great families of Cyprus had been buried. Its remnants lie somewhere underground near the Paphos Gate.

The new defences must have seemed impregnable. The Turkish siege of 1570, not long after their completion, proved otherwise. The defending Venetian Cypriot troops and the civilian population suffered fearfully when the Turks broke through – it is said that altogether about 20,000 men, women and children were killed, and under the most horrific circumstances. The churches were wrecked and used for storage, great breaches in the walls made them useless, and much of the city was ruined.

Nicosia took almost three centuries to recover any degree of prosperity, let alone pride. Visitors from Europe in the seventeenth, eighteenth and nineteenth centuries found the place a virtual slum, only a few private gardens making a pleasant refuge from the stinking filth of most of the city. And it was not only the fabric of the place that was in a state of wreckage; the citizens were demoralised and often infernally treated – occasionally to such a degree that they revolted against their rulers, as in 1764, when they turned on the Turkish governor and killed him. But the Turks for the most part kept the upper hand: in 1821, for instance, another governor rounded up 200 Christians and slaughtered them, confiscating their property.

Whatever some patriots may have thought at the time, it must surely be asserted that it was only after the raising of the British flag in Nicosia in July 1878 by Vice-Admiral Lord Hope that reasonably civilised government returned to the city and the island. Not that

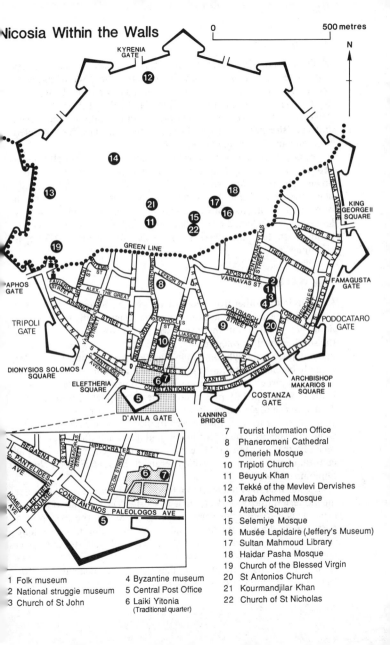

Nicosia Within the Walls

0   500 metres

KYRENIA GATE

⑫

N

⑭

⑬

ATHENA AVENUE

KING GEORGE II SQUARE

⑱
㉑ ⑰
⑯
⑪ ⑮
㉒

⑲

GREEN LINE

APHOS GATE

ARTEMIS ST
PANIKRATIS ST
ANTIEROS STREET
ALEX. THE GREAT
LEFTON ST
PHANEROMENI STREET
APOSTOLOS VARNAVAS ST
PENTADAKTYLOS
THESEUS STREET
FAMAGUSTA ST

②
①
③
④

FAMAGUSTA GATE

TRIPOLI GATE

ARSINOE STREET
VASILEIOS VOULGAROCTONOS STREET
⑧
SOPHOCLES ST
LIASIDES STREET
⑩
TRIKOUPI STREET

PATRIARCH GREGORIOS STREET
⑨

KORAES ST
SOLONOS ST
⑳

IPHICRATES ST

PODOCATARO GATE

DIONYSIOS SOLOMOS SQUARE

PANTELIDES AVENUE

HIPPOCRATES ST
XANTHIS
SOLON STREET
CONSTANTINOS PALEOLOGOS

AGHLAUROU AVENUE

ARCHBISHOP MAKARIOS II SQUARE

ELEFTHERIA SQUARE

⑥⑦
⑤

COSTANZA GATE

D'AVILA GATE

KANNING BRIDGE

REGAENA ST
C. PANTELIDESA AVE
HOMER AVE
ELEFTHERIA SQUARE
TRIKOUPIS
ONASAGORAS ST
HIPPOCRATES STREET
SOLON STREET
⑥⑦
CONSTANTINOS PALEOLOGOS AVE
⑤

1 Folk museum
2 National struggle museum
3 Church of St John
4 Byzantine museum
5 Central Post Office
6 Laiki Yitonia (Traditional quarter)
7 Tourist Information Office
8 Phaneromeni Cathedral
9 Omerieh Mosque
10 Tripioti Church
11 Beuyuk Khan
12 Tekké of the Mevlevi Dervishes
13 Arab Achmed Mosque
14 Ataturk Square
15 Selemiye Mosque
16 Musée Lapidaire (Jeffery's Museum)
17 Sultan Mahmoud Library
18 Haidar Pasha Mosque
19 Church of the Blessed Virgin
20 St Antonios Church
21 Kourmandjilar Khan
22 Church of St Nicholas

trouble ceased, of course; the British may have been, on balance, less oppressive than the Turks, but all Cypriots did not see it that way, and in 1931 Government House was burned down by mobs supporting the Bishops of Citium and Kyrenia. In the 1950s anti-British demonstrations gave way to that open hostility between the Greek and Turkish citizens which still simmers today as they live separated from one another by the Green Line.

The city within the ancient walls is neither dapper nor well-preserved: many old houses near the Green Line have fallen or been torn down, and there are what look like bomb-sites (actually simply neglected patches of ground in which no one is interested). Yet much of Nicosia retains its character, and if the southern half of the city looks in part neglected rather than preserved, much of the old city is being renovated, and Laiki Yitonia (*Map* 6), devoid of traffic, is charming.

THE WALLS

Once, as in that other troubled walled town of Londonderry, it was a splendid experience to pace out the whole length of the walls; this is no longer possible, but the visitor will find it worth walking around the southern walls, which remain much as they were when they were laid out in 1570, though sometimes (they are so substantial) they have actually become part of a ring road! Some parts of the moat below have been turned into pleasure gardens and parks. The *Paphos Gate* is the most completely preserved of the original city entrances (the *Famagusta* and *Kyrenia Gates* have suffered as a result of modification in order to cater for modern traffic – the latter is now set like some extraneous monument in the middle of a traffic island). But recently the Famagusta Gate has been restored as a municipal cultural centre – a project which received the 1986 Europa Nostra Diploma of Merit.

Just south of the Famagusta Gate, on the ramparts, is an interesting modern statue, *The Poet*, made by Costas Varotsos out of broken glass. It is a strange but very successful piece. On the *Podocataro Gate* stands the Liberty Memorial, commemorating Cyprus's long struggle for independence, and the martyrs of that struggle. It is perhaps over-grandiloquent, but undeniably effective: two soldiers raise a portcullis, and lifesized figures struggle dazedly towards freedom from the darkness of their prison cells. On the *Costanza* bastion, to the south, are the remains of a mosque said to mark the spot where the first Turkish standard was set up at the siege of 1570 by a man called Bayraktar, whose tomb is close by. The Central Post Office (*Map* 5), the nearby Municipal Library and the town hall (c.1930) stand actually on the other southern bastion, the *D'Avila*.

MUSEUMS

The Cyprus Museum (Outside the Walls, *Map* 1)

The Cyprus Museum lies outside the walls in Museum Street, not far from the Paphos Gate. It grew out of a private collection established in 1883 by Captain H. H. Kitchener, a thirty-three year-old British army officer employed on survey work on the island, who was its first curator. Later he was to be famous as the conqueror of the Sudan and, as Earl Kitchener, Secretary for War between 1914 and 1916. In 1908 his small collection became the core of a national museum supported out of public funds as a memorial to Queen Victoria. It has been twice enlarged, most recently by the building of an annexe and the roofing of a courtyard. A project for an entirely new museum building was shelved at the time of the Turkish invasion, when a number of the best and most valuable exhibits was removed to Athens for safekeeping; they have now been returned.

It would be unhelpful to provide a room-by-room description of the exhibits, because (as with so many museums at a time when all curators are much concerned with improving their displays) they are very often moved about, and are rarely in the same place for very long. A descriptive leaflet and guide should be available at the information desk, and there are short explanatory essays posted at the entrance to each room.

The museum is certainly crucial to an understanding of the island's history, and there are many fascinating things to be seen here, the earliest dating from the Neolithic Age (stone, bone and flint tools and religious objects). Many of the most fascinating exhibits are of religious origin, amongst them the votive figures found at Ayia Irini: minotaur fertility-symbols; male and hermaphrodite figures wearing helmets, from the seventh and sixth centuries BC.

Some of the bronzes (dating from the early Bronze Age to the Roman period, and most often of bulls, stags and birds) are extremely sensitive and, interestingly, seem related to other similar bronzes which have survived from other cultures.

There are many statues, too – Cypriot sculptors seemed to prefer carving 'in the round' to relief-work. There are some wonderful limestone heads dating from the fourth century BC, a fine nude Aphrodite from Soli (second century BC), and a huge and magnificent figure of Septimus Severus – the Afro-Roman emperor who died at York in AD 211 – ploughed up by a farmer at Kythrea. Much material from Salamis is exhibited, including some handsome life-size and more than life-size figures: the Apollo with his lyre found in many pieces in a swimming-pool, and carefully reconstructed; the Farnese Hercules from the second century AD; Asklepius, god of medicine; a grave, poised head of Aphrodite carved by a Greek sculptor working at the court of the king of Salamis in the fourth century BC, her lips half-parted as if to speak. The Aphrodite of Soli is a lovely little figure: a girl who might be seen today, if one was lucky, strolling along the beach at Petra tou Romiou – though for all her beauty she has the air of an independent spirit with whom it would be unwise to take liberties. On a smaller scale still there is a beautiful little carved chalcedony gemstone found in the palaestra of the gymnasium at Salamis: a finely carved lion, signed by Hyllos, the well-known jeweller who made it.

Here, too, is much material found in the necropolis of Salamis, including a handsome throne which was one of three found in Tomb 79. It is impossible, looking at it, not to compare it with some of the more fabulous treasure from Tutankhamun's tomb – and indeed there is an Egyptian connection. The wood of this throne was completely decayed, but it was entirely covered by thin ivory plaques, which survived, so that it has been possible to reconstruct it as a handsome piece of furniture, part of which is a carving of a sphinx in gilt cloisonné work inlaid with blue and brown paste, wearing the crowns of Upper and Lower Egypt and walking in a field of stylised flowers. This chair is surely one of the most interesting single objects to be seen in Cyprus: a direct and vivid link to the past, reminding one irresistibly of Homer's description of Penelope's throne. Near by is what must have been an equally magnificent bed, and there are other beautiful carved ivory plaques, some of which formed part of it. They show among other things the seated figure of the god Heh, holding a branch of a palm-tree from which hangs the Egyptian good-luck symbol the *ankh*. Much of the decoration of the ivory furniture is highlighted by thin sheets of gold. There is a magnificent bronze cauldron near by, and some trappings from the funeral chariots and the harnesses of the horses that drew them. Below this room are some excellent reproductions of rock-tombs, just as they were found, in which some of the items found in them – including skeletons – are placed.

The Bronze Age terracotta figures are specially worth noting: some for their social interest – there are three small representations of women giving birth, the midwife kneeling in front of them while a friend supports them from the rear. In the same room are simple but undeniably comic figures of men and women relaxing – one in what seems to be a deckchair – and there are some crude representations of women, some holding children, which are uniquely tender and touching. Elsewhere is an extraordinary representation of a religious scene, a whole round courtyard or corral in which a ceremony is taking place: mysterious figures stand or sit, there are beasts waiting to be slain, and perhaps a human child, held in its mother's arms worryingly near the sacrificial enclosure. A man has climbed the wall and peers over it, as eager as we are to discover just what is going on. In a near-by case is a model of oxen, ploughing. Equally revealing of its time, ages hence, and in another way, is a Grecian pot on which there is a little scene of seduction – a man makes a pass at another's boyfriend, while a third looks on quizzically. The attempt to censor the pot by painting out the seducer's phallus hasn't worked. Do not miss, incidentally, another landmark in erotic art – the mosaic of Leda and the swan, from a Roman house at Palea Paphos, Leda looking unmistakably miffed at the attentions of an extremely persistent bird.

There are one or two facsimiles for sale in the museum shop, but postcards and reproductions are infuriatingly few, and the Cypriot Antiquities Department's habit of sloppy and poor labelling is almost as prevalent here as elsewhere. All the same, this is not a collection to be missed.

The Byzantine Museum (Within the Walls, *Map* 4)

This museum forms part of the Cultural Centre in Archbishop Kyprianos St, and should certainly be visited for its collection of icons, one of the finest in the world. It consists of 144 icons from the whole island, covering the period from the eighth century to the eighteenth, each one a wonderful example of Byzantine art. Those who complain that icons 'all look alike' miss the point: the icon was always primarily a religious rather than an artistic object – a medium through which the worshipper could communicate with the person shown: Christ, the Virgin or the Saints. The artist was particularly concerned to depict a *likeness*, so he always copied faithfully the characteristics of previous portraits; and indeed one can recognise, say, St Peter, from icon to icon.

Nevertheless, inevitably the icons also reflect their periods: seeing Flemish hats in a sixteenth-century icon of St Nicholas, we realise that at the time it was painted Flemish merchants were visiting Nicosia. The pictures of the donors also reflect fashions in jewellery and clothing.

The earliest icon here dates from the eighth or ninth century – the Virgin painted in melted wax mixed with colours; but it was in the twelfth century that icon-painting reached its apogee – the wealthy military governors brought famous painters from Constantinople whose work endures in a few examples.

Every visitor will have a personal favourite: among the most beautiful icons are those of Christ, St Eleftherios and St Paraskevi, painted in 1356 (Nos. 46–8), and the fifteenth-century processional icon of the Virgin and the Deposition of Christ (Nos. 65a, 65b)) from Kalopanayiotis; but it is difficult to resist St Mamas (No. 29), painted in about 1500, riding on a somewhat quizzical lion, the tip of its tongue protruding as though it is not entirely sure that lunch may not, after all, yet take place.

The collection of European pictures upstairs may safely be ignored: those that are not insignificant are copies.

The Folk Museum (*Map* 1)
Near the Byzantine Museum, and just north of the Church of St John, is a Folk Museum, established on the ground floor of a fourteenth-century monastery building known as the Old Archbishopric (notice the sheep dozing happily under a palm tree in the marble panel at the head of the outside staircase). Perhaps most interesting are the costumes and embroidery, showing just how ancient and established this art is on the island; but there is plenty to show how the Cypriots of only a couple of generations ago were still living.

CHURCHES AND MOSQUES

The Church of St John (*Map* 3)
Also known as Ayios Ioannis, this is the church of the Orthodox archbishopric, and lies next to the archiepiscopal palace and the

Byzantine Museum. It stands on the site of the Benedictine Abbey of St John of Bibi, which was left empty when the Benedictines departed in 1426, taking with them one of St John the Evangelist's fingers, of which they were the custodians. The Orthodox Church adopted the building, and in 1665 it was repaired; later, the walls and ceiling were decorated with paintings which – though very late by Cypriot standards – have a colourful exuberance; the terrifying Day of Judgment above the south door and the delightful Creation on the north side are worth seeing, as is the graphic account of the discovery of the tomb of St Barnabas, on the right of the archbishop's throne. These paintings have, over the years, been blackened by candle-smoke until they are almost indecipherable; restoration has now started, and where it has been completed (entirely without repainting, it should be emphasised) the paintings are seen in all the glory of their original colours.

The Omerieh Mosque (*Map* 9)
This was originally a fourteenth-century Augustinian church, the shrine of St John de Montfort, who accompanied Louis IX (St Louis) to the Fourth Crusade but died here in 1249. The church was badly damaged during the siege: the west door and a chapel on the west side, now used by Muslim women, are the remains of the original building. Mustapha Pasha recognised the church, the moment he set eyes on it in 1571, as the site of the resting-place of the prophet Omar, and designated it as such.

The Phaneromeni Cathedral (*Map* 8)
Built in the seventeenth century, this cathedral was repaired in 1872, using old stone and making use of various fragments of earlier buildings, including some fairly obnoxious gargoyles. The bishops slaughtered by the Turks in 1821 (see p. 66) are buried here.

The Tripioti Church (*Map* 10)
This is one of the most impressive Greek Orthodox churches, and dates – as may be seen in an inscription over the door – from 1690; as with the Phaneromeni Church, its builders used many pieces of stone from earlier buildings.

St Antonios Church (*Map* 20)
A church with a nicely carved gallery and a pulpit reached by a stone staircase so narrow as to be barely negotiable by a choirboy, let alone

a bishop. Ticking time away in a corner is a rather endearing clock with a wooden ship rocking its way across a painted ocean. (A solemn tick-tock is to be heard in most Cypriot churches.)

There are several other churches in Nicosia, but none of such note that the tourist need feel bound to visit them.

LARNACA

Hotels

Five-star: the Palm Beach (tel. 57500) is a large hotel 7 km. from Larnaca, and has its own private beach. It offers regular live music, as does the Golden Bay Hotel (23444), on the beach 3 km. east of Larnaca. Besides the usual amenities, it has 'studio suites' available at a supplement.

Four-star: the Sandy Beach Hotel (24333), on the beach 8 km. from the centre of the town. The Sun Hall Hotel (53341) is on the promenade opposite Larnaca marina.

Three-star: the Beau Rivage Hotel (23600) is on the beach 6.5 km. from the town centre. The Lordos Beach (57444) is on the beach 7 km. from the town centre. The Karpasiana Beach (55001) is 8 km. from Larnaca, and offers conventional rooms, luxury suites, and first-floor 'bungalows'. It has a resident band. The Four Lanterns (52011) is on Athens Avenue, overlooking the promenade and virtually in the main shopping area. It was the first real hotel to be built in Larnaca, and retains a pleasantly Edwardian air. The Flamingo Beach Hotel (21621) is relatively small, ten minutes' drive from the airport and half an hour's walk from the town shopping centre. The Sveltos Hotel (27100), 6.4 km. from Larnaca, is fifteen minutes' walk from the beach.

Two-star: the Cactus Hotel (27400) is ten minutes' walk from the beach, but only twenty minutes from Larnaca promenade and Castle, and is nearest to the centre of town. The Three Seas Hotel (0442 291) is in the country on the road to Cape Kiti near the village of Perivolia, twenty-five minutes from the airport. The Miriandy Hotel (23333) is on the Larnaca–Dhekelia road ten minutes' motoring time from town.

Apartments

Class A: Michael's Beach Hotel apartments (21100) are next to the Karpasiana Hotel. The Atrium Zenon apartments (21400) are right in the centre of town, and opened in 1987. There is a swimming pool on the roof. Stavros Hotel apartments (23000) are 300 metres from the sea, 6.5 km. from Larnaca. Corinthia Beach Hotel apartments (24037) are 11 km. from Larnaca airport, on the beach next to the Larnaca–Dhekelia road.

Others: Sun Hall Hotel apartments (21400) are attached to the hotel (above). The Paschalis/Golden Bay apartments (27222) are 300 metres from the beach 7 km. from the centre of town. Tsialis Hotel apartments (24550) are 100 metres from the beach in the centre of Larnaca Bay, near the main Larnaca–Dhekelia road. Adonis apartments (56644) are 1.6 km. south of Larnaca, next to the Adonis Fish and Kebab Taverna. The Acropolis Hotel apartments (23700) are in Larnaca, five minutes' walk from the sea. Pasithea apartments (54980) are on a hill overlooking the Salt Lake almost 5 km. from the town. Golden Bay Hotel apartments (21377) are also 5 km. from Larnaca, 350 metres from the beach. Constantinia Beach apartments (21300) are 3.2 km. from Larnaca, in a tourist area with many tavernas and bars. Socoriky Sea Gardens (0442 2401) are on the beach in a small complex of their own.

Some restaurants
Eracles, in the Municipal Gardens; the Flamingo Restaurant on the salt lake, near the Tekké; the Militzis, Niale Pasha St; Monte Carlo, Niale Pasha St; Cyprus Sky, 1st April St, has marvellous kebabs in pitta bread – extraordinary value at 50c.

Some tavernas
Arhontico, Athens St; Scala Tavern, Artemidos Avenue.

Some nightclubs
Golden Night (bouzoukia), Galileos St; Acapulco (cabaret), Hermes St; New Chiquito (cabaret), Timayia Avenue; Fantasia Cabaret, Timayia Avenue; the Pink Piano, Limassol road.

Cinemas
Attikon, Kyr, Matsis St; Othellos, Ay Eleni St; Rex, Democria St; Vassiliades Andreas, Z. Kitieus St.

The marina
Larnaca has the most accessible marina in the island, close to the centre of town. About 400 boats are permanently moored there, some never having put to sea since the marina opened in 1976. Berthing charges range from 13c to 17c per metre per day, plus water and electricity charges. Telephone 53110; telex 357.4500 Cytmar; VHF call-sign LARNACA MARINA, Channel 16 (work ch. 8), 07.30–20.00 local time. Reservations must be made at least eight months before estimated time of arrival. Security is extremely tight at the marina, where Arab terrorists murdered two Jews a few years ago.

Tourist Information Office
This is in Democratias Square, near the north end of the seafront (54322) (*Map* 2).

HISTORY

The population of Larnaca has more than doubled during the past twenty years, and since its airport – once a small field on which shaky landings were made in the 1930s, now best-known as the major point of communication with the war-torn Lebanon – has become the main entry-point for most of Cyprus's tourists, it has become perhaps the island's most important town.

This is not a fact you would readily assume on sight of the 'promenade' – Athens St – which leads from the Customs House at its north end to the charming little fort at the south. The straggling palm trees fringe a decidedly unattractive beach, and the many beachside restaurants and tavernas have a seedy look about them (though there is good Greek food to be had at most). Perhaps the best time to visit the area is after dark on a warm evening, when the lights and the bustle give it a gay and friendly air, and there are certainly some excellent restaurants west of the fort, still on the seafront.

Town Plan of Larnaca

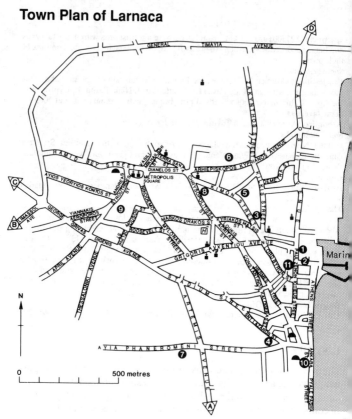

1 Central Post Office
2 Tourist Information Office
3 District museum
4 Church of St Lazarus
5 The Citium acropolis
6 Ancient Citium site
7 Phaneromeni Church
8 Ancient Citium site
9 Ancient tomb
10 The Fortress
11 The Pierides Collection

Routes to
A Larnaca International Airport
B Limassol
C Nicosia
D Ayia Napa, Paralimni, Dhekeli

Ⓗ Hospital
◣ Mosque
✝ Church

Nevertheless, it is difficult to visualise Larnaca as the elegant Citium of ancient Cyprus, a Mycenaean city founded on trade with the Phoenicians. The city took the wrong side in the Graeco-Persian war on the island, and was sacked by forces under the great Greek statesman and general, Cimon, who was killed during the siege (in 450 BC).

During its less prosperous period, Larnaca was distinguished as the birthplace of Zeno, a Phoenician born here in 335 BC, whose father sent him to Athens on business. There he studied philosophy and applied severe commonsense to the theories of the time, mistrusting (as it were) the reality of any philosophical concept he could not actually kick. He virtually founded the Stoic school of philosophers, and his bust – copied in 1921 from the only known likeness, found in Herculaneum – stands in his home town.

When Famagusta fell under the rule of the Genoese, Larnaca became additionally important, and it was from its port that most pilgrims embarked for the Holy Land. It was in the mid-1600s that a small English colony was established here, and since then the town has maintained its connections with the English who obviously set out to enjoy themselves from the start, joining happily in local festivals – a group of young chaps were arrested in 1681 for racketing around the bazaars in women's clothing. Others were happier to enjoy experimenting with the local food, and gathering for evenings of music and polite conversation.

The history of Larnaca from 1700 onward is one of steady growth in trade and tourism; trade has much increased since the Turkish invasion, though Limassol also has a large share.

MUSEUMS

The District Museum (*Map* 3)

The District Museum is at the north end of Lord Byron St, at the junction with Kimon St and Kilkis St. It is a small, modern building, where the exhibits are well lit and displayed (some, as we write, are still in course of arrangement). In the gallery to the left of the entrance is a collection of sculpture, with some fine male heads (one, lively and humorous, from Pergamos), a sensitive head of Tyche from Arsos (of which she was goddess), and a stern veiled head of a woman with dark, deep-set eyes – an obvious portrait. Some of these heads still bear traces of bright paint. A case near by holds a very abstract terracotta mother and child which might have been made by Picasso; among other items is a lovely little sixth-century sphinx.

Across the hall, two rooms have cases of Bronze Age seals. There is a wonderful ninth-century BC king and queen in a chariot drawn by three horses – the left-hand one tossing its head slightly; and here too is an ivory Bes – the ugly Egyptian dwarf-god of childbirth – from a Citium temple, and very fierce he looks.

The Pierides Collection (*Map* 11)

The tourist interested in history should also visit the Swedish Consulate in Paul Zenon Kitieus St, which runs parallel to the harbour front. It houses the Pierides Collection, which was gathered in the second half of the last century by Demetrios Pierides and enlarged by other members of the family until, in 1974, it was completed. It contains over 3,000 pieces and is open to the public on weekday mornings between 9 a.m and 1 p.m.

Here is all the impedimenta of the enthusiastic and civilised nineteenth-century amateur collector fascinated by the history of his country. There are many terracotta figures, including some displaying the usual robust Bronze Age humour: the most important – perhaps the most important in the country, and certainly the largest Chalcolithic figure yet found – is the model of a nude man, *c.* 3900–2500 BC, seated on a four-legged stool with his elbows on his knees, his hands at his cheeks, and his mouth open. Water (or wine?) poured into his mouth would emerge through his prominent penis. Other terracotta figures show a slyer but no less infectious enjoyment of cartoon or caricature; or sometimes just a joyful sense of pleasure in life – see the pot with antlered deer perched on its sides. (This humour and extravert pleasure are a great feature of the Bronze Age terracotta figures at the Cyprus Museum in Nicosia – especially in Room XV, where men lounge in deckchairs or reel drunkenly about, and several of the female figures are so touching and amusing that one has to laugh aloud with them.) But there are extremely serious figures here, too – a seventh-century BC goddess, for instance, hands uplifted to bless, and an eighth-century BC warrior with a club almost as big as himself.

Some of the carvings are fine: the fourth-century BC funerary statue of a seated young man, for instance, holding a dove; the head of an equally handsome boy of the same period, crowned with fruits; and a Hellenistic limestone head of a sombre woman.

CHURCHES

The Church of St Lazarus (*Map* 4)

After Lazarus had been raised from the dead, he was thrown out of Bethany by the Jews (perhaps troubled by the publicity?) and sailed in a rather untrustworthy boat, accompanied by his sisters Mary and Martha, to Citium, where he became Bishop before eventually dying for the second and last time. He was buried in a tomb which was miraculously revealed to local churchmen eight centuries later, when his body was exhumed and sent to Constantinople, whence it was eventually stolen by the French and shipped to Marseilles. St Lazarus Church was built in the ninth century by the Emperor Leo VI over the empty tomb; you can descend to see two marble sarcophagi which some experts unsportingly allege were an import from a near-by necropolis; one is told firmly that on one of these – the larger of the two – are carved the Greek words: LAZARUS, THE FRIEND OF CHRIST. But since the phrase is actually nowhere to be seen, there is no telling what the truth may be.

Though the Turks banned bell-towers on the grounds that they might be used to signal uprisings, there is one here, and a very handsome one, too, nicely decorated and glowing pale gold in the sun. It stands above a sturdy cloister with strong columns, square on the outside but with threefold round pillars on the inside, and rough vaulting. The church has a pretty wooden balcony for women at the west end, three aisles and four heavy columns with Corinthian capitals presumably installed during the seventeenth-century renovation, some time after the church had been repurchased from the Turks to be used for both Latin and Orthodox rites. The columns are all split, and the gilt rococo pulpit is reached by a stairway within the thickness of one of them. At the front of the pulpit a carved hand supports a fluttering dove, and, opposite, above a fine icon of the Virgin and Child, a serpent stretches out its head to support a lamp. After a fire a few years ago, the insensitively plastered interior was stripped and the original stonework revealed; this is now a noble and dignified church, and one of the most beautiful on the island.

Other churches

There are several other churches in Larnaca – the seventeenth-century *Church of St John the Divine*, and those of *Santa Maria della Gratia*, *Chryssopolitissa*, *Chryssostiros* and *Phaneromeni*. Although they are less interesting than the *Church of St Lazarus*, *Chryssopoli-tissa* has some good nineteenth-century icons and a pulpit reached by a vertiginous ladder; and the new *Church of St George*, on the Nicosia road, completed and opened in March 1987, which holds 1,800 worshippers, has good modern icons and carvings brought from Greece.

CITIUM

Ancient Citium (sometimes spelt Kitium) lies beneath the modern town of Larnaca, peeping above ground only where excavation has proved possible – built-up areas make excavation difficult, and it has only been at isolated intervals that work has been able to proceed. In 1930 *figures of Hercules* were found amid the remnants of what seems to have been an open-air temple; in 1963 a Hellenistic *bath-house* was discovered near St Chryssopolitissa Church (with evidence of much earlier, Bronze Age activity), and between 1967 and 1968 excavations uncovered twelfth-century *Mycenaean workshops* and an eighth-century BC Phoenician *Temple of Astarte*, the fertility goddess who was worshipped under various names throughout the Middle East, and was so disliked by the Christians that she ended up as a demon, and one of the fallen angels in *Paradise Lost*.

The most interesting site, where work is continuing, is to be found at the top of Kilkis St; turn left behind the English cemetery through Pampulas St and a housing estate. The site is an incoherent one (though an excellent guide is obtainable). The earliest remains seem to be of about the thirteenth century BC, and there are several temples, the first built in about 1200 BC. All these buildings were probably destroyed during a severe earthquake in 1075 BC; *Temple I* was eventually reconstructed as a temple to Astarte. The god and goddess of the Copper Ingot were worshipped here, too, and there is a direct reference to Hephaistos, the lame Smith-god to whom Zeus gave Aphrodite in marriage, and who forged a gossamer-thin net in which to catch her betraying him with her lover Ares.

There have been excavations near by which in the 1960s produced some of the pottery, alabaster and jewellery to be seen at the District Museum, but the whole site of Citium was very badly damaged by the British in 1879, who ploughed up the entire upper strata to fill in a near-by marsh where malaria mosquitoes were breeding.

The fact that the site of the five temples which have so far been

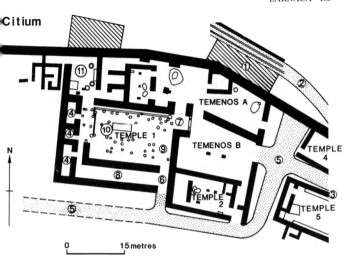

Citium

TEMENOS A

TEMENOS B

TEMPLE 1

TEMPLE 4

TEMPLE 2

TEMPLE 5

N

0   15 metres

1	City wall	6/7	Ceremonial entrances
2	City street	8	Corridor
3	Site of city gate	9	Courtyard
4	Holy of holies	10	Sacred pool
5	Street	11	Copper workshops

found has been so often-re-used makes it all the more difficult for us to comprehend it. But there can be no doubt of its importance. At the north edge of the site (**1**) run the remains of Citium's *city wall*, originally made of mud bricks bastioned with limestone blocks. *Temples 2 and 3*, the latter not shown on the plan because it was later built over, were contemporary with this first wall, and had a small courtyard to the east and a holy of holies to the west. Walking in *Temple 2* you can still tell that it was divided into a central aisle with two porticoes and two rows of three columns (their bases remain). Inside the courtyard of *Temple 1* there are a number of small circular pits connected to a water system; these probably held the roots of the plants and trees of a sacred garden or grove (as at the *Sanctuary of Apollo*, see p. 133).

These remains are all of buildings abandoned by the end of the thirteenth century BC. Other, more substantial remains are of buildings erected in about 1200 BC, when the mud-brick city wall was replaced by one of huge stones – and a street ran around it (**5**). Between *Temples 4 and 5* was a city gate, now entirely vanished. Temple 2 was rebuilt at this time, on the original plan, and on the site of *Temple 3* rose Temple 1, an impressive building with a three-roomed holy of holies (**4**) to the west, each room of which could be entered from the courtyard – which itself could be entered through ceremonial gates (**6**) from the street (**5**) or from *Temenos B* (**7**). A corridor to the south (**8**) was probably used for ceremonial religious processions and there was a sacred garden in the courtyard itself (**9**) where a pool (**10**) may, like the sacred lakes of Egyptian temples, have contained sacred fishes.

North of Temple 1 were *copper-smelting workshops* (**11**) directly communicating with the temple – metallurgy and religion were very closely connected during the late Bronze Age in Cyprus. It was in a well in Temple 4 that the ivory plaque of the Egyptian goddess Bes was found (now in the District Museum), together with an opium pipe.

These buildings were in turn abandoned towards the end of the twelfth century BC; a century and a half later the Phoenicians moved in, and Citium was a Phoenician city until 312 BC; this site remained sacred, and parts of the Temples have Phoenician elements – but not many, for the stones were later looted and used for private building.

EXCURSIONS FROM LARNACA

Remember that any car journey to the north-east of Larnaca will bring you up eventually against the Green Line which separates Cyprus proper from the occupied part of the island. Your car will be stopped at the line, and your only recourse will be to turn back. Do not attempt to photograph the area near the line, or any checkpoints. For bus and taxi services see pp. 20–2.

Larnaca to Ayia Napa and Protarus

Route   Take the coastal road, eastwards around Larnaca Bay for 38 km.

Ayia Napa is now an extremely popular, horrendously overdeveloped tourist resort; the reason for an excursion – apart from the magnificent beaches – remains its beautiful monastery.

Three km. from Larnaca one passes through **Livadhia**, and shortly afterwards a turning on the left leads to the village of **Voroklini**, where olives are grown, and where there are the remains of a quarry once supervised by the French poet Rimbaud, the author of the extraordinary *Le Bâteau Ivre*, who after a brilliant period of creativity in his youth gave up the literary life and vanished from France for sixteen years, during part of which time he worked here. A further 2 km. brings a turning to **Pyla**, where there is a pretty Medieval tower, now a UN observation post. This is the one village in Cyprus where Greek and Turkish Cypriot people live together in perfect amity. Shops here specialise in fashionable international sportswear, though it is technically illegal to buy from Turkish shops. The main coastal road continues to **Dhekelia** past some of the impressive hotels built within the past ten years – the Palm Beach, the Beau Rivage, the Lordos Beach – and passes the British army base, near which is a turning for **Xylotymbou**, a small market-town. In a further 7 km., on the left, is **Ormidhia**, which used to be a popular spring and autumn retreat for Western Europeans in the early nineteenth century. Another 11 km. brings one to **Ayia Napa**, and **Protarus** lies a further short drive east.

Ayia Napa
Hotels
The village has now become a major tourist centre, full of fast-food restaurants and souvenir shops. It has some excellent hotels, amongst which are the following:
  Five-star: the Grecian Bay Hotel (037 21301) is on a beautifully sandy beach in the centre of the bay, set in gardens with mimosa and fruit trees, fifteen minutes' walk from the village.
  Four-star: the Grecian Sands Hotel (21216) is 300 metres from the Grecian Bay, and under the same management. The Nissi Beach Hotel (21021) is five minutes' drive from Ayia Napa, but there are shops near by, a discotheque, taverna, and 'frequent music' – there is also the popular Nissi Beach itself. The Florida Beach (21821) is fifteen minutes' walk from the village and has a freshwater swimming pool. The Asterias Beach Hotel (21901) is 5 km. from Ayia Napa, on Makronissos Beach, backed by open country. The Dome Hotel (21006) is also on Makronissos Beach.
  Three-star: the Mermaid Beach Hotel (21606) is fifteen minutes' walk from the village and monastery, overlooking the beach. The Bella Napa (21601) is 1.6 km. from the village, overlooking the beach.
Apartments
There are perhaps more apartments for rent at Ayia Napa than at any other resort, and the following is an arbitrary selection. The Anesis Hotel apartments (21104) are 200 metres from the beach and harbour. The bungalow-style Karystos Bungalows (21201) are near Sandy Bay Beach, and a restaurant is available. Karas/Eleana Hotel apartments (21640) are opposite the Grecian Bay Hotel, whose bars can be

used. Anthea Hotel apartments (21450) are 500 metres from the harbour. Karousos Hotel apartments (21116) are 'a few minutes' from the sea, and fifteen minutes' walk from Sandy Bay Beach. The complex includes a disco. Takkas Hotel apartments (21026) are five minutes from the sea. Castalia Hotel apartments (21106) are fifteen minutes' walk from sea and village, Kallenos Hotel apartments (21201) somewhat closer. Monte Napa Hotel apartments (21826) are twenty minutes from the beach.

Restaurants and tavernas

There are probably more restaurants and tavernas to the square kilometre here than anywhere else on Cyprus, and they change hands so quickly that it would be pointless to recommend any; apart from which the general view is that while you can perhaps eat more cheaply here than at any other resort, it is equally true that what you eat is unlikely to be memorable. 'Cheap and cheerful' is an accurate description. The near-by beaches often serve one better: above Anemos Beach in Fig Tree Bay, for instance, is one of the best restaurant-bars in the area, open all hours (031–31488).

Monastery of Ayia Napa

Ayia Napa Monastery is architecturally unique, and was among the last buildings to be erected by the Venetians before they left the island in 1570. It sits like a little oasis in the middle of pizza parlours and 'pubs' – the Monastery Café Bar is just opposite! It has been suggested that its design, with a high wall, was contrived to convince any pirates casting avaricious eyes from seaward that it was a fortified castle or palace rather than a place of prayer. There is a free-standing, slim campanile above a church in pinkish stone guarded by a squat and solid two-storey gatehouse. In the courtyard in the middle of this a beautiful fountain spouts water from the four volutes of an Ionic column protected by a dome supported by four more columns, beneath which is shade and rest for the traveller. The water arrives via a fascinating Roman-type aqueduct and, apart from the fountain, also flows from the mouth of a Roman boar's head. There is a tiny folk museum off the cloister, which among other things has some examples of the threshing boards used on the island since prehistoric times – boards set with many flints, which, face-downwards and with the farmer standing on them, were drawn by oxen.

The church has a wide entrance passage with seats along it, whence one goes downstairs into the body of the building, which was partly excavated from rock.

Protarus

At Protarus, immediately to the east of Ayia Napa along the main coastal road, there is another tourist development. Four-star **hotels** are the Sunrise Beach (tel. 031–21501), 500 metres from Fig Tree Bay, from which the area takes its name, and where there are several good tavernas. The hotel is elegant and relatively quiet. The Virissiana Beach Hotel (21216) is one of the few on Cyprus with a moderately interesting design; its beach is excellent, and it is within easy reach of the villages of Ayia Napa and **Paralimni**, to which there is a bus service. The Capo Bay Hotel (22101) is the newest hotel here (1985). **Apartments** for rent include those at Ayios Elias Village (22300), outside Protarus which have a marvellous panoramic view, and there is entertainment in the 'village square', which also has a coffee shop, market and pottery. Melini Hotel apartments (21460) are more conventional. Green Bay Hotel apartments (23333) are 100 metres from a sandy beach, and are quiet, though with some evening entertainment. Panale Hotel apartments (21460) are three minutes from the beach; near-by hotel swimming pools may be used.

FOR WALKERS

There is a very pleasant, easy coastal walk from Potamos – a small estuary west of Ayia Napa – to the town, past **Ayia Thekla**, Makronissos Beach, Nissi Beach and Sandy Bay, turning inland at Ayios Yeoryios to Ayia Napa itself. Three hours should do it: the total distance is about 10 km.

After leaving Ayia Napa you might like to give yourself the melancholy pleasure of driving north to **Dherinia**, then west through **Phrénaros**. Turning right here will bring you on to a road which for 14 km. runs parallel to the border with Occupied Cyprus, a few paces from the Green Line, overlooked by UN troops from their little boxlike lookout posts. A kilometre away, the small town of **Akhyritou** looks grey and deserted.

Larnaca to the Tekké of Hala Sultan and Kiti

Route The Tekké lies 6 km. south of Larnaca off the road to the airport. Kiti is a further 6 km. to the south. To go there from the Tekké drive back to the main road and then turn right.

Take the road south out of Larnaca, which skirts the shores of the large lake which a sixteenth-century traveller, Marco Zuellart, described as 'of about nine miles circuit, in which are springs of salt water which, with waters from the winter rains, and kept enclosed during the summer, by the heat and ardour of the sun, they harden and congeal into a very beautiful salt, white like snow.' Salt is still produced here, and the phenomenon is credited to St Lazarus, who when passing this way was refused some grapes by a local woman and turned the area into a salty marsh as a mark of his displeasure. The lake is the haunt of much bird-life (see p. 42). With its weird landscape of sparkling conical salt-heaps, it also makes a remarkable setting for the *Tekké of Hala Sultan*, standing amid palms and cypresses. To reach the shrine, take a right-hand turning 6 km. from the centre of Larnaca.

The Tekké of Hala Sultan

Ummul Haram (Hala Sultan is the Turkish form of the Arabic name, meaning 'respected mother') was for centuries believed to be the Prophet Mohammed's aunt, but turns out merely to have been the aunt of his secretary, Ana Ibn Malik. She accompanied her husband, Maoayah, governor of Syria, to Cyprus with the Arab army which invaded the island in the late seventh century AD, apparently as a nurse, but also somewhat as a propagandist. Coming ashore, she fell from her mount, broke her neck, and was buried on the spot. For some time, it is recorded, a fifteen-ton meteoric stone brought to Cyprus by angels from Mount Sinai hovered miraculously in the air over her grave, but eventually settled into position on top of two almost equally large upright stones (also supernaturally transported to the spot). The shrine as we now see it, beautifully set in an Eastern garden with flowering shrubs and trees and sounding with bird-song, was landscaped in 1816 by Seyyit Mohammet Emin, then Turkish governor of Cyprus. The mosque he built lies under an eighteenth-century dome now in rather poor condition, containing the mihrab and with the pierced wooden shelter for women worshippers on its balcony. The inner sanctuary contains the tomb itself, covered by gold-embroidered cloths. Also buried here, in the arcade of the mosque, is the Turkish second wife of King Hussein of the Hedjaz, who died in 1929, and there is a commemorative monument to Baldassare Trivizani, the Venetian lieutenant-governor of the island between 1489 and 1491.

Until comparatively recently, all Turkish ships passing the island close enough to see the dome of the mosque would dip their flags and fire a salute, for this is one of the three holiest Muslim shrines (Mecca and the shrine of Mohammed at Medina are the other two).

Kiti

Kiti is a village which has claimed association with Citium, but in reality it was nothing to do with that ancient city. The *Church of Panayia Angeloktisti* is a handsome building with a high nave and a lantern dome beneath a conical cap. It was originally built in the eleventh century on the foundations of a fifth-century building said to have been constructed with angelic assistance, and it contains the finest mosaic in Cyprus, and one of the finest anywhere. This great mosaic – surviving from the fifth-century building – shows the Virgin and the Child on her arm, guarded by the Archangels Michael and Gabriel, bearing orbs and sceptres as a sign of rank, their wings a sheen of feathers. The Archangel Gabriel is, sadly, much damaged. There has been some controversy about the dating of the mosaic, but it is unlikely to be later than the eighth century, and is probably two centuries older.

The church was badly damaged by fire some time ago, and villagers, repairing it, painted over some of the fine frescoes. These are now being painstakingly uncovered and restored, where possible – a wonderful, wild St John can be seen on the east face of the northern pillar of the nave. In the little fourteenth-century chapel of *Ayii Anarghyri*, on the north side of the church, is part of a splendid fresco of St George and the Dragon. The southern Latin chapel (used as a school until 1908) contains a fine selection of rather damaged icons, including an impressive St John the Theologian (apparently suffering from a serious toothache) and an Archangel Michael repainted since the fourteenth century, but wonderfully original, with an asymmetrical, oval face which gives the pose life. There is also here a tombstone bearing a portrait of the Lady Simone, who died on 5 November 1302.

The church should be open between 8 a.m. and 5 p.m. If it is closed, the key may be had from the owner of the house which faces the south side of it, who should also be prepared to switch on the lights so that you can see the mosaic properly.

Larnaca to Stavrovouni Monastery, Pyrga and Kornos

Route For Stavrouvouni take the main road to Limassol, passing the Roman aqueduct on your left, then the turning for Klavdhia (9 km.), driving on through Anglisidhes (19 km.), and taking the sharp right-hand turning just before Kophinou

(29 km.). In 11 km. there is a right-hand turning which in 10 km. leads to the monastery itself, on the summit of a hill. [NB: Though visitors are always welcome, women are only allowed to enter the monastery buildings on Sundays between 10 a.m. and 12.30 p.m. However, the magnificent view alone makes the visit worthwhile.] Returning to the main road, turn right, in the direction of Nicosia, and in 2 km. take the right-hand turning signposted Pyrga (1 km.). Pleasant driving here, among the olive-groves. Turn back to the crossroads, and continue over the main road to Kornos.

Stavrovouni Monastery

High on one of the three hills in Cyprus called 'Mount Olympus' – over 600 metres above sea-level – the monastery is reached by a road which twists and turns through hairpin bends which demand a driver's full attention. The lower slopes of the hill are often used by the army, and a soldier may well leap from the hedge and order you to stop for a while, while he radios his colleagues to cease spraying the area with live ammunition. He will probably speak no English; it is advisable to obey without argument whatever you take to be his instructions.

Stavrovouni Monastery was built on the site of a Temple to Aphrodite, traces of which are still to be seen. But the goddess gave place to a superior force when St Helena brought the True Cross to the island in AD 327. The story of Helena and the True Cross is a fascinating one, though it originated only at the end of the fourth century, and is therefore likely to be largely fictitious. Whatever the truth of the matter, it is said that this humbly born woman who became the wife of the Emperor Constantius I Chlorus and the mother of Constantine the Great found the Cross on which Christ was crucified and the Cross of the Penitent Thief in Palestine, and brought them both to Cyprus on her way back from Jerusalem to Constantinople. Her voyage was a troubled one, and after surviving a particularly vicious storm she donated a piece of the True Cross and the entire second cross to a group of monks, with instructions that they should build a monastery in which the relics could be deposited. This was done, in 327, and the monastery of 'The Mountain of the Cross' has been a place of pilgrimage ever since, some visitors being vouchsafed the sight of the entire Cross suspended miraculously in the air above the monastery.

It is of course impossible to trace the pedigree of the cross still venerated here; the original was at one time stolen by a monk, and the monastery was severely damaged by the Arabs in 1426, the remains being burned by the Turks in 1570; the site was only reoccupied in the seventeenth century – so the original cross seems unlikely to have survived (unless of course it was hidden, and if that were so one would have expected the fact to be proudly recorded). One is shown a cross which is dated 1476, but still claimed to be that of the Penitent Thief (there seems to be a mistake somewhere). It is set in silver with a gold frame containing a tiny fragment of wood alleged to be a piece of the True Cross. (There are several of these on the island, and it is fair to point out that enough of them are preserved in various parts of the world to build a small church.)

Parking below the monastery (in a car-park which must have one of the best, most panoramic views of any in the world), walk up a fairly steep flight of stone steps to the monastery itself, entering the courtyard where a door on your left should be open. Whether or not there is anyone around, walk boldly in and up the facing stairs, which lead through a doorway into a tiny courtyard where three bells hang from a tower. Ahead is the *Church of the Cross*, a nineteenth-century building, though there are older fragments of masonry about it – including a piece of wall on which an eleventh-century monk scratched a prayer. A monk is at present at work frescoing the whole interior, a task which will no doubt take some time (see p. 40). The small chapel of the monastery seems to be permanently closed, and there will probably be no point in taking the advice of a large notice advising you (in Greek) to ring the bell outside if you wish to see it.

The monks here are said to have 'invented' the sultana – or at least to have been the first to cultivate the sultana grape; the fine clear honey they produce is almost as famous as the Stavrovouni cats, originally brought in to control the snake population. Icons are also painted here, and make acceptable souvenirs of a visit.

For Walkers

There is a fine walk from a point near the little *Monastery of Ayia Varvara* to the *Monastery of Stavrovouni*. You need a car or taxi to reach Ayia Varvara, as there are no buses; the walk starts opposite the signpost marked '**Spitoudhia**'. It should take no more than an hour, partly on a rough track and partly on the motor road. The hill up to the monastery is not in fact as vertiginous as it appears. The total distance to the monastery is 6.5 km.; you can return either along the same route, or by the motor road.

Pyrga

The 'Royal' *Chapel of St Catherine*, a sweet little nut of a church built in rough stone by King Janus in 1412, stands next to the large modern church of St Marina (completed in 1982). Its barrel-vault is marked with the Lusignan coat-of-arms, and there are three doors, the south one with a little belfry above it. The building must have been a brave sight in its heyday, with a bell hanging in its belfry, a gallery running around three sides, and flags flying from posts on the west face, above the main door. Most of the wall-paintings were, sadly, destroyed in 1426, after King Janus's defeat in battle at Khirokitia (see p. 63). The remnants suggest that the originals were masterpieces: if you need convincing, look in the north-east corner at the glowing, youthful face of St Damien, a wonderfully subtle and convincing piece of painting. Below the central east window was a Crucifixion. Only the lower quarter now remains, but at the foot of the Cross kneel a king and queen who can only be Janus and his second wife Charlotte de Bourbon. Other fragmentary scenes represent King David (below and between the windows of the east wall), the Raising of Lazarus, the Last Supper and the Washing of the Feet (also on the east wall), and sections of the Dormition of the Mother of God and the Martyrdom of St Laurentius (on the west half of the vaulting).

Kornos

Here, huge red jars are produced from the characteristic clay of the area: good, sound jars, without pretensions, and meant for storing oil or wine. Most tourists simply have to admire them, for the thought of transporting them home is, alas, a nightmare. (Beware, incidentally, of the awful plastic replicas sometimes on sale locally.) It is worth seeking out a pottery, usually just a lean-to-shed against the wall of a cottage, and watching the jars being turned out on a rough wheel driven by foot-power – though the very largest jars are simply moulded by hand without a wheel.

Larnaca to Dhali (Idalion) and Perakhorio

Route Dhali lies on the main Larnaca-Nicosia road 23 km. from Larnaca. Perakhorio is about 3 km. from Dhali, to the west.

Dhali (Idalion)

This is a small and uninteresting village, and the only reason for
visiting it is that in antiquity, as *Idalion*, it was an important religious
centre – with, it is said, as many as fourteen temples, and associated
not only with Adonis (supposed to have been killed in the vicinity and
commemorated every year by a floor of red poppies on the hills) but
with Aphrodite, Aphrodite Kourtrophos, and Athena. The city was
founded by emigrants from Salamis and settled later by Phoenicians.
There are references to Idalion in antiquity – in Virgil's *Aeneid*, for
instance, when Venus

> ... showered a dew of peaceful sleep on the limbs of
> Ascanius, snuggled him in her breast, and divinely bore him
> Up to Idalian groves, where the tender marjoram puts him
> To bed in a cradle of flowers and shade and entrancing
>   fragrance.

The site as a whole is thoroughly disorganised, but the city lay
originally between the two limestone peaks that can still be seen:
Aphrodite's Sanctuary was on Gabriel's Hill, to the east, and between
the two peaks lay the *Sanctuary of Athena*. Two more sanctuaries
were some distance away, and from one of these came the stone
votary statuettes to be seen in the Cyprus Museum. Phoenician and
Graeco-Roman graves have been found here, but pillaged and
destroyed by a series of pirates. Permission to look over the site must
now be obtained from the near-by military post.

Unfortunately, the site has been ransacked over the ages by
amateur archaeologists and thieves, and only the most comprehensive and disciplined excavations would be likely now to turn up anything of similar interest to the fine eighth-century BC statue of King
Sargon of Assyria, found here, and now in the Berlin Museum. Some
work is in progress on the remains of what seems to have been a large
building.

Perakhorio

The Medieval *Church of the Twelve Apostles* in Perakhorio is just
south-west of the village; the murals are much damaged, but among
them is a fine corps of flying angels.

LIMASSOL

Hotels

Five-star: the Amathus Beach Hotel (tel. 051.51152) is on the beach 8 km. from the centre of Limassol, with private rooms and suites available, a 'village' taverna, private beach, two swimming pools, sauna/massage/gym and other first-rate amenities, including a resident band. The Poseidonia Beach Hotel (21000) is 6.4 km. from town, again with its own private beach. The Apollonia Beach (23351) is a little closer to Limassol, with its own beach and marina and resident band. Aerobic classes and tennis may be followed by a sauna and massage.

Four-star: the Curium Palace Hotel (63121) is near Limassol's shopping centre and a short walk from the beach. It is being interestingly refurbished, and is hanging some good modern paintings and etchings. Limonia Beach 'family' Hotel (21023) is a fifteen-minute bus ride from town. Elias Beach Hotel (25000) is near ancient Amathus, 7 km. from the centre of town; uniquely, it has a horse-riding centre offering trekking and equestrian schooling. The Miramare (21662) is 4 km. from the town centre, facing the sea. The Churchill (24444) is between the city centre and tourist areas; its restaurants offer *nouvelle* and classic French cuisine. A swimming pool overlooks the sea. The Marathon (21111) is a new hotel (1986) 6.4 km. from the centre of town, and near the beach.

Three-star: the Ariadne Hotel (59666) is just across the road (there is an underpass) from the beach, within walking distance of the town centre. The Crusader (21333) is on a quiet beach which is near the town centre. The Asteria Beach Hotel (21177) is on the seafront 4.8 km. from town, with pleasant gardens stretching down to the beach. The Avenida Beach Hotel (21122) is on a beach half-way between Limassol and Amathus. The Alasia (71747) is somewhat to the north of the town centre, but specialises in catering for British visitors. The Golden Arches Hotel (22433) is 5 km. from Limassol, on the Nicosia road. The King Richard Hotel (21330) is 8 km. from the town centre; it has a small swimming pool.

Others: the small Aquarius Beach Hotel (only 11 rooms, 22042) has a garden facing the sea; TV and video can be supplied on request.

The three-star Pissouri Beach Hotel (052–21201) is on the coast half-way between Limassol and Paphos, out in the country, and with genuinely quiet sandy beaches very near at hand. It has all the usual facilities. A hire-car is probably essential (once you get there, the hotel has its own fleet).

Apartments

L'Onda Beach apartments (21821) are described as 'super de luxe': they are suites with designer bathrooms and an adjoining restaurant serving Cypriot dishes to the accompaniment of a live orchestra; there are facilities for riding, squash, tennis and other exercise. The Azur Beach apartments (22667) are numbered One and Two: they are at Potamos Yermassoyias, 4.8 km. from the centre of Limassol; Two has air-conditioned apartments; One, next-door, has not. The Balmyra Beach apartments (22600) are ten minutes from town; Essex apartments (78808) are 100 metres from the sea; Old Bridge Hotel apartments (21200) lie amid citrus trees at Yermassoyia, ten minutes' walk from the beach; the Estella Hotel apartments (21922) are 200 metres from the public beach. Others include the Drakos apartments (21508), in the tourist area; Atlantica (21141), 6 km. from the town centre and ten minutes from the beach; Roussos Beach (22322), 4.8 km. east of Limassol, with a swimming pool and a disco open until early morning; and Tasiana

No. 2 Hotel apartments (21214). The Ser Criso apartments (21411) are 4.8 km. from the centre of Limassol, 'a stone's-throw from the sea'.

Some restaurants
Lucullus, Limassol-Nicosia road; Aphrodite's Garden, Ser Criso Hotel; Neon Faliron, Gladstone St; Blue Island, Limassol-Nicosia road; Bridge, Limassol-Nicosia road; Oasis, Gladstone St; Scotti's, Makarios III Avenue, has the reputation of serving the best steaks in Cyprus.

Some tavernas
Lemonies, Chr. Cranos St; Sykamies, Limassol–Nicosia road; Klima, Yermassoyia Avenue; Alakati, Yermassoyia Avue.

Some nightclubs
Bird Watcher's Club, Makarios III Avenue; Salamandra, Polemidia Village; Archontissa, Makarios III Avenue; Maxim, Stassinos St.

Cinemas
Ariel (open-air), Makarios III Avenue; Othello, Thessaloniki St; Pallas, Aristophanes St; Regal, Macedonia St; Rialto (open-air), Heroes Square; Galaxios, M. Michaelides St; Apollon, Meskit St; Crystal, Thessaloniki St; Rio (open-air), Hellas St; Yiordamli, E. Paleogina St.

Tourist Information Office (*Map* 5)
This is at 15 Spyros Araouzos St, on the promenade (62756).

Like Larnaca, the importance of Limassol has increased enormously over the past two decades – its population has trebled since the 1960s, and it is now Cyprus's largest port.

It is not, frankly, a very interesting town, but excellent modern hotels have made it a popular tourist resort, and visitors find much to enjoy in the innumerable discotheques and nightclubs of the Potamos Yermassoyias district (5 km. west of Limassol along the old Nicosia road, and the scene of a recent spy scandal allegedly connected with the near-by British base at Akrotiri). The town has a number of excellent small shops, and jewellery and made-to-measure suits are excellent buys. Anexartisia St, once the main thoroughfare, straggles north from the seafront. Off it to the east is Heroes' Square, once the centre of a lively red-light district which is now grubby, sleazy, expensive and unattractive.

HISTORY

It was in the Middle Ages that Limassol took the place of its neighbour Amathus as a prominent port. The town was severely damaged by the Genoese in 1373 and by the Saracens in 1426; in 1539 the Turks took their turn in devastating it. Earthquake and flood also contributed to its desuetude, so that by the end of the fifteenth century the whole area was a ruin. Between the sixteenth and eighteenth centuries the town was of little repute, and its fortunes

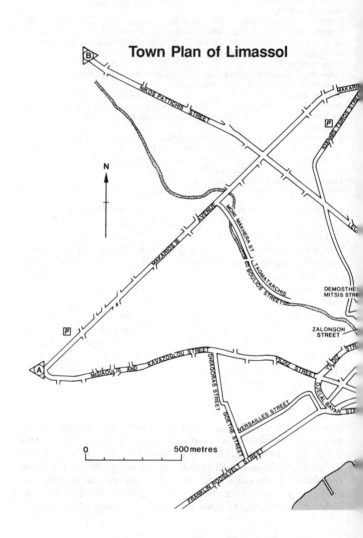

Town Plan of Limassol

B

NIKOS PATTICHIS STREET

MAKARI

P

DANNIS ISIDOS STR

N

MAKARIOS III AVENUE

MONI MAKHERA ST

AGMATARCHIS

BOULIOS STREET

DEMOSTHE
MITSIS STR

ZALONGON
STREET

A

MISIAOULIS AND KAVAZOGLOU STREET

DHIAGORAS STREET

YILDIZ STREET

STR

DJELAL BAYAR STR

GOETHE STREET

VERSAILLES STREET

FRANKLIN ROOSEVELT STREET

0   500 metres

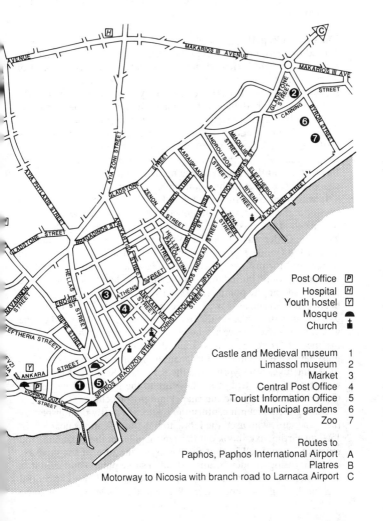

Post Office   P

Hospital   H

Youth hostel   Y

Mosque   ♠

Church   ♦

Castle and Medieval museum   1

Limassol museum   2

Market   3

Central Post Office   4

Tourist Information Office   5

Municipal gardens   6

Zoo   7

Routes to

Paphos, Paphos International Airport   A

Platres   B

Motorway to Nicosia with branch road to Larnaca Airport   C only began to rise again with the growth of commercial activity in the 1880s. Above a sand and pebble beach (its facilities run by the town) rises a promenade, recently refurbished and now extremely attractive.

The Castle (*Map* 1)

It used to be said that it was in the chapel of Limassol's fourteenth-century castle that Richard the Lion Heart married Berengaria of Navarre, and here, too, that she was crowned Queen of England. It is now supposed that these events actually took place at Amathus.

The castle has had (like most similar buildings) a chequered career: in the early thirteenth century it was enlarged, and a church of the Knights Templar added when it became the headquarters of the Order after the fall of Acre in 1291 and was much improved; the walls were made so thick that passages, some secret, could run within them. It is said that some strange marks on the masonry of the east chapel may be clues to the Templars' hidden treasure.

It was from here that, in 1303, Jacques de Molay, last Grand Master of the Order, was summoned to Paris by Pope Clement V (to be burned at the stake in 1309). The Lusignans took over the castle when the Order was banned in 1308, and unsuccessfully defended it against the Genoese in 1373; with the help, it may be, of a Scottish mercenary, for just over twenty years ago the skeleton of a six-foot soldier was found buried in the castle, his right hand on his heart and his left hand on the pommel of a long-vanished sword. His skull had been split by a single blow. Local experts suggested that 'his height and conformation suggest that he was a Scot'. He still lies where he was found – and the castle holds other bones than his: those for instance of former prisoners, some of them so broken that torture must have killed them. The Lusignans took control of the castle when the Mamelukes left Cyprus, and the Knights of St John of Jerusalem were placed in control of it; they turned the great west hall into a Gothic-style church, and the chapel into prison cells.

During the sixteenth century the castle was partly demolished by the Venetians, who used the fabric to build fortifications near by. In 1567 an earthquake shook out the central pillar of the great hall, and much of its roof fell in; but the Turks, at the turn of the century, rebuilt it (using wooden beams instead of stone pillars) and used it as a prison; it was a prison, indeed, until as recently as 1940. The central arch of the hall was replaced in 1950, and the castle continues to be refurbished as a monument and museum. A guidebook will soon be available.

MUSEUMS

The Medieval Museum (*Map* 1)

Limassol Castle now houses the town's Medieval Museum, with arms and armour, wood carvings and ceramics and pottery. Look out for the fourteenth-century tombstone of a pregnant woman, the child shown in her womb; a ceramic plaque of two colourful knights; a unique marble relief icon of David in the Lions' Den, and not far away three scenes from his life on silver plates – including his marriage, with two attendant flute-players. In the cellars are some carvings from Famagusta and Nicosia, and many photographs of some of North Cyprus's many fine medieval buildings that are now impossible to visit because of the Turkish occupation.

The Limassol Museum (*Map* 2)

Opened in 1975, this museum has a great deal of material from Amathus. In one show-case a graphically vigorous phallus with a plump and phlegmatic mother near-by nursing an enormous baby with a pointed cap; a lovely, slightly damaged head of a child is in the next case; and a horizontal case in the same room holds some fine jewellery, including a delicate head-dress of leaves and berries in gold. A huge and threatening Bes is in the next room, squat and bearded (the stone bears traces of colour) and in a near-by corner is a smaller, more approachable carving of the god, with a curled beard. A portrait head on a fifth-century tomb could have been carved fifty years ago by Eric Gill; but in the same gallery is a fascinating capital bearing a very Egyptian head of Hathor – the sky-goddess who gave birth to the world, was patroness of music and the dance, and was later to be identified with Aphrodite and then Venus.

There are other treasures in the Limassol Museum, too, including amazingly delicate Bronze Age pottery, some of which makes a sort of visual pun: a woman sits holding a pot on the side of the pot you're holding (in Larnaca Museum is a pot with pots on it). This is a fine collection altogether, even if one could (again) wish for more informative labelling: to be told that a case holds 'jewellery from the Middle Bronze Age to the eighth century BC' is interesting without being helpful.

OTHER PLACES OF INTEREST

At 253 Ayios Andreas St is a *Folk Art Museum* with peasant costumes, jewellery, ceramics, hand-woven materials, and so on.

The *Municipal Gardens* (*Map* 6) near the Limassol Museum, are pleasantly cool. There is a small *Zoo* here (20c, 10c for children) which one views with very mixed feelings – the cages which contain, among pelicans and other birds, some moufflon (the national animal of Cyprus), an old elephant (who not long ago accidentally killed his devoted keeper) and a pair of beautiful lions are cramped and old-fashioned. On the other hand the animals appear in good condition and are clearly well cared for.

For those who are interested, it is also possible to tour the local *winery and distillery*, just outside the town on the Paphos road.

There are no notable churches or mosques to be seen in Limassol.

EXCURSIONS FROM LIMASSOL

Limassol to Colossi Castle, St Nicholas of the Cats and Curium

Route Take the Paphos road westwards out of Limassol. The Castle of Colossi (or Kolossi, as it is sometimes spelled) is signposted on the left after 11 km. If you drive on for another 10 km. or so after visiting the castle, you will come to the Monastery of St Nicholas of the Cats, which lies just outside the north border of the British Military Airfield east of Akrotiri village. For the Curium Museum return to the main road and follow the signpost for Episkopi village. The museum is in the village. For Curium itself, return again to the main road; in approximately 3 km. you will find the site on your left. Continuing westward on the Paphos road, within 1 km., on your right, is the Greek stadium used by the inhabitants of the area. The Sanctuary of Apollo lies a further few hundred metres along the main road.

The Castle of Colossi

When Richard the Lion Heart landed in Cyprus, Isaac Comnenus had his camp here, and this is where they met. The site was always a military one – so much so that the previous building was a wreck by the end of the fourteenth century. The present castle dates from about 1454, when it was built by the Knights Hospitaller; the insignia of the Grand Commander of Cyprus, Louis de Magnac, with references to Cyprus, Jerusalem, Lusignan and Armenia, are to be seen on its east wall. In 1468 an Englishman, John Langstrother, was

Grand Commander, though whether he actually spent any time here is open to question; Edward IV had his head off after the Battle of Tewkesbury. The castle and its estates were confiscated by the Turks in 1570, but the title of Grand Commander survived, and was held by the Cornaro family until the end of the eighteenth century.

Colossi is not a large castle, but it is a very traditional, four-square one, such as any child might draw – and an extremely elegant one, with its drawbridge and Gothic keep (its walls 3 metres thick) and with some charming rooms: two first-floor chambers, one of them a kitchen; and two upper, one the Grand Commander's room, with a beautifully carved fireplace which would not look out of place in a French château (the arms are those of de Magnac), and handsome round-arched windows; he also had his private privy. A nicely proportioned spiral staircase leads on up to the terrace with its battlements and arrow-slits, a classic example of its kind, with a *mâchicoulis* from which debris could be thrown on any attacker who gained the drawbridge below. There is a nice view of the Salt Lake. On the ground floor are dungeons (or, more likely, storerooms). In the gardens, notice the aqueduct which still bears water from the hills.

St Nicholas of the Cats

The Monastery of St Nicholas of the Cats is said to have been founded by monks sent to Cyprus by the Emperor Constantine (*c*.325AD); the present ruins are thirteenth-century. It was the cats that attracted most visitors – cats introduced to the monastery by St Helena to deal with local snakes. Around 1900, one visitor still saw them at their military best:

> nearly all are maimed by the snakes; one has lost a nose, another an ear; the skin of one is torn, another is lame; one is blind of one eye, another of both. And it is strange that at the hour for their food, at the sound of the bell, all those scattered in the fields collect in the said monastery. And when they have eaten enough, at the sound of the bell they all leave together and go to fight the snakes.

The monastery was abandoned soon after the 1571 Turkish occupation. Only a single arch of the cloister now remains, but the church is plain and handsome (note the Lusignan coats-of-arms above the door). There is the occasional cat to be seen, but no snakes: the latter have all gone to live on the Cape Zevgari golf-course.

The Curium Museum

The Curium Museum (in Episkopi village) has some material from the Sanctuary of Apollo and some fine statuary from the Roman villa at Curium excavated in the early 1960s: Hermes Pastor – protector of shepherds – with a beautifully modelled back; Asklepius, god of medicine; a fine lion fountain. There are also household goods: lamps, strigils, mirrors and pottery. The lack of proper labelling is again infuriating.

Curium

If it is sad that one cannot for the time being visit Salamis, Curium – now frequently referred to as Kourion – is some compensation; it is a very splendid and notable site indeed – an acropolis looking down over the sweeping coast, and ruled by Apollo, whose cult was celebrated here and at the Sanctuary not far away. Apollo is a relatively young Greek god, and there is almost complete ignorance of his provenance (see p. 132). There are other mysteries: though he is not a god of hunters, he appears holding bow and arrow; he is also associated for no known reason with the stag or the roe, and even has a lion in his train. His arrows signify pestilence – so the god of healing is also the god of plague.

But we know something of the rites that would have been performed at his Sanctuary near by: they celebrated youthful renewal and the banishment of disease (by song and dance); and the god was also said especially to protect all poets, so he was invariably summoned to his festival through the paeon (a special metrical form of verse), and would appear on a swan-drawn carriage while nightingales and swallows sang and crickets chirped. Choruses of boys and girls would celebrate his presence with music, and there would often be competitions for voice and lyre, voice and flute, and solo flute, as well as sporting events, particularly horse-races. The victors would receive laurel wreaths.

Curium was first explored by General di Cesnola in 1873, who claimed to have discovered a splendid collection of gold and silver artefacts (which he sold to the Metropolitan Museum in New York). Whether he actually found these things at Curium is still open to question; he may have plundered them from elsewhere on the island. But between 1933 and 1950 serious archaeological work really got

The Greater Curium area

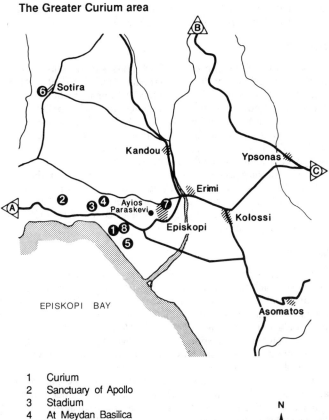

1 Curium
2 Sanctuary of Apollo
3 Stadium
4 At Meydan Basilica
5 Ermoyenis chapel
6 Teppes
7 Bamboula
8 Early Christian Basilica

Routes to
A Paphos
B Troodos
C Limassol

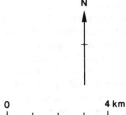

going, and the great *Villa of Eustolios* and the *Theatre* were excavated. And there has been much work since then.

HISTORY

The site of Curium was occupied 6,000 years ago; Herodotus mentioned it as the home of the Peloponnesian Argives in 1200 BC (they settled on a Bronze Age site) and Strabo, writing in the first century BC, described how those ill-advised enough to touch Apollo's altar were hurled from a near-by headland. During the Graeco-Persian wars Curium's forces played an important part in the outcome of the Battle of Salamis, and its support for Alexander the Great at the siege of Tyre contributed to the Persian defeat.

Apollo was displaced by Christ in the earliest centuries of the new religion, and an early Bishop of Curium, Philoneides, was martyred under Diocletian. The city was badly damaged by earthquakes in the first half of the fourth century, but was deserted only after the Arab raids in the seventh century.

THE SITE

Having driven down the path to the car-parking space near the entrance to the site and paid your entrance fee, it is best to turn sharp left and double back inside the boundary fence, walking along the rough track until just at the corner by the main Limassol–Paphos road you find the *Building of the Achilles Mosaic*. This seems to have been a ceremonial reception area: it had a colonnade with a marvellous mosaic showing Odysseus's surprise as the hero Achilles throws off the female disguise he had adopted to court his mistress Deidameia, daughter of King Lycomedes of Skyros. There are rooms at the side with lesser mosaics – though one, of Ganymede (the boy stolen away by an admiring Zeus to become the original Aquarius of the zodiac) must have been charming. It is now almost destroyed. A clearer treatment of the same subject can be seen at the House of Dionysus in Paphos.

Now, walking back along the same track, you come to the *House of the Gladiators*, a once elaborate building in the central courtyard of which are the only mosaics in this part of the world to depict scenes from gladiatorial games – perhaps games held in the near-by theatre. One shows two men, Hellenikos and Margaritis, practising combat with blunted swords; the other is less peaceful, for in it Lytras, in full armour, rejects the peacekeeping gestures of his friend Darios, and launches a vicious attack on his antagonist. (Darios holds a green baton, and may have been a sort of referee.) The house to the east, above this one, was obviously important – it has been suggested that it might have been the meeting-place of the local governing body.

Further south, passing the small *Fountain House* which was a public place for the drawing of water, you find a large excavation site, where work has been in progress since 1975. An elaborate water-supply system has been uncovered, with cisterns and pipes; but as to the buildings, one major one features an impressive colonnade which may have been part of the Forum (though an inscription suggests it may also have been a gymnasium). There was a row of shops near by, and many private houses stood around the site.

To the east are the remains of what clearly was once a *Nymphaeum* – a building consecrated to the nymphs, especially the Naiades, who were the spirits of springs of water. It would have been not only a sanctuary, but also a reservoir for water-supply and an assembly room, used among other things for the celebration of marriages. From the fragments which remain, it must have been a specially beautiful building.

The Early Christian Basilica (*Plan*)

To the right of the Curium site entrance is what was probably the fifth-century Basilica of the early Christian bishops of Curium – a substantial cathedral with two rows of six granite pillars set on bases of marble (1), and with four more pillars which once supported a baldachin (2) or canopy over the altar. (Some of these pillars were originally part of a temple to Apollo which stood on the same site.) Very little remains of the building, which seems to have been systematically spoiled over the centuries. There are a few broken fragments of mosaic pavement (5). Near by, the baptistry (3) had a nave and two aisles; a little marble-clad baptismal basin is in the south wall. New excavations south-east of the site recently revealed a small courtyard (4) with a wrecked feeding-trough near which the skeletons of a mule and a young girl were found; they died at 5.30 a.m. on 23 July AD 365, in a famous earthquake. The remains of four other people were found, and enough material – coins, oil-lamps, lampstands, pitchers – to promise a fascinating study of Curium at that particular time. Excavations continue in this area, and it is plan-

The Basilica at Curium

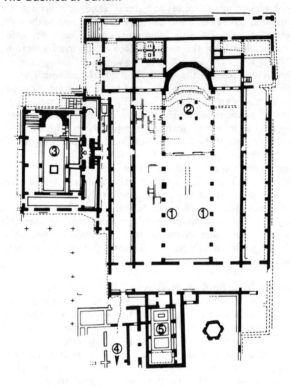

1   Bases of pillars
2   Position of baldachin
3   Baptistry
4   Courtyard
5   Mosaic

0   10
metres

ned to remove the excellent tourist pavilion in order to extend them towards the west.

The Theatre
The Theatre was very considerably reconstructed in 1961, and performances of various sorts are given in it. It was originally excavated in 1949–50, and a familiar curved auditorium was uncovered, and with the kind of view theatrical designers would find it difficult to counterfeit. Spectators entered through a vaulted corridor behind the auditorium, and went to their seats along gangways. The theatre held about 3,500 people, so was considerably smaller than its counterpart at Salamis, where no less than 17,000 could gather. Nevertheless, in its heyday it must have been fine, with the 'scene-building' behind the stage rising to the height of the highest seat, so that a vellum awning could be stretched out over the whole auditorium to give cover from the sun. Perfumed water was sprinkled to alleviate the heat, and during the interval the audience could go around to the back of the scene-building to buy cakes and honey-wine from small shops there.

As with most Roman theatres, the auditorium and stage areas were remodelled several times; in the third century or so AD, grand spectacles became popular and the theatre was adapted for the display of wild beasts – traces were found of iron bars which protected the audience from the animals, and the little niche right at the centre front of the stalls (helpful in providing shade in which to change the film in one's camera) may have provided a place of refuge for hard-pressed animal-trainers. The theatre returned to conventional use before it finally fell into disrepair in the fourth century. The foundations on which the scenery was built can be seen behind the present orchestra pit. It is a tribute to the original architects and their choice of setting that the theatre remains as impressive as it must have been when the first performance took place there over 2,000 years ago.

The Villa of Eustolios
From the theatre one walks up the hill to a later building or series of buildings: according to an inscription set in mosaic, one Eustolios built 'this cool refuge, sheltered from the winds' as a tribute to Apollo – though elsewhere the name of Christ has been added (see *plan*). The rooms one first enters (**2**) – which include servants' quarters (on

the left), but seem chiefly to have been meant for pleasant relaxation (and there are lavatories on the right, **9**) – were probably in the first instance part of a luxurious villa built in about 150 BC, but were later (from perhaps AD 457) opened to the public. A flight of stairs (now concealed beneath the wooden walkway) leads up to the *Baths* which were evidently extremely civilised and up-to-date, with a central room (**3**, perhaps the exercise-room) with mosaics showing Creation as a female figure holding a measuring-rod. To the north and east of this room are smaller ones which were approached through a hygienic footbath: these contained frigidaria, or cold baths (**4**). To the west was the tepidarium, or warm room, and behind it the caldarium or hot room (**5**), heated by hypocausts – hollow channels running beneath the floor, which may still be seen. There is some doubt about the bathing procedure: but it is supposed that, having undressed and been oiled, one exercised, then, perspiration having mixed with oil, went to the caldarium, where strigils were used to scrape off the dirt, before relaxing in the tepidarium and having a final inspiriting plunge in the pool of the frigidarium (often, though not here, it would be large enough for swimming). The water, from a cistern which still exists, came from an aqueduct to be seen at the entrance site.

There are various interesting mosaics besides the welcoming inscription and the image of Creation: in the central hall (**3**) is a picture of a red-legged partridge; the cold plunge-bath has a beautiful rippling abstract pattern; and there are fine abstract designs elsewhere, too, often of considerable elegance and intricacy. But it is in the south-east hall (**6**) that the finest mosaics can be seen. The southern panel has a pattern of Greek crosses meeting in an eight-pointed star, inside which is a splendid guinea-hen, while on each side a smaller panel contains a bird and a fish. Elsewhere a fine grey goose can be seen, and a plump duck. The east hall (**10**), thought to have been a dining-hall with folding doors opening on to a garden, has perhaps the best abstract mosaics.

The Chapel of Ayios Ermoyenis (*Map* 5)
Down the hill south of the main Curium site is a little eighteenth-century chapel to St Hermogenes, a Turk whose Christian parents instructed him. He became Bishop of Samos, where he performed miracles but was tortured and finally decapitated by a heathen governor. Christian supporters placed his head and body in a coffin

The Villa of Eustolios

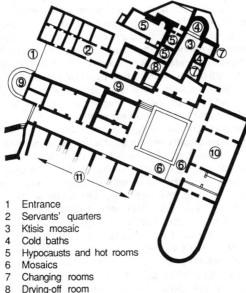

1 Entrance
2 Servants' quarters
3 Ktisis mosaic
4 Cold baths
5 Hypocausts and hot rooms
6 Mosaics
7 Changing rooms
8 Drying-off room
9 Lavatories
10 Dining room
11 Men's and women's rooms

and floated it away on the tides, which brought it to Curium, where the chapel was built to receive it. The good saint is said to protect young lovers and to effect a cure for the common cold. You may find the chapel completely encircled by a piece of string – local women do this to protect the saint from inquisitive intruders and perhaps from the souls of the evil dead. There is sometimes a shepherd near by who has a key to the chapel.

The Stadium (*Map* 3)
The Curium stadium was built in the second century AD, at a time when the Greek passion for physical fitness was spreading through the Roman Empire. Many of the greatest Greek athletes toured the

Empire much as professional athletes do today, performing at identical sports grounds – for a *stadium* was in fact a unit of length: about 186 metres. The walls of the stadium are six metres thick, made of giant blocks of limestone quarried near by. Three entrances led into the arena, one in the middle of each side and one at the rounded end, where two stone post-holes mark the starting-line for races. The athletes probably entered at the sides and marched in procession to the start, each no doubt cheered on by his supporters – and there was room for plenty of supporters, for in seven rows of stone seats 6,000 people could watch the games (some of the seats have been replaced in position on the south side of the arena).

All sorts of activities took place here: usually organised to celebrate special occasions, such as a great victory, or the birthday of the emperor; games may also have been dedicated to Apollo. This stadium was not big enough for chariot races, but certainly there would have been foot-races and probably javelin- and discus-throwing, jumping and wrestling. The athletes often appeared naked, though sometimes they wore loincloths and sandals. The stadium fell into disuse after the earthquake of AD 370 – though an early biographer of St Barnabas records that the saint, passing by, was so shocked at the pagan display of nudity that he provoked a landslide which swept away the stadium and killed all the athletes and spectators. This is thoroughly in character, but was surprising, since the site is entirely flat and there is not a hill in sight; however, a miracle is a miracle.

And where did they live, those thousands who inhabited Curium and flocked to the stadium? The answer is that, largely, we do not know, for almost no private houses have as yet been found; they lie somewhere under the soil of the peninsula, awaiting the trowels of the archaeologists.

The Small Basilica (*Map* 8)

Just north-east of the stadium, reached by a track from the parking-place, is a small basilica, At Meydan, probably built in the sixth century AD but perhaps on a site where there was a shrine as early as the fourth century BC. The original building was very possibly a nymphaeum, for two marble plaques have been found, used by the Christians as paving-stones, on whose underside are beautiful mythological scenes showing Anadyomene, Poseidon and a satyr, and a water nymph.

The Sanctuary of Apollo

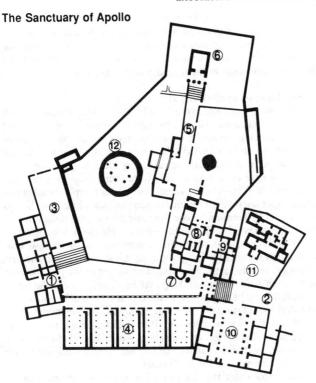

1 Paphos Gate
2 Curium Gate
3 Lodging-house?
4 Dormitories
5 Approach to temple
6 Temple
7 Votive pit
8 Priest's house
9 Treasury
10 Palaestra
11 Baths
12 Circular site

N

0 _____ 40
metres

Fragments can still be seen of the marble paving-stones which covered the floor of the nave and chancel in a geometrical design. Some of the fluted columns were clearly brought here from the Curium theatre. This small basilica was in use for about a century and a half, probably only on the feast day of a local saint.

The Sanctuary of Apollo (*Map* 2)

This lies among pines and cypresses a little east of the stadium. Of all the Cypriot archaeological sites perhaps it is the most beautiful and the most moving. When the first modern writer, an American missionary, came here in 1839, he found that the local people still called the place Apollonas – though they did not know why; and beneath an altar excavated in 1980 were found fragments of a jug dated about 2000 BC – so the ground on which the temple complex was built in about the seventh century BC had been used by human beings for at least a millennium before that; and for the next millennium it was to be associated with Apollo Hylates – 'He of the Woodland'.

Apollo Hylates, god of prophecy, music and archery, also protected flocks and herds. The geographer Strabo, writing in the first century BC, recalled a tradition that deer sacred to the god swam to Cyprus from Asia Minor to take refuge here; and in a circular space to the north-west of the site priests danced in a grove of laurel, myrtle and palms – trees specially sacred to Apollo (terracotta models have been found, showing such scenes). Burnt offerings were made here, and terracotta figures left as dedications – over 10,000 of them have been found in the sanctuary, which was continuously used for dedication and worship for 1,000 years.

Visitors now enter the site (see *plan*) near the eastern, Curium Gate (2); and it is best then to walk along the south side of the southern buildings and enter the Sanctuary itself by the western, Paphos Gate (1). On your left, up a flight of stairs, are the remains of a building (3) which originally had two aisles with stone benches and pillars. Worshippers may have lodged here or have displayed their votive offerings: or maybe the rooms were dormitories – though this was more likely the case with the range of five rooms (4) to the south, behind a handsome colonnade, each one having an open paved area surrounded by benches and columns.

Walking on past the colonnade, a street opens out on your left which led – leads – to the temple itself (6). Two columns have been re-erected to give some idea of the elegant, slim structure as it originally was, approached by a flight of steps which led beneath the columns and portico to the *pronaos* or outer chamber, and then the *cella* or inner sanctuary.

Turning to walk back down the open street, strike out westward to the circular site (**12**). Soil would have covered the bare rock which now shows, but in that rock pits were cut which almost certainly held the roots of the sacred trees. West of this magic circle is a great oblong cistern which supplied the Sanctuary with water – it held over thirty-seven metric tonnes.

On the other side of the street is a range of houses at least one of which was a kitchen. To the north of this range is a small courtyard in front of a house (**8**) which probably belonged to a priest; next to it (**9**) was the treasury; note in the uprights of the window-frames the holes which once held bars.

At the south end of the street, on your left, is the semi-circular votive pit (**7**). Hundreds of terracotta figures of people and animals were found, carefully and reverently stored here when there was no longer room for them in the sacred precincts of the temple itself.

Outside the Sanctuary proper, near the present entrance to the site, is an elegant small courtyard with columns around it (**10**). This is the *palaestra*, the exercise area where youths kept themselves fit to serve Apollo (god of manly beauty). In one of the two niches of the west wall of the courtyard was found a statue of a young athlete with a ball in his hand – so ball games of some sort were presumably played here; and when the heat of the day became oppressive, cold water could be drawn from the huge stone jar which, though broken, still stands in a corner of the yard. Then, only a step from the *palaestra*, the athletes could repair to the baths (**11**), throwing off their vestigial garments in the changing-rooms before a plunge in the cold pool and a relaxing half-hour in the hot, hotter and hottest rooms, the hot air circulating beneath the floor from the furnace-room at the west end of the building.

The walls of the Sanctuary fell to the ground in AD 370, during an earthquake the epicentre of which was about 50 km. south of Petra tou Romiou. Work on the site has taken place over a century, from the activities of Cesnola in the 1870s to the work done between 1934 and 1953 by the University of Pennsylvania, and continuing excavations sponsored by various American sources. The whole site is a tribute to meticulous work and tactful, imaginative reconstruction and landscaping.

Time Scale

To put the buildings of the Sanctuary in an historical context, the earliest altar found here dates from the late seventh century BC, when a fertility god associated with the Bull was worshipped. The earliest inscription to mention Apollo dates from the fifth century BC. Some of the houses to the west of the site (around the Paphos Gate) were built in about the fourth and fifth centuries BC. The earliest inscription to Apollo Hylates dates from the third century BC. During the first century AD the temple (**6**) and circular space (**12**) were added, and under the Emperor Nero the 'dormitory' buildings (**3** and **4**) were erected. By the beginning of the second century AD the Emperor Trajan was associated with Apollo Hylates, and the baths (**11**) were built.

Limassol to Teppes and Bamboula

Route For those interested in the earliest history of Cyprus, these two sites are attractive. The first, Teppes, is a Neolithic settlement near the village of Sotira, reached by turning to the right off the Limassol–Paphos road just after Erimi, towards Kandou, then after about 3 km. turning left as signposted to Sotira. Bamboula is found by returning to the Kandou road and turning right, to the south. Take the turning signposted Episkopi; the late Bronze Age city and cemetery will be found on your left.

Teppes (*Map* p. 123, **6**)

In these Neolithic houses 5,000 years BC lived Cypriots, their sheep, goats, pigs and dogs (dogs strangely like fox-terriers). They hunted deer and gathered nuts, wild olives and grapes. They chose the site of their village well: there are good views to the Troodos, and over the sea. One can still see the walls of their forty-seven flat-topped houses (finally demolished by earthquake) facing south to catch the best of the winter sun. Inside the houses were found stone tools, storage jars, handmade pots, bone needles and fish-hooks.

Bamboula (*Map* **7**)

Around 1600 BC the true ancestors of the inhabitants of Curium lived in this Bronze Age city and the site is particularly interesting because the people there produced really very sophisticated 'grave gifts' such as the 'window krater', to be seen at the Cyprus Museum – a pot with beautiful drawings, including a famous one of a girl holding a flower.

Bamboula was protected by a great wall and a tower, and its

inhabitants were relatively wealthy. They lived in real houses, spread along narrow streets; they had no furniture, but doubtless made themselves comfortable on animal furs; they lit their rooms by hanging lamps. No 'shops' have been found, but potters' wheels, great jars for storing oil and wine, and blacksmiths' implements have turned up – and the tombs near by have yielded beautiful objects of faience, ivory, glass, bronze and gold; some, however, imported.

Limassol to Amathus, Khirokitia and Pano Lefkara

Route Take the coastal road (*not* the motorway) eastward from Limassol, passing innumerable tourist hotels. In about 11 km. watch, on your right, for the Avenida Beach Hotel. In 500 metres there is a valley on your left. Park here and climb the eastward hill to the major visible remains of Amathus. Leaving Amathus, and continue along the coastal road until you see signposts to the motorway. Khirokitia on the left is well signposted after approximately 25 km. From Khirokitia you can take a circuitous and picturesque road to Pano Lefkara by simply following the minor road to the north of the site, but this is not advised for nervous drivers, or those without an infallible sense of direction. Better return to the motorway and follow the signpost (to Skarinou) in 2 km. which indicates a first-rate new road to Pano Lefkara, a further 12 km.

Amathus

Amathus was once one of Cyprus's city-states, with a famous Temple to Hercules (worshipped by the Cypriots as Melkarth) and a joint Temple to Adonis and Aphrodite. Every year, the *Adonia* games were held here – in celebration of Adonis. These opened with a commemoration of the god's death and descent into Hades; next day his resurrection was celebrated with dance and song (the parallel with the Christian resurrection is instructive); there would be ritual slaughter – particularly of boars, for it was a boar that killed Adonis. Finally, athletic competitions and awards.

In the seventh century AD the first patron bishop of the Knights of St John of Jerusalem was born here; when he was buried (also at Amathus) it is recorded that the bodies of the two previous bishops courteously turned upon their sides to make room for him. It was here, too, that Richard the Lion Heart stepped ashore.

Much of Amathus lies under the sea, and the site is not so much badly signposted as not signposted at all. It is a fairly steep climb, very trying in the heat of summer; start early in the morning. The hillside is scattered with blocks of stone and remnants of walls; there has been much archaeological activity here in recent years, but the site remains incoherent and as yet no guidebook has been produced.

At the top of the hill, however, is what must have been the *Forum*; some rooms, with beautiful flagstoned floors, have been cleared; there is a pediment here, a column base there – an earthenware drainpipe still lies snugly in its channel, a capital is beautifully carved with a dragonfly. It is a wonderfully romantic site, hanging dizzily over the Nicosia motorway.

At the foot of the hill once more, cross the road. Along the beach a few traces of old wall protrude from the earth; the rest of Amathus is below the water-line. It is a tempting place not only for philosophical reflection, but for a swim – and impossible, while swimming, not to dive and see what fragments of the great city may lie within reach. Remember, it is illegal to remove so much as a single mosaic stone from Cyprus; the ordinary Cypriot people jealously guard their heritage – and, incidentally, do not be concerned at those you see apparently conducting private archaeological digs on the hillside. They are actually searching for edible snails – especially during Lent, for some arcane ecclesiastical law exempts snails from the general interdict against eating meat.

Khirokitia

From Amathus, it is a drive of 25 km. (see directions above) to this Neolithic site, one of the earliest settlements so far discovered on Cyprus, where there was a thriving settlement of about 1,000 houses in at least 5800 BC. Forty-eight houses have so far been excavated, and they were quite elaborate: round buildings, with domed, mud-brick roofs and windows, hearths, and special sleeping-platforms supported on stone pillars (which formed the earliest upper floors yet to be discovered in the history of architecture). There were cupboards in the walls or pillars. In some cases the buildings made small complexes: a house for living, with a courtyard (paved with stone) around which were grouped smaller buildings used as kitchens or workshops for grinding corn. Sometimes there were stone tables in the courtyards at which meals could be eaten.

The several thousand people who lived on this hillside over seven millennia ago, tended cattle and cultivated fields, experimented rather clumsily in the relatively new art of pot-making, and even decorated their pots (there are examples in the Cyprus Museum at

Nicosia). But they concentrated on making vessels of polished stone: spouted stone bowls and square or roughly rectangular dishes have been found. These were mostly plain, but some were decorated with bands and knobs; and some animal-shaped vessels and some human heads have turned up. The Khirokitians worked well with wood, too, and were no mean builders. The large wall they constructed through their village (rather like a railway embankment) still stands; on each side of it, the little beehive houses clustered, each built on the remains of several others, on circular stone foundations above which rose mud-brick walls. Sandwiched between the floors of the generations of tenements, the bodies of the inhabitants were buried, personal jewellery and household utensils with them, and each body with a heavy weight placed upon it, to discourage it from rising up to haunt the new tenants on the floor above. As many as twenty-six bodies have been found in various strata underneath one hut.

Understanding a site as early as this one requires a certain amount of application on the part of the uninformed visitor; but this is one of the easiest of its period to take in, and it does not require too much creative imagination to be able to construct a picture of how life was being lived here when civilisation was still struggling to its feet. It is a marvellously interesting site, as well as perhaps the most important early example of the remains of a human community.

Pano Lefkara

There are marvellous views over hills and valleys driving along the new road to Pano Lefkara, a hill village twinned with Kato Lefkara, just down the hill. The home of St Neophytos, this is one of those little villages – like Polperro, or Sidi bou Said, or Eze – which immediately grasps the heart, with its sound, stone, pastel-coloured houses under roofs of ancient tiles, its little wooden balconies almost meeting across the narrow streets. For centuries its men have travelled far and wide through Europe selling the lace for which their womenfolk are still famous. It is said that even Leonardo da Vinci was impressed by their art, and bought lace here as a gift to the cathedral at Milan (not a likely story, since there is no record of his ever visiting Cyprus). Besides lace, the women do drawn-thread work on linen or cotton, and table-linen from Pano Lefkara makes a splendid souvenir of the place and the island.

The other thing for which Pano Lefkara is celebrated is *lokoum*, or Turkish Delight. Search for a modern factory, and you will search in vain; copper cauldrons of sugar bubble away over wood fires while nuts roast gently in flat pans near by. Good figs grow in the area, too. There is a cheerfully unkempt tourist pavilion at the top of the village, and near by the shop of Michael Rouvis, who designs and sells silver and embroidery a cut above that you may find elsewhere in the village. The church here is fairly plain, but the cool interior is fresh and attractive in its light blue and cream colours; an elegant stair coils around a pillar to the high pulpit, and there are some interesting icons.

Leaving Pano Lefkara it is worth driving through the little village of **Kato Dhrys** (unless you are nervous of streets which seem at least six inches narrower than any known make of car) to the *Monastery of Ayios Minas*. One monk and several nuns keep it, spending their time painting icons for the tourists. Rejoin the motorway via Khirokitia.

Limassol to Makheras Monastery, Phikardou, Tamassos and the Monastery of St Heracleidos

Route   Drive east along the coastal road to Amathus (11 km.) and there turn left and continue due north for 24 km. to Melini, and follow the main road for 5 km to Ora. Turn left and in 3 km. at Vavatsinia, continue straight ahead on a minor road for 15 km. to Makheras Monastery. After visiting the monastery, take the road for Gourri – a thoroughly indifferent, not to say terrifying, road, which is however gradually being improved. At Gourri turn right and in 3 km. you will arrive at Phikardou, a preserved village monument to life in the sixteenth century. From there, return to Makheras, and, if you wish to continue the excursion further, drive north-east on the main road for 10 km. to Kambia, then on through Pera, 4 km., to the site of Tamassos. Just south of Tamassos is the monastery of St Heracleidos. (The most northerly of these sights can also be visited from Nicosia.)

Makheras Monastery

In the middle of the twelfth century, two monks – Ignatius and Neophytos – discovered a cave near here in which, protected by a naked sword, was an icon of the Virgin Mary. (There is a Holy Well, from which clear water continually springs, near the site of the original cave.) The monks decided to build a monastery in which to enshrine the miraculous object, and Ignatius travelled to Constantinople and returned with a grant of land and the promise of an annual donation from Emperor Manuel Comnenus of Byzantium. 'The

Convent of the Sword' was founded in 1148, and the first abbot – later to become Archbishop Ninos – took charge of the community in 1172. There are various stories of the holiness of the place, including one which will not commend itself to the women's movement: for when Hugues IV's wife, Queen Alice, decided to ignore the traditional rule that men only should enter the monastery's sanctuary, she was struck dumb, and recovered her speech only in order to testify to the authenticity of a piece of the True Cross.

The original monastery buildings (but not the miraculous icon, which is still to be seen – or, rather, its container is) suffered two disastrous fires, and little remains of them; the present building is not particularly beautiful, but the setting is spectacular, not only because of the splendid landscape stretching below, but for the surrounding wooded hills with vineyards on their lower stretches. One may see, close by, the hide-out used during the EOKA troubles by Gregory Afxentious, General Grivas's second-in-command, who died here. There is some accommodation at the monastery for male visitors and an excellent liqueur is distilled here.

Phikardou

The whole of the village of Phikardou has been specified as an ancient monument. Apart from the intrusive electrical wiring, it is easy to believe that one is back in the sixteenth century as one walks along the narrow streets cobbled with large, rough stones. Phikardou once belonged entirely to a family of that name; now the family has departed and only ten people live in the village. The *House of Katsinioros* has been restored, and is now a museum of local life – the ground floor has a wine press, storage jars for wine and oil and a still for making local 'whisky'; upstairs, a bed, a loom, brass licence plates issued to shepherds, the one glass used by an entire family …

Near by, all white and blue, is the *House of Achillea Dimitri*, with its workroom, its two looms (each family made cloth and embroidered it, not only for use but as a source of income); its living-room with a huge bed, homemade chairs; and another separate bedroom (or 'house' – each room is called a 'house'), almost a cave, with the bed made up on a stone shelf.

The keys for the two houses are kept by Mr Yiannakos. If you telephone him in advance of your visit (there is one village telephone, 0263–2353), he will be pleased to cook you a good Cypriot meal, and serve his own 'whisky', 90 per cent proof, and lethal. He will provide a simple meal, perhaps an omelette, without prior notice. He speaks no English, so get an interpreter to help you with your call.

Tamassos

Although there is now practically nothing to be seen of the extensive remains, there has been life in and around Tamassos for at least 6,000 years, mainly because of the copper for which it was famous (it is mentioned in Homer and by Ovid); Alexander the Great knew the mines, and so did Herod the Great, who brought Jewish slaves from Palestine to work them. In AD 115–16 the Jews revolted against their Roman masters, and there was wholesale slaughter; as many as 250,000 people are said to have perished at Tamassos and Salamis.

The place was a centre of population much earlier than that: and there were concentrations of priests here serving various deities, among them Venus and Apollo. It is said that it was at Tamassos that Atalanta lost her marriage race because of Aphrodite's trick with the golden apples, and that it was near here that Adonis was gored by the wild boar: and all around

> No flow'r was nigh, no grass, herb, leaf, or weed
> But stole his blood and seemed with him to bleed

– hence the plethora of commemorative poppies.

There are no temples to be seen now, though their sites have been identified; a handsome life-size bronze statue of Apollo was un-covered in 1836, but the peasant who found it chopped it to pieces for the value of the metal. A sword found close by the village is in the Cyprus Museum, and resembles Agamemnon's sword as described by Homer. St Paul and St Barnabas are said to have come here and ordained Heracleidos as first Bishop of Tamassos.

Two sixth-century BC tombs may be seen, though they are frankly not very interesting apart from the carving of the stone at the entrances to make them resemble wooden doors (even with imitation bolts). A silver dish with a raised carving of a horse was one of the few things that evaded centuries of tomb-robbers; it is now in the Cyprus Museum in Nicosia, and its value encouraged some archaeologists to believe that the tombs were originally those of 'kings'.

The Monastery of St Heracleidos

The skull of the patron saint is preserved in the church, but does not seem to dampen the spirits of a cheerful little community of nuns who sell homemade jams. Your guide will point out the entrance to a Roman tomb which it is asserted was the burial-place of St Heracleidos himself and his friend St Mnason, who according to Acts played host to St Paul. In 1769, Yannis, a young Cypriot possessed of devils, was brought here, and subsequently 'was moved to vomit and cast forth from his mouth a snake a span long and two crabs, and he was healed from that hour'. The dried snake used to be on view to visitors. More worthy of attention are the paintings in the dome and vaulting, bright and lively, almost cartoon-like.

THE TROODOS MOUNTAINS

The Troodos mountains are crossed by a tangle of minor roads which are a positive invitation to get lost; even the most detailed map is difficult to follow, quite apart from possible inaccuracies. Nevertheless, the suggestions that follow should be taken as general, and you should not hesitate to investigate any sideroads which take your fancy, for each valley seems more dramatic and beautiful than the last – and subtly different from it. The scented pine forests of the Troodos are dotted with monasteries and churches most of which are worth visiting, and it is still true that the Cypriots are a generous and hospitable people whose attitude to strangers has remained the same for centuries. Many villages have their own local wines, which invite a tasting, and there is always the local *kafenion* at which to sit with a cup of coffee and watch the world amble timelessly by. You will certainly achieve only a fraction of the experience by attempting a 'day-trip'.

Limassol to the Monasteries of Omodhos and Troodhitissa and to Troodos

Route Take the Paphos road out of Limassol, and just before Episkopi fork right just past the bridge at Erimi for Kandou and a further drive for 15 km. to Ayios Amvrosios past excellent valley views (note, too, the good dry-stone walls). Following the signposts you will arrive after another 12 km. of hill driving at Omodhos and its monastery. Leaving Omodhos, drive on through Mandria (4 km.) to Kato Platres and turn left; in 4 km. you will come to Troodhitissa Monastery. Returning to the main road turn left at Kato Platres and a few more kilometres of mountainous roads will take you through Pano Platres to Troodos.

Troodos and the Hill Resorts

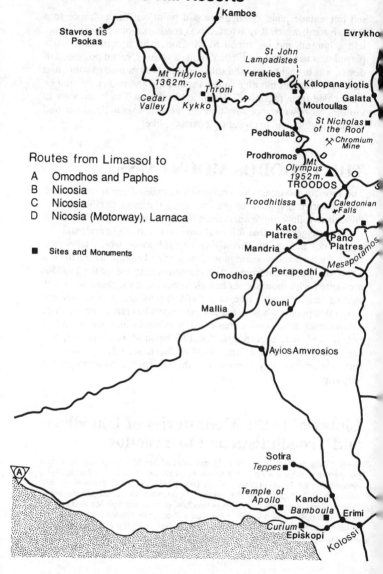

Kambos

Stavros tis
Psokas

Evrykho

St John
Lampadistes

Mt Tripylos
1362 m.

Yerakies

Kalopanayiotis

Throni

Galata

Cedar
Valley

Kykko

Moutoullas

St Nicholas
of the Roof

Pedhoulas

Chromium
Mine

Prodhromos

Mt
Olympus
1952 m.
TROODOS

Routes from Limassol to

A   Omodhos and Paphos
B   Nicosia
C   Nicosia
D   Nicosia (Motorway), Larnaca

■   Sites and Monuments

Troodhitissa

Caledonian
Falls

Kato
Platres

Pano
Platres

Mandria

Mesapotamos

Omodhos

Perapedhi

Vouni

Mallia

Ayios Amvrosios

Sotira

Teppes

Temple of
Apollo

Kandou

Bamboula

Erimi

Curium

Episkopi

Kolossi

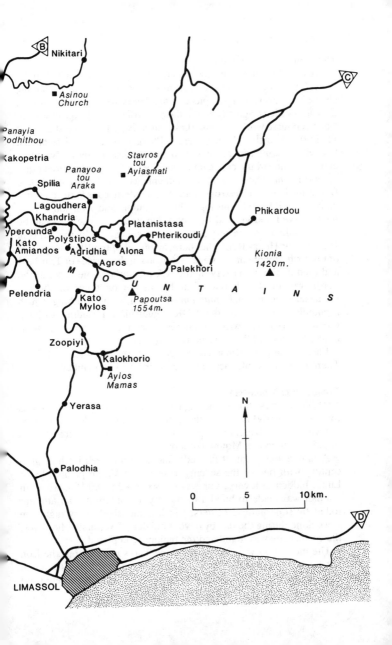

The Monastery of Omodhos

There is no longer a 'working' monastery here, but the Church of the Holy Cross (built on the site of an earlier and famous Byzantine church) retains its relics; a piece of the True Cross, but also parts of the ropes which originally bound the hands of Christ. Large crosses of silver repoussé work enshrine these relics. Here too is the skull of St Philip the Apostle, who preached in Phrygia and died at Hierapolis, but whose skull was presented to this monastery by a Byzantine emperor. Indeed the case containing it bears the seals of three other emperors, all testifying to its authenticity. The church has fine Byzantine icons and also one of the best modern icons in the country, painted in 1984. The bishop's throne, pulpit and icon-stand were finely carved and guilded by Abbot Dositheos, whose bust can be seen outside the monastery entrance. He was hanged by the Turks in 1821. Major Henry Rooke lies here, an officer of the 100th Regiment of Foot who fought at the siege of Ancona in the service of Tsar Paul and died at the monastery in 1811. A memorial stone is set in the north wall of the church. Near by, in the buildings of the ex-monastery, is a small *museum* in which some clothing which reputedly belonged to the EOKA guerrillas, including Colonel Grivas, is treasured with no less reverence than the more religious relics. The roof of the museum is finely carved.

Lace is made in **Omodhos** village, and can be purchased here. There is an enjoyable local fair each year on 14 September.

Troodhitissa Monastery

At 1,300 metres, this is the highest monastery on Cyprus. It was founded as early as the tenth century AD, and is also sometimes known as the Olympia or Aphroditissa Monastery (Aphrodite was once worshipped on Mount Troodos).

A miraculous pillar of fire led a monk to this area in the eighth century with one of the seventy icons of the Virgin painted by St Luke; hidden in a cave, this was rediscovered in AD 990, when an attempt was made to build a monastery to contain it – an attempt foiled by supernatural powers, which demolished every night the work done during the day by devout builders. Eventually, however, the correct site was found and the building completed.

The monastery was destroyed by the Turks in 1585, but the icon was later found intact under an apple tree in the garden. The church was rebuilt, but burned down in 1842, to rise again in its present form the following year. It now supports nine monks, who guard the icon, a stone which fell from the church and would have killed a child had the icon not moved to protect him and a belt which, donned by a sterile woman, guarantees conception.

The church has two splendid carved walnut thrones for abbot and bishop completed in 1986; and in 1951 Abbot Pancratios removed the St Luke's icon from its covers and had it photographed. From the photograph he painted a copy, which hangs over the south door of the church and proves that the original must be spectacularly beautiful: the Virgin (like so many of the island's icons) is peculiarly human, and a rather adult Child sits enthroned in the crook of her right arm, gowned in gold and studying his Book.

Pano Platres

Clinging tenaciously to the hillside above a deep-cut valley, Pano Platres is a popular health resort and the largest of the Troodos hill resorts in this area. It has good sporting facilities and several hotels, including: *four-star*, the well-known Forest Park (tel. 054–21751), with a heated swimming-pool and sauna; *two-star*: the Edelweiss (21335) and the Pendeli (21736); *one-star*: the Grand (21331), the Lanterns Cottage (21434), the Minerva (21731) and the Splendid (21425). The Yiolandel restaurant is extremely reliable. It is next to Michael Pastellis's supermarket, who also manages it. The vegetables are always fresh, and the Troodos trout are excellent.

This is a good centre for walking and riding: and even perhaps for exploring the part of Cyprus between the Troodos mountains and the Green Line. The countryside here has been compared to that of Scotland – one local beauty spot is actually called the Caledonian Falls. To the north is Mount Olympus, which at 1,715 metres is the highest peak on the island. Strabo said that there was a temple to Aphrodite Areia on its summit; now there is a TV tower. New gods for old.

Troodos

Hotels: Two-star: the Jubilee (054–21647), the Troodos (21635).

Troodos is an admirable sporting resort with excellent skiing during the first three months of the year. The poet Rimbaud, who had left the quarry at Voroklini (see p. 105) to return to France for a while, worked here in 1880 in charge of the building of a rather strange house which was to be the summer home of the High Commissioner. A plaque commemorates the fact.

Troodos is a convenient centre from which to explore the mountain area as a whole, and for those who can afford to spend a day or so here we give below a couple of useful circular routes. These can of course be taken from Limassol, although they would make for quite a long drive.

For walkers

A nature trail starts at the north end of Troodos main square, for which a leaflet is provided by KOT. The walk is to **Chromion**, and is 4 km. long; towards the end there are fine views towards **Prodhromos**, of *Kykko Monastery* and of **Throni** (where Archbishop Makarios is buried). Another KOT walk starts 1.5 km. south of Troodos on the Platres road, and leads for 4.8 km. past the *Caledonian Falls* to *Psilon Dhendron trout farm.* The falls are especially attractive.

Troodos to Kakopetria and Asinou

Route From Troodos drive 7 km. east to Pano Amiandos and in 2 km. turn left at the crossroads for Kakopetria (11 km.). Continue on the same road and in 10 km. turn right on to the main road from Nicosia. In another 12 km. turn right for Vizakia and drive a further 2 km. to Nikitari, where the priest holds the keys to Asinou church. The best way to contact him is through the coffee-house opposite the church right at the end of the village; the little blue-and-white house where he has lived since 1950 is only a few yards away. He will accompany you to Asinou, but will want you to drive him back to Nikitari afterwards. After visiting the church you could make a little excursion into the hills above Asinou, where especially in autumn the scenery is magnificent. On the way back to Troodos there are two calls worth making, the first at Galata and the second near Kakopetria.

Asinou Church

This church is so tiny that it is difficult to believe that the journey will have been worthwhile. But it is like a jewel box, containing wonderful things – the finest frescoes in Cyprus, painted (or rather repainted) in 1331, are rightly known and admired by specialists in Byzantine art. Their colours are spectacular (especially since the excellent restoration carried out in the 1960s by experts from the Centre for Byzantine Studies at Dumbarton Oaks, a department of Harvard University), and they crowd every square foot of the interior of the building.

Starting at the west end of the nave, see in the south-west arcade a portrait of Nikiphorus Magister, the donor of the church in 1105–6, and in the north-west arcade a picture of the scene of the Forty Martyrs of Sebastea about to be thrown into a frozen lake, their arrow-wounds bleeding freely, bloody footprints staining the ice. At the right of the picture a soldier volunteering to take the place of a fleeing man and being rewarded by the fortieth crown of martyrdom. The whole scene has a graphic chill of horror. Above the west door of the church, leading into the narthex, is a major painting of the Death and Assumption of the Virgin, with Christ holding his Mother's soul in the form of a child.

The paintings in the narthex, the little room at the west end of the church, are dated c. 1333, with the Last Judgment as a central theme, with Christ the Ruler of the World and medallions of the Virgin, angels and saints surrounding him; 'saved' men are near Him, but below are sinners, tortured by fire and snakes. St George is in the south apse of the narthex, his spirited horse's caparison glittering with jewels and his own with shining gold. There are well over 100 paintings altogether, and a booklet describing them should be, but is not always, available.

Galata
Hotel: *One-star*: the Rialto (0292–2438).

Retracing your steps, just before Kakopetria is the town of Galata with its *Church of St Sozemenos*, completed in 1513. This has a sequence of paintings showing the martyrdom of St George and the life of the Virgin, with striking likenesses of (among others) SS Paraskevi, Kyriaki, Varvara and Catherine. The little *Chapel of Panayia Arkhangelos* (1514) also has some fine paintings (by the local artist Symeon Afxentis), with a charming Nativity showing a balding shepherd befriending Joseph, and that of *Panayia Podithou* (1502), a wonderfully rich Last Supper and Annunciation.

Kakopetria
Hotels: There are four in the town: *three-star*, the Makris (0292–2419); *two-star*, the Hakali (2501), the Hellas (2450); *one-star*, the Krystal (2433).

Kakopetria has grown considerably in recent times, and there are several good restaurants there. South of Kakopetria (by about 3 km.) is the *Church of St Nicholas of the Roof (Ayios Nikolaos tis Steyis)*. The original dome of the church is concealed by a later roof; but the interior still shows its marvellous eleventh- to thirteenth-century frescoes, and a unique fourteenth-century icon of St Nicholas painted on vellum. The oldest frescoes show the Raising of Lazarus and the Entry into Jerusalem, and the twelfth-century Apotheosis of the Sea, showing a half-naked nereid riding a fish, reminds one how often the old pagan legends became associated with later Christian lore (it is notable, for instance, that on Cyprus the Virgin seems half-sister to Aphrodite, with a greater emphasis on her femininity, even sexuality, than almost anywhere else in Christendom).

Troodos to Kalopanayiotis and Kykko

Route   North-west from Troodos, in 5 km. you pass through Prodhromos (at 1,400 metres the highest village in Cyprus); a further 3 km. leads to Pedhoulas. Drive 3 km. further to Moutoullas, and then north to Kalopanayiotis. In just over 1 km. turn left to Yerakies along a mountain road, and at Xistraroudhi junction (in 13 km.) turn right and drive 4.8 km. to Kykko Monastery.

Pedhoulas
Hotels: There are four at Pedhoulas: *three-star*: the Churchill (0545–2211); *two-star*: the Marangos (2657); *one-star*: the Central (2457) and Jack's (2350).

The village grows excellent fruit, and in spring is drenched with cherry-blossom. The 1474 Church of the Archangel Michael (*not* the big church with the white dome, but a smaller building near by) has good but damaged frescoes.

Kalopanayiotis
Sufferers from indigestion, rheumatism and skin afflictions still travel to this town to take the benefits of the sulphur springs (either drinking the waters, or sitting in them). Here is a beautiful *Church of St John Lampadistes* – or rather, three churches, for beneath one roof are an eleventh-century church of St Heracleidos (with thirteenth-, four-teenth- and fifteenth-century paintings, including a Triumphal Entry into Jerusalem), a north chapel built especially for the celebration of the Latin rite, with some particularly lovely sixteenth-century frescoes, and the main church (greatly restored) containing the tomb of St John Lampadistes himself, of whom next to nothing is known.

The Monastery of Kykko
This monastery was always said to be the richest in Cyprus, and certainly amassed a considerable fortune over the centuries, partly

because of an affectionate and profitable relationship with Tsarist Russia. It was founded in 1080 after a spectacular gesture by the Byzantine Duke of Cyprus, Manuel Voutomitis, who had been cured of an illness by a local hermit, Isaiah, and somehow persuaded the emperor of Constantinople, Alexius Comnenus, to part with an icon of the Virgin which was one of three said to have been painted by no less an artist than St Luke (more celebrated, it will be recalled, as a doctor). Some authorities suggest that it was the emperor's daughter who had been cured, of sciatica; but what would she have been doing in the mountains of Cyprus? Others assert that the painting was of a less distinguished subject, one Eleousa the Compassionate. Anyway, one way or another an original artwork by St Luke was acquired – and is still at the monastery, having miraculously survived several fires (which completely destroyed the monastery in 1365, 1542, 1751 and 1831), and, now placed centrally on the iconostasis, is so thoroughly covered by a cloth decorated with seed pearls and encased in silver-gilt that it cannot actually be seen. It is particularly revered as an object which, if treated with proper respect, will bring rain; the local people also point out that the trees of the mountains around bow towards the monastery as a sign of respect for the icon. The prevailing winds are not thought to have anything to do with this fact. There is another endearing relic here: a bronze arm which was once flesh and blood and attached to a Negro gentleman who tried to light a cigarette at one of the lamps illuminating the icon. The Virgin immediately severed the arm and turned it into bronze. Smoking is not now encouraged.

The monastery's traditional function as a place of sanctuary was so enthusiastically upheld during the EOKA operations of the 1950s that it was for a time occupied by British anti-terrorist troops (Commandos and Gordon Highlanders). After the final settlement, an enormous cache of arms was removed from the monastery buildings. President Makarios served time here as a novice monk. Regular rebuilding after fire has ensured that the monastery buildings are relatively modern and relatively uninteresting. There are, however, some well-executed and moderately well-designed mosaics at the entrance and around the monastery's interior walls; and even a short stay in the church will show that it is frequently visited by the faithful, for there is a constant trickle of worshippers – young boys in leather jackets, girls in bright skirts, the old in rusty black – kissing the icons on the iconostasis. Non-worshipping visitors, incidentally, should not step behind the rail which protects these.

The monastery's *museum* (20c entrance fee) has some eighteenth-
and nineteenth-century reliquaries containing sundry pieces of bone
from various saints, a fine eighteenth-century embroidery of the
funeral of the Virgin, some embroidered stoles, amber and alabaster
bishops' staffs, a twelfth-century bible and fifteenth-century icon of
the Crucifixion.

Not 200 metres from the monastery is an excellent tourist pavilion
serving decent basic dishes and with a fine panoramic view of Mount
Troodos (in winter, capped with snow) at its centre.

Some 27 km. from Kykko (via Cedars Valley, south of Mount
Tripylos, and by a particularly beautiful route) is the *Stavros tis
Psokas Forest Station*, with its moufflon enclosure (see p. 44).

Troodos to the Pitsilia District

Route From Troodos to Pano Platres (7 km.), and leave by the upper road past
Mesapotamos, a disused monastery; in 21.7 km., at Kato Amiandos, turn left
(signposted Nicosia) and in another 4 km. turn right and follow the road to
Kyperounda; in 10.4 km. at Khandria, turn right for Agros (9.6 km.). A drive
eastwards from Agros leads to Palekhori after 18 km. Alona is a 13 km. drive from
Agros. To visit the Church of Panayia tou Arakou, drive westward from Alona,
turning right after Polystipos for Lagoudhera (3 km. farther on).

This whole area, in pleasantly hilly but not really mountainous
countryside, would make a delightful, quiet holiday retreat; the hills
are covered with vines, and it is here that the grapes are grown for the
Commandaria dessert wine first produced by the Knights Hospitaller
(see p. 80).

At **Palekhori**, the little houses cluster around the poplars by the
waters of the Peristerona River; good local wine has been served here
since the days when the Templars ruled (indeed, owned) it. Though
there are some passably interesting seventeenth-century paintings in
the local churches, there are more interesting buildings not too far
away. To see these start again at Agros and drive to **Alona**, turning
right there for the delightful *Church of Stavros tou Ayiasmati* near
Platanistasa. Here there are good wall-paintings done in 1446 by an
artist called Philip (retouched since, but not too radically) showing
events in the life of Christ and the Virgin, and portraits of saints –
including (at the west end of the south wall) St Mamas riding his lion,
and St Demetrios. (NB: for the key, apply to the priest at Platanistasa,
2 km. to the north.)

Return to *Alona* and drive to **Lagoudhera**. Here, above the village, on the right-hand side of the road and looking like a farmhouse, is the *Church of Panayia tou Arakou*, whose late twelfth-century wall-paintings are regarded as second only to those at Asinou. The whole church is covered by a wooden trellis, shielding even the little round tower. The brilliantly coloured paintings centre on a great Christos Pantokrator, Ruler of the World, up in the dome, surrounded by angels and prophets. There are biblical scenes, too, and saints and martyrs decorate the walls, arches and vaults, and a very stern Virgin and Child, rebuking rather than blessing. All the designs are splendidly vigorous, the colours rich and satisfying, specially since the fine restoration work done here in the early 1970s by the Dumbarton Oaks team from Harvard.

PAPHOS (KTIMA)

Hotels

Five-star: the Annabelle (tel. 38333) is a first-rate hotel with most desirable amenities. It stands on the site of a number of Hellenistic and Roman tombs, in one of which was found a complete, unique set of ancient surgical instruments. Some of the tombs have been preserved and may be seen in the forecourt and basement of the hotel.

Four-star: the Cypria Maris Hotel (38111), about 2.4 km. from the old harbour of Paphos, is near a sandy beach, but there is also rock bathing close by. There is a kindergarten to care for children; live entertainment includes folk-dancing, and there are the usual facilities. The Paphos Beach Hotel (33091), currently being renovated, has eight acres of landscaped gardens and its own sandy beach, and is ten minutes' walk from the harbour. There are 'mountain-view' and 'sea-view' rooms.

Three-star: the Cynthiana Beach Hotel (33900) is in a rocky cove five minutes' drive from town. The Dionysus Hotel is at the centre of the tourist part of Paphos, 300 metres from a good beach; it is described as 'homey'. The Aloe Hotel (34000) is a small and modern, fifteen minutes' walk from Old Paphos. The Veronica Hotel (36333) is 500 metres from the sea, 2.4 km. from Paphos harbour.

Two-star: the Theofano Hotel (33666) is 400 metres from the sea, at some distance from the centre of Paphos.

One-star: the smaller Pyramos 'family' Hotel (35161) is in the centre of the tourist area; the beach is ten minutes' walk away.

Apartments

The Sofianna Hotel apartments (35111) are next to an ancient church, three minutes from the sea and near the old harbour. The Daphne apartments (33500) are in the same area. Paphos Gardens apartments (37031) are conveniently near to two large hotels, but ten minutes away from other restaurants. The Leda Gardens (35909) are 2.4 km. from the beach. The Basilica Gardens (35737) are near a pebble beach; the Miofori Hotel apartments (34311) are in New Paphos, near the tavernas and discos. Thelma Holiday Apartments (34353) are fifteen minutes' walk from New Paphos and the sea. The Marina apartments (35838) are on the seafront and near the archaeological sites. The Helios Bay apartments (35656) are 6.5 km. from Paphos harbour, in a small, sandy cove. Stephanie Villas (34363) are near Tala village, 8 km. inland; there are splendid gardens, and use of the Kamares Club's swimming pool. Kamares Villas apartments (34495) are 800 metres north of Tala, 1.5 km. from St Neophytos Monastery. There is a swimming pool and a sunbathing area.

Some restaurants
King's and Theo's are half restaurants, half tavernas along the old harbourside, and serve decent Cypriot food. Others include Pegasus, Apostolos Pavlos Avenue; Mousallas, Akropolis; Dolphin, Poseidonos St.

Some tavernas
The Pelican, Paphos harbour; the Castle, Paphos harbour; Mandra, Poseidonos St.

Cinemas
Atheneum, Kiazim Osman Pasha St; Taliotis Nicolas, E. Pallikarides Avenue; Titania, N. Antoniades St; Zena, Geroudis St.

Tourist Information Office (*Map 5*)
This is at 3 Gladstone St (32833).

Cypriots who speak of the town sometimes refer to it as Ktima: in fact, Ktima is the modern, administrative centre. About 3 km. to the south is Nea (New) or Kato (Lower) Paphos, the port, while 15 km. to the east is Palea (Old) Paphos. The tourist need not be confused, however: a map makes everything quite clear (see p. 154). There is now little to choose between Ktima and Nea or Kato Paphos – the once pretty harbour bay has been visually raped by indiscriminate overdevelopment, though the harbour itself is lively enough in summer, when the little tavernas lay their tables in the open air above the lapping water. The two pelicans once such a feature of the waterfront have long since died as a result of eating litter.

HISTORY

The area was inhabited in Neolithic times, and it used to be suggested that Nea Paphos was founded in the fifteenth century BC by members of an Arcadian expedition to Troy. Paphos certainly existed in Homeric times, for in the *Odyssey*, after the break-up of the affair between Aphrodite and Ares,

> To the soft Cyprian shores the goddess moves
> To visit Paphos and her sacred groves
> Where to the Powers an hundred altars rise
> And breathing odours scent the balmy skies.
> Concealed she bathes in consecrated bowers,
> The Graces unguents shed, ambrosial showers,
> Unguents that charm the gods: she last assumes
> Her wondrous robes, and full the goddess blooms.

There are certainly records to show that the town was thoroughly established by the seventh to eighth centuries BC – sufficiently so for Arab raiders to pay it regular attention. Earthquakes subsequently devastated the town, and as Salamis grew in importance so Paphos declined, until by the fifteenth century AD it was little more than a disreputable camp. It was, in its day, however (and particularly during Ptolemaic and Roman rule on the island), an important guardian of the Greek tradition: it was governed by a *demos* or popular assembly and a *boule* or council, and under Septimus Severus was given the title *iera metropolis ton kata Kypron poleon* – 'the sacred metropolis of all Cypriot towns'. The Cypriot mint was at Paphos, and the city was responsible for supervising the cults not only of Aphrodite and Apollo, but of Zeus, Leto and Artemis. It seems always to have been an extremely civilised town: where else have sacred doves been trained to flutter about the head of the king, to cool him in the heat of summer?

THE ARCHAEOLOGICAL SITES

During the present century Paphos harbour has been dredged, while, following the Turkish invasion, an airport has been opened and the area has become a centre for tourism. Apart from the pleasures of sea and sand, however, there are interesting archaeological sites to visit and amateur archaeologists began to show an interest in Paphos as far back as the nineteenth century.

Most of the sites lie within the Roman city wall, which embraces the old town. Starting at the harbour, you can follow the wall along the line of the coast to the west and north, then, turning inland just outside the modern lighthouse, reach the coast again south of the *Church of Panayia Theoskepasti* (*Map* 23), at a point at which SS Paul and Barnabas are thought to have embarked.

The House of Dionysus Mosaics (*Map* 11)
This, too, lies down near the old harbour. In 1962 a plough turned up some fragments of mosaic, and excavation uncovered the remains of a palatial Roman villa of twenty-four rooms grouped in two storeys around a central colonnaded open courtyard. An earthquake toppled the walls in the fourth century – one of them falling conveniently on a slave making his escape with a hoard of his master's coins; these dated the villa (together with those found, in mint condition, in a

Town Plan of Paphos (Ktima)

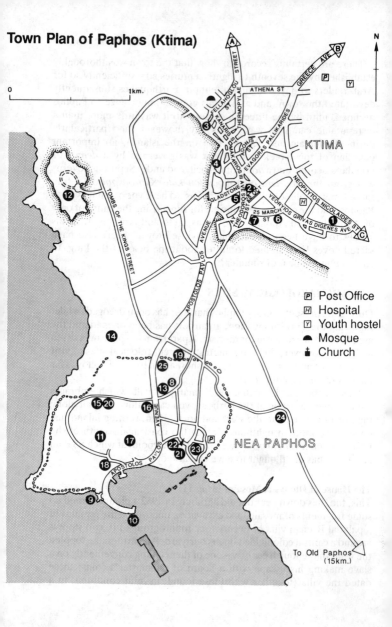

N

0   1km.

KTIMA

P Post Office
H Hospital
Y Youth hostel
⬤ Mosque
⬥ Church

NEA PAPHOS

To Old Paphos
(15km.)

large amphora). The mosaic floors are wonderfully complete, and in fourteen rooms offer a series of mythological subjects, each one carefully captioned in Latin. Inside the main entrance sits Narcissus, on a rock, gazing wistfully into the middle distance. Turning right, the floor of the *Hall of Mother Earth* has portraits of Spring, Summer, Autumn and Winter surrounding the Earth Mother herself – the heads enclosed within a cleverly devised border of cubes which deceive the eye into believing them three-dimensional.

An excellent illustrated handbook available at the site describes the other mosaics in detail: among figures to seek out are that of Dionysus driving in triumph in a chariot drawn by panthers, with a lively Pan following behind, and two naked, bound African slaves. Another panel shows Dionysus drinking with the nymph Akme, a wonderfully solid cart drawn by oxen bringing more wine, and two youths falling-down drunk.

Perhaps the most beautiful of all the panels shows the nymph Daphne being chased by Apollo, their figures so supple that it is difficult to believe that they are composed of pieces of stone. Some fierce hunting scenes show Cypriot moufflon, dogs, leopards and boars. The tableau of the young Ganymede being carried off by an eagle – and looking not entirely dissatisfied with his fate – has been often reproduced, but like the others rewards careful study; the colours are dim with dust, but splashes of vivid red, green, blue can still be seen.

There was a building on this site before the House of Dionysus, for

Town Plan of Paphos (Ktima)

KTIMA
1 Paphos District museum
2 Cyprus Handicrafts Service
3 Market
4 Central Post Office
5 Tourist Information Office
6 Byzantine museum
7 Eliades Collection

NEA PAPHOS
8 Ayia Solomanii Tomb
9 Castle
10 Nea Paphos Fortress
11 House of Dionysus Mosaics
12 Tomb of the Kings
13 Christian catacombs
14 Rock-cut tombs

15 Odeon, Gymnasium
16 Old Latin Cathedral
17 Byzantine Fortress
18 Panayia Limeniotissa
19 Rock of Dighenis
20 Roman Theatre
21 Church of St Kyriakis Chryssopolitissa
22 Site of Gothic Cathedral
23 Panayia Theoskepasti
24 Cave Sanctuary of Apollo Hylates
25 Ayios Lambrianos

Routes to
A Coral Bay, Ayios Yeoryios
B Stroumbi, Polis
C Yeroskipos, Paphos Airport, Limassol

a few years ago a piece of earlier pebble-mosaic flooring was found one metre below the level of the more ambitious mosaics. Showing Scylla, the mythical sea-monster, it has been lifted and may be seen in a corner near the entrance.

North-west of the House of Dionysus is the *Villa of Theseus*, a building which must have been of great magnificence. It has been tentatively identified as the official residence of the Roman governor. It contains a mosaic showing an elegantly complex labyrinth complete with Minotaur, Theseus and Ariadne. Near by, another shows an unidentified scene with a pugnacious, armed Cupid in a corner.

The Basilica of Panayia Limeniotissa (*Map* 18)

Between the House of Dionysus and the harbour lie the meagre remains of a fifth-century basilica probably destroyed by piratical Arabs in AD 653; the Arabs then took over the site, though after their departure in the seventh century a smaller basilica was built here. St Neophytos describes its destruction by earthquake in the second half of the twelfth century.

Nea Paphos Fortress (*Map* 10)

This neat little Turkish fort, built in 1592 by Hafouz Ahmed Pasha, then governor of the island, protects the harbour. It reinforced the Venetian fortifications which themselves had replaced Byzantine walls, and was built on the site of two earlier forts (the second, built in 1391, had been blown up by the Venetians). But it is not of great interest; some prison cells and a single central room. Good views from the roof. The Fort is usually open on weekdays between 7.30 a.m. and 2 p.m., on Saturdays until 1 p.m.; it is closed on Sundays.

The Roman Theatre (*Map* 20)

A Roman wall embraces the site of Nea Paphos; follow this around east and then north from the fort, and just south-east of the lighthouse you will find the remains of a Roman theatre with fourteen rows of seats – their marble cladding has vanished, presumably removed by local builders. But they have been refurbished, and the theatre is now once more occasionally used for performances.

The 'Byzantine' Fortress (*Map* 17)

This stood near the harbour just east of the basilica and the House of Dionysus. It was obviously a site of very considerable importance, but for many years confused inexpert attempts to understand it, for as usual much of the fallen stoneware had been carried off for use elsewhere, and fallen columns had been broken up or shifted about. The building which stood here was for years referred to as 'The House of Forty Columns', marking the number of granite pillars which still lay around. Recent work has revealed that it was in fact a Frankish castle destroyed, not too long after its erection, by the earthquakes of 1222. It had a square keep with towers at each corner, and an open courtyard around which columns supported an upper floor. A wall and moat surrounded it, protected by more towers. There is some suggestion that this was 'a Crusader castle', and indeed records show that several Crusaders died at Nea Paphos, among them a duke of Bavaria, a count of Savoy and a king of Denmark. This is a fascinating site – a wonderful place for children of all ages, full of strange corners, dark, deep wells and staircases leading nowhere.

The Old Latin Cathedral (*Map* 16)
Only two toppled walls mark the position of the sometime Latin Cathedral of Paphos, just on the right of the road leading down to the harbour. That this was an important building of peculiar sanctity is testified by the belief that earth taken from the site, mixed with water, and swallowed, miraculously improves the flow of milk in nursing mothers.

The Tombs of the Kings (*Map* 12)
These lie to the north of the lighthouse, some way from the above sites. It is certain that no kings were actually buried here; but the tombs were used for burials between the third century BC and the third century AD, and later by early Christians who took refuge here as they did in the catacombs of Rome. In spring then as now, the hardy cyclamen blossomed, clinging to the surface of the rocks and contributing to the somewhat melancholy, romantic air of the place.

These tombs, despite the occasional Christian graffito, are not much like those of the catacombs – they are more like those of the kings and queens of Egypt, 500 miles to the south. And before time had stripped away the frescoed plaster which once covered their walls, the resemblance must have been much closer. It is safe to assume, indeed, that the original inhabitants were Ptolemaic officials.

Some of the burial-places are simple holes in the rock, but the more elaborate ones are worth descending into – particularly perhaps Nos. 3 and 4 (the latter is the best-preserved on the site) and No. 5, which was recently excavated and is one of the largest tombs on Cyprus, with twelve sturdy pillars. Near Tomb No. 7, preserved under glass, lie the bones of a horse, presumably sacrificed after drawing its master's body to its last resting-place (see p. 190).

Ayia Solomonii (Map 8)

This is a catacomb dug into the rock of Fabrica Hill opposite the Apollon Hotel, and lies in the shadow of an enormous and ancient fig tree whose branches are still more often than not decorated with tattered handkerchiefs brought as votive offerings to St Solomonii, whose seven sons were martyred in 168 BC for their Jewish faith. Originally just one of a number of tombs, the place was singled out in the fourth century BC as a synagogue, and then became a chapel complete with ninth-century frescoes (the earliest in the island) and a tenth-century picture of the Distribution of the Dismembered Christ (or the Eucharist). The well off the courtyard next to the cell used to be known for curing diseases of the eyes. This catacomb will probably only be lit by one or two flickering candles. Take a torch if you have one, and watch your step.

The Cave Sanctuary of Apollo Hylates (Map 24)

The Cave Sanctuary lies at the east of Nea Paphos, and while it has little to show must have a sentimental value for those who wish to pay their respects to the ancient mysteries of the island, for, dated 600–296 BC, it is an unmistakable counterpart of the famous shrine of the Oracle at Delphi – and of the other oracle sites like those in Malta. There are two underground chambers from which the Oracle spoke to the Guardian of the Sanctuary, who in turn interpreted the gnomic utterances to the faithful.

CHURCHES

The Church of St Kyriaki Chryssopolitissa (Map 21)

An eleventh–twelfth-century Byzantine church converted from Latin to orthodox rites, the building is less interesting than the adjoining site, at the extreme west of which some granite columns still stand, part of an earlier basilica. Unsupported tradition says that St Paul was chained to one of these (the taller, rounded one at the gateway to the site) to receive the punishment known as 'the forty stripes save one': assault with a whip with thirty-nine lashes. He recovered, and it was at Paphos that he confronted a sorcerer named Elymas, who under the name of Bar-Jesus was regaling the governor, Sergius Paulus, with various prophecies. St Paul, never short of a pungent phrase, set about Elymas with his tongue and threatened him with blindness. Whereupon, Acts tells us, 'there fell upon him a mist and a darkness, and he went about seeking someone to lead him by the hand'. The governor was converted.

Some beautiful patches of mosaic – some of them extensive – can be seen here, with lovely half-buried acanthus capitals, scraps of carved marble and an occasional tombstone.

The Church of Panayia Theoskepasti (*Map 23*)
The most interesting thing about the Church of the Shrouded Madonna is the fact that, when the Arabs invaded, a church-shaped cloud descended and hid it (alas, only temporarily) from their eyes.

MUSEUMS

The Paphos District Museum (*Map 1*)
In Grivas Dighenis Avenue, on the right-hand side of the Limassol road as you enter Ktima, this is an excellent collection. Among the miscellaneous pottery of which there are many counterparts elsewhere, there is some fine jewellery (including a lovely pair of earrings, two tiny, exquisite winged cherubs). A fourth-century BC tombstone shows a small child bidding farewell to its dead father, who holds its hands with one of his, and with the other grips that of his mourning wife. A lively lion from Nea Paphos pounces in the neighbouring room, and there is a case of items from the House of Dionysus, including perhaps the owner's own sword and a brazen head and shoulders of Dionysus himself. A perfect, undamaged statuette of Asklepius (from the Villa of Theseus) holds the staff and serpent which were the signs of his devotion to healing, and – the most surprising item in the museum, and one of the most surprising in all Cyprus – there is a set of Roman hot-water bottles carefully shaped to warm all the separate parts of the body: left hand, right hand, left side of face, genitals . . .

The Byzantine Museum (*Map* 6)
There are some fine icons in this museum, which is in 25 March St.

The Eliades Collection (*Map* 7)
The collection is housed at 1 Exo Vyrsis St. It is a private one, but visitors are welcome; there are costumes, coins, kitchen utensils and a few other artefacts.

EXCURSIONS FROM PAPHOS

Paphos to Yeroskipos and the Temple of Aphrodite at Palea Paphos

Route Leave Paphos by the main Limassol road, which leads in 4 km. to Yeroskipos. From here, continue along the main Limassol road for 11 km. to the village of Kouklia. The site of Palea Paphos lies to its north. Petra tou Romiou is 7 km. further east along the coastal road to Limassol.

Yeroskipos

The village's name, in the original Greek, meant 'the Sacred Garden'. Here, the pilgrims who had landed at the harbour of Nea Paphos and were making for the spring festival at the Temple of Aphrodite would pause for rest among trees and flowers specially nurtured for this and other similar occasions. In more recent times, Turkish Delight has been a speciality here.

The village itself is relatively modern, dating from Byzantine times, and the main reason for stopping here is to call at the *Church of St Paraskevi*, whose saint was a Roman convert born in the second century and martyred under Marcus Aurelius. This church and the one at Peristerona are the only two on the island with five Byzantine domes, three of them on the main axis of the church and the other two, at a lower level, over the north and south transepts – the style imitates that of St John's Church at Ephesus and the Coronation Church of the Holy Apostles at Constantinople. There is a famous icon here – double-sided, probably fifteenth-century, with the Virgin and Child on one side and the Crucifixion on the other. Inside the church is plain, with a stone balcony for women; a few tatters of fresco survive on the north wall of the nave: a peculiarly Roman Last Feast with the disciples looking like Roman citizens, a Betrayal with watching soldiers in medieval armour, and a Washing of the Feet.

A *Museum of Folk Art* has been established in a house which once belonged to a brilliant Greek Cypriot youth called Zinbouli, who was made British vice-consul in 1800 and called himself Haji Smith as a compliment to his patron, Sir Sydney Smith. The museum is devoted to local costumes, farming implements, pottery, domestic implements and naïve art.

FOR WALKERS
There is a pleasant walk to be had from Yeroskipos back to Paphos harbour, cutting south from the village to the coast, then following it back to the town – a distance of about 8 km.

Palea Paphos

HISTORY

Pausanias, the second-century AD Greek traveller who wrote a history of all things Greek, says that Old Paphos was founded by Agapenor, the hero of the Trojan Wars; and the city is certainly associated with King Pygmalion (see p. 75). His child by Galatea was named Paphos.

To turn to more positively recorded history, though the site had been occupied as early as the sixteenth century BC, Palea Paphos is first mentioned on an Assyrian tablet (now in the British Museum) which refers to a seventh-century BC king named Ithuander; later, the city-state was ruled by priest-kings, successors of Kinyras (Adonis's father, who was said to have lost an unwise musical contest with Apollo) who practised Egyptian religious rites adapted to the worship of Adonis and Aphrodite. After a rebellion against Ptolemy I, in 295 BC, Paphos forfeited its power, though it remained a religious centre until the Romans took over government in 56 BC. During the fourth century AD, a decree of the Byzantine emperor Theodosius (AD 346–395) forced all pagan temples to cease their religious practices, and it was at this time that the Temple of Aphrodite fell into disuse after many centuries as a centre of worship of the old gods.

The village of **Kouklia** achieved some importance under the Lusignans as the site of a royal pavilion (see below); but by the beginning of the fifteenth century Saracen raids had reduced it to a desuetude equal to that of the near-by temple complex.

Serious excavations started here in 1887, when the British School in Athens sent an expedition; and there has been intermittent work ever since. There remain enormous opportunities for excavation, for Old Paphos was a great deal larger than present-day Kouklia, and the whole of the ground between the present village and the main road could be one large archaeological site.

The Temple of Aphrodite

The Temple of Aphrodite is part of a rather confusing site which conveys little of its original importance. Some archaeologists consider that the great temple of the goddess remains to be discovered, and that what we have here are simply outbuildings. Paphos was already Aphrodite's home in the *Odyssey* (i.e. about 1000 BC). But this site dates from the twelfth century, when Mycenaean Achaeans settled here, and there are various signs of Mycenaean occupation – the tripartite temple façade with cult horns shown on coins found here, for instance.

The building thought at present to be the Temple consisted of a series of courtyards in a Phoenician style, but built using Greek techniques. The use to which many of the rooms and courtyards was put can only be guessed at; but it is fairly clear that processions of pilgrims approached from two directions – eastward from the harbour of Paphos and westward from Curium – and entered by two ceremonial gates on the eastern and southern sides, from which they would probably have progressed to the large central court with its two adjoining halls, the centre of the complex where was the *naos* in which a statue or symbol was placed for worship (see site plan, p. 165).

The site must always have been open and airy – breezes scented by flowers and herbs were usually features of Aphrodite's temples, blowing gently through landscaped gardens in which there were often pleasure-benches or pleasure-booths where visitors could pause to make love.

The precise forms of the rites practised here are unknown, but scraps of information suggest that pilgrims and priests took part in the festivals (particularly the great spring festival) according to their rank and degree. There were, it seems, public games which were simply festive, and in which the generality took part; these would be followed by purification ceremonies involving sea-bathing – still fun, but obviously with serious undertones. (Aphrodite's association with the sea has always been strong, and psychiatry has shown how consistently the sea, and water, is connected in the collective unconscious with sexuality and motherhood.) Sacrifices would be offered to Aphrodite, culminating in the High Priest's offering of *Pyramous*, or ritual cake.

The more serious parts of the festival would involve commemorating the premature death of the golden youth, Adonis, by ceremonies of mourning; and these would be followed by celebrations of our resurrection – which probably meant more or less orgiastic activities in which sexual rites played an important part. Phallic symbols would be carried and shown, encouraging fertility, and salt would finally be presented at the altars, symbolising Aphrodite's sea-birth.

It is in one of the poems of Sappho (c.seventh century BC) that the worship of Aphrodite is most charmingly portrayed, with a circle of young girls awaiting marriage, lying on couches bathed in the aura of the goddess and decked out with rich head-dresses, garlands of flowers, sweet fragrances. Aphrodite is summoned to the festival, and descends to her sacred grove:

> In that chariot pulled by sparrows reined and
>   bitted
> Swift in their flying, a quick blur a-quiver,
> Beautiful, high. They drew you across steep air
>   Down to the black earth;
>
> Fast they came, and you behind them, O
> Hilarious heart, your face all laughter,
> Asking, 'What troubles you this time, why again
>   Do you call me down?'

This site more perhaps than any other in Mediterranean history has been associated with religious sexuality, and disapproving writers throughout the ages have tended to see the rites here as excuses for blatant displays of lust, and for 'religious prostitution': Martial suggested that the place was 'infamous through too much heat'. Herodotus reported that here, as in Corinth, every woman in the district must once in her lifetime come to the temple and sit, wearing a plaited bandeau about her head, until a man threw a silver coin into her lap and claimed her in the name of Aphrodite. The priests took the silver; the man took the woman. Historians have suggested that the only reason why pilgrims came here was to indulge themselves. But the truth is that the Temple was a life-asserting centre where congregations praised Aphrodite as the bestower of all fruitfulness, and in particular as goddess of the sexual impulse, and celebrated human sexuality as the source of our being, praising it for that reason. It is interesting, incidentally, that the pilgrims' and priests' homage was paid not to a statue of the goddess in all her earthly beauty, but first to an unshaped, natural stone, and later to a simple cone-shaped stone and to smaller reproductions of it, which priests and worshippers would anoint with oil. Not that there are not figurative 'portraits' of the goddess. Some of the earliest – Bronze Age statuettes – show her naked and with a repulsively frightening bird-face, linking her with Astarte. The statuary of the first half of the seventh century, in which she wears long, sumptuous robes and a high goddess's crown – fine clothes seem at that time to have been her peculiar pleasure – show her in a rather oriental light. It was in about 340 BC that Praxiteles created his famous nude statue of her for the sanctuary in Cnidos which for centuries remained the model of beauty for all European womankind.

THE SITE

Having paid your entrance fee at the ticket office just inside the archway of the Lusignan Manor House, or Chiftlic, to the south of the site (*Map* 1), walk back to the north, passing on your left a platform (2) on which there are innumerable fragments of stone once part of the two sanctuaries. Excavation here has proved difficult because of the wreckage of centuries (including the use of the site as a sugar refinery). The first, southern sanctuary (rebuilt by the Romans on a Bronze Age site) was largely destroyed in medieval times. Originally there was a Temenos, or sacred enclosure (3) and a covered hall (4). A few of the huge stones of which the protective wall was built can still be seen, but the altars which must have stood in the Temenos have vanished. The hall probably stood on the site of the Bronze Age temple: it was here that an enormous twelfth-century BC storage jar was found, which can be seen in the museum. The central shrine or *naos* was probably of light wood and cloth – some sort of canopy which has left no trace.

The second sanctuary was rebuilt in AD 77 after an earthquake: there are two halls (5) and an east wing with an open courtyard (6). A large monolith of dressed limestone near the south-west corner of the north wall (7) marks the position of what the guidebooks still

The Temple of Aphrodite

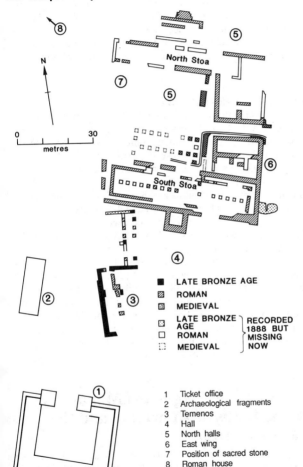

0 ____ 30
metres

North Stoa

South Stoa

■ LATE BRONZE AGE
▨ ROMAN
▩ MEDIEVAL

▫ LATE BRONZE AGE   ⎫ RECORDED
□ ROMAN   ⎬ 1888 BUT MISSING
⸬ MEDIEVAL   ⎭ NOW

1 Ticket office
2 Archaeological fragments
3 Temenos
4 Hall
5 North halls
6 East wing
7 Position of sacred stone
8 Roman house

modestly call 'a conical stone' – the phallus anointed and worshipped as representative of the god. The layout of the north sanctuary bears a close resemblance to that of the Sanctuary of Apollo at Curium (built at about the same time; see p. 134). There are fragments of mosaic and of Doric columns. Other nice, if fragmentary, mosaics can be seen in the remains of a house just west of the north sanctuary (8),

The Lusignan Manor House (Chiftlik)

There is a *museum* in the manor house (also known sometimes as the Royal Pavilion, or La Covacle) in which are some objects found here, and in particular the phallic symbol of Aphrodite which once stood at the centre of the site; there are also two baths, one of which has a beautifully designed, practical soap-dish. The *hall* below the museum is a fine example of Frankish architecture.

Up the hill north-east of Kouklia are the remains of a ramp built by the Persian army which attacked the area in 498 BC; beneath it were found many pieces of Roman masonry and carving.

At **Petra tou Romiou**, a crop of rocks juts into the sea, marking the small beach of Achni where Aphrodite is supposed to have stepped ashore (see p. 72). 'Soft foam' still dances on the waves here, and it is a beautiful spot for a bathe – with the added advantage that the sea beautifies the bather (though it must be said that Aphrodite had the reputation of liking, in particular, to confer irresistible seductive beauty on men, which too often led to trouble on Olympus). The beach is pebbly, and the modern Aphrodites who have posed here for photographs have paid with many a bruise. There is an excellent tourist pavilion on the hill above the bay.

Paphos to Ayios Neophytos Monastery, Polis, the Baths of Aphrodite and the Fontana Amorosa

Route Leaving Paphos by the direct road to Polis on the north coast, in 5 km. turn left to Trimithousa, and in 5 km. north come to Ayios Neophytos Monastery. Thence, turning back to the main road, drive on northwards through Stroumbi (9 km.) to Polis and a further 19 km. on, 7 km. west of Polis by the coast road, you reach the parking place for the Baths of Aphrodite (Loutra tis Aphroditis). From here it is a 5 km. walk to Fontana Amorosa.

Ayios Neophytos Monastery

St Neophytos was born at Kato Dhrys (near Kato Lefkara) in 1134, and taking exception to his parents' choice of a bride ran away from home to become a novice at the Monastery of St Chrysostomos, near Buffavento (see p. 182). Illiterate, at first he cultivated the vineyards; but he taught himself to read and write and eventually rose to become sacristan. However, he obviously felt unsuited to community life and decided to find a convenient cave somewhere in Asia Minor in which to set up as a hermit. Reaching Paphos, from which he was to set sail, he was arrested (for what reason we are not told) and put into prison. Released at the age of twenty-five, he made for the hills above the sea north of the town, and there excavated his own cave, in which he was to live for sixty years. His desire for the solitary life was frustrated, for Christians hearing of this remarkable man who had dug himself a home in the sheer rock with his bare hands, continually descended on him, and eventually formed a community around him, so that he was virtually forced to found his own monastery. He later wrote several books of theology, including an Introduction to the *Song of Solomon* and a tirade against Richard the Lion Heart ('that wretch the English king').

The setting of the monastery is beautiful; there is a handsome small garden first cultivated by the saint himself, with olive, lemon and pomegranate trees. The cave or caves in which the saint spent his life are fascinating. In one of them is a coffin (which may also have been his bed) cut out of the rock, and a cupboard once filled with the skulls of his followers. Communicating are a little sanctuary, a table and chair carved out of the rock, with a tiny niche for pens and paper, and a chapel with a rough wooden cross and some simple but affecting frescoes – including one of Christ Washing the Disciples' Feet (they sit on the ground removing their sandals and waiting their turn). The paintings on the north side of the chapel are perhaps 700 years old. In the sanctuary is a portrait of the saint, supported by angels, and in his cell is the Resurrection, with St Neophytos kneeling at Christ's feet. There is another cave somewhat up the hill which, driven out of his rooms by crowds of admirers, he evidently used for solitude and contemplation. This is usually closed to visitors.

The monastery itself, east of this little complex of caves, has a few guest rooms facing the sea (it has always been an hospitable community), and a church built in 1435, with three aisles and a barrel-vault roof supported by columns with delicate acanthus-leaf carvings on the capitals. The paint with which the monks had covered these carvings has now been removed by the Cypriot Ministry of Antiquities, which is also working to restore the frescoes which remain – the salt from water seeping through the roof has unfortunately done irreparable damage, and though originally the whole interior of the church was covered with paintings, only a few – of high quality – remain. On the south barrel of the roof of the sanctuary can be seen the rough preparatory drawings done by the original anonymous artist (see p. 40). The removal of the plaster from the dome has revealed, at least, the remarkable masonry.

St Neophytos died in 1219 and was buried in the coffin he had carved for himself next to his writing-desk. For some years pilgrims came to gaze at his body, but during the sixteenth-century Turkish occupation a wall was built and decorated, to conceal the corpse, and eventually its whereabouts were forgotten. It was in 1715 that a monk, told in a dream of the presence of hidden treasure behind the wall, broke it down to reveal St Neophytos's body, still entire and sweet-smelling. It was removed from the tomb in 1750, and the bones now lie here, in a wooden sarcophagus; his skull is near by in a silver reliquary. There are also some early icons which are well worth examination: a fine Virgin and Child of 1450, a 1505 portrait of the saint, and the famous Great Deisis which originally consisted of seventeen panels ranged on the iconostasis – Christ in the centre, the Virgin and St John the Baptist on her right and left, the Archangels Michael and Gabriel, and the twelve Apostles (one of whom is now missing). Outside the monastery is a useful souvenir shop, and a number of cats some of whom have emigratory ambitions, for they insist on climbing into one's car.

Stroumbi

Stroumbi was devastated by an earthquake in 1953, and subsequently rebuilt in a rather monotonous style. The village is said to be named after a Medieval landlord who was inordinately fat (*stroumbos*); it is an excellent place to stop for a glass or two – even a bottle or two – of the local wine. Your sober companion may then be encouraged to drive on through a valley with fine views of the mountains to the east, and then opening out to a patch of sea to the north, where you may either turn right, bypassing **Polis**, or enter the town.

Polis

A centre of the lemon-producing trade, Polis has felt the brunt of the Turkish occupation, now being cut off from Morphou and Nicosia, its closest large markets. *Marion*, a town founded by Athenians in the seventh century BC, was just east of here, and exported copper. In 312 BC Ptolemy's army destroyed it, and its inhabitants were forcibly deported to Paphos; the town was then rebuilt by Ptolemy Philadelphus as *Arsinoe*, just south of the present Polis, which came into existence under the Lusignans.

Polis is surrounded by 400 tombs, most of them excavated under Richter in 1886, when many artefacts were discovered and sold at auction in Paris. Later amateurs and professionals scraped the platter so clean that there is little left here to interest anyone.

West of Polis, drive through **Lachi**, with its cosy little harbour with quays of piled rocks, take the right-hand fork and park near the tourist shelter looking towards Pomos Point (a pleasant spot for a picnic) and walk 300 yards or so through beautiful fertile countryside overlooking the Bay of Khrysokhou.

The Baths of Aphrodite (*Loutra tis Aphroditis*)

The landscape surrounding the Baths of Aphrodite was described by Lodovico Ariosto, the sixteenth-century Italian poet, in his *Orlando Furioso*. It has not changed much since his day:

> Six miles ascending gently from the flood
> Stands on a beauteous hill a verdant wood
> Where cedars, myrtles, bays and orange grow,
> With various plants that grateful scent bestow.
> Wild thyme, the lily, crocus and the rose
> Perfume the air, while every wind that blows
> Fresh from the land, far o'er the surgy main
> Wafts the sweet gale to greet the sailor-train,
> Clear from a spring a murm'ring riv'let pours
> Its winding tribute to the meads and flowers.
> Well may this spot be named the favourite soil
> Of lovely Venus, where with roseate smile
> Each dame, each virgin shines in bloomy pride
> Of charms unequall'd through the world beside,
> Whilst the soft goddess youth and age inspires
> And ev'n in life's last stage maintains her amorous fires.

Aphrodite not only once bathed here, but chose this spot in which to make love to the Greek hero Akamas, who was one of the warriors inside the famous Trojan horse. A British consul once remarked that in his experience the effect of the waters was merely 'to make the spirit willing while the flesh continues weak'. However, that is a matter visitors may safely be left to decide for themselves.

The Fontana Amorosa
The upper, paved path leads to the Baths, the lower by a larger footpath to Fontana Amorosa. The walk around the coast from here towards Cape Arnauti offers the most magnificent views of the bay, and the rough track is usually unpeopled – only the occasional herd of goats with perhaps a young herdsman in attendance may be seen in the distance, their bleats contesting with bird-song. All around, in season, cyclamen, narcissi and cistus and innumerable wild orchid. The walk must surely be the most beautiful in all Cyprus, and even if you do not wish to tackle the whole 5 km. to Fontana Amorosa, do stroll for a hundred metres or so, just to taste its pleasures.

Paphos to the Monasteries of Chrysorroyiatissa and Ayia Moni

Route Leave Paphos by the Polis road, and in 14 km. take a right-hand turning just before Stroumbi, passing through Polemi in 2 km. and joining a splendid new road which courses over the hills with majestic mountain and valley views on to Kannaviou in 10 km.; a fork to the right soon after leads in 9 km. to Pano Panayia (the birthplace of Archbishop Makarios). A sharp right-hand turn here brings one in 2 km. to Chrysorroyiatissa Monastery. Ayia Moni monastery is 3 km farther along the same road.

An excursion to Kykko may be made from Pano Panayia (3 km.) rather than from Limassol (see p. 00). The winding road has marvellous mountain prospects. Allow for an average speed of no more than 6 k.p.h. for the journey of 15 km.

The Monastery of Chrysorroyiatissa
The monastery of 'Our Lady of the Golden Pomegranate' hangs on a terrace over a valley backed by wooded hills. There is total silence except for a chatter of birdsong. The last monks – only two or three of them – left in 1985, and there is now only a caretaker, though Mass is said regularly by a visiting priest. The monastery was allegedly founded by the hermit Ignatios, who lived on Mount Kremaste. One day, looking out from the mountain towards the sea, he saw what

seemed to be a fire burning with peculiar brightness, and when he went to investigate found a miraculous luminous icon which was the handiwork of St Luke. The icon had originally been kept at Isauria, south of Iconium and Lystra in Asia Minor. During the eighth-century Iconoclastic Wars (the result of Pope Leo III's edict against the veneration of pictures) a woman threw the icon into the sea, for protection, and it made straight for Cyprus and Ignatios, who was supernaturally directed to build a shrine for it on Mount Royia – named, it is claimed, after the 'golden breasts of the Virgin' (though some, scandalised by the suggestion, held that the name was derived from the word for pomegranate). As soon as the Christians of Cyprus heard of the icon, they beat a path to the mountain, and the monastery was founded. Whatever reason lay behind the choice of site, it is spectacularly beautiful, almost 1,200 metres above sea-level, with forest to the north, and looking westward over heavily wooded countryside to the sea.

The monastery prospered until the Turkish occupation, when it was deprived of much of its property: the Turks knew the place as the Monastery of the Bell, since its abbot had somehow managed to gain exemption from their prohibition against bell-ringing. Four bells still hang from the little bell-tower. It was in the second half of the eighteenth century that Bishop Panaretos of Paphos encouraged restoration, and since that date the monastery has been one of the most successful and venerated in the island. There is a small church within a beautifully kept unique triangular cloister, and the icon is still kept here inside a silver-gilt case made in 1762, so it cannot be seen; but it is shown in a copperplate engraving done by a famous Greek icon-painter of the late nineteenth century, John Cornaros. The icon itself has always been specially associated with the forgiveness of condemned criminals. Wine with the monastery's own label may be bought here.

The disused *Monastery of Ayia Moni*, protected by Kykko Monastery (see p. 148), has a medieval church built on the site of a much earlier Temple to Hera, at once sister and wife of Zeus and Queen of Olympus: the apse of the pagan temple remains part of the church, which was restored in 1885.

Paphos to Emba, Coral Bay, Peyia Basilica and Ayios Yeoryios Church

Route Emba lies 3 km. north of Ktima. Coral Bay, about 8 km. from Emba, is reached by driving back towards Paphos and taking a violent right-hand fork to bypass Khlorakas. Return along the road leading into the Bay, taking the road up to Peyia, a pleasant hill-village, and following the road to its end, about 7 km., to Peyia Basilica and the Church of Ayios Yeoryios.

The dual-domed large Byzantine *Church of the Blessed Virgin Mary* at **Emba** has three aisles and a narthex from which an outside stairway leads to the roof. The frescoes were over-enthusiastically repainted in 1886. The original fine painting of Christ Pantakrator on the inside of the dome is to be admired. A sixteenth-century icon with two panels, preserved under glass, shows the Twelve Apostles, and with it is a much-damaged copy of the Gospels bound in Venetian leather in 1539. The countryside around Emba is particularly celebrated for spring wild-flowers.

Coral Bay is a famous coastal landmark (on some maps the Bay is called Maa). Originally it was celebrated as a secluded bathing-place, with beautiful coral-pink sands. It cannot now be said to be secluded, though much of the development in the area (hotels and self-catering apartments) is of a high standard. In a cave near by, the bones of early Christian martyrs were found by local inhabitants and venerated for some years – until scientists identified them as being the remains of pygmy hippopotami.

The remains of *Peyia Basilica* – really, those of no less than three churches, one lying above the other – were uncovered in 1951 when archaeologists were excavating some near-by baths. There are enjoyable mosaics of wild beasts. Near by is the *Church of Ayios Yeoryios*, with an altar formed by two Byzantine capitals. These buildings stand near the centre of what was once the Roman city of *Drepanum*: the square mile of ruins has never been properly excavated.

THE OCCUPIED NORTH

In the pages that follow, we give a somewhat truncated description of North Cyprus, which comprises the part of the island occupied after the Turkish invasion in 1974. We underline once more the fact that the Turkish occupation is not recognised by any country in the world other than Turkey, and that though you may enter the northern territories, via Nicosia, for one day, if you enter the island via a northern port or airfield you will not be permitted to enter Cyprus proper.

Though it is very sad that most of the best Byzantine buildings on the island, and many remarkable archaeological sites – including Salamis – are in the occupied sector, we cannot recommend that you undertake any considerable journey over the Green Line. It is for this reason that we concentrate in this section on the history, rather than the topography, of the places mentioned.

It should be understood that it has been impossible to check much of the information given here, which is mostly taken from Hazel Thurston's original *Travellers' Guide to Cyprus*, last revised in 1971. We apologise if this is now in some respects faulty; churches, in particular, have often been pillaged since the invasion, icons stolen and paintings and mosaics defaced or removed.

NICOSIA

Places of historical interest in the Turkish-occupied sector
The map references below are (with one exception, indicated) to the map of 'Nicosia Within the Walls' on p. 89.

The *Tekké of the Mevlevi Dervishes* (*Map* **12**) is on Kyrenia St, just south of the Kyrenia Gate. It was originally a monastery of the whirling dervishes, but was closed when Kemal Atatürk suppressed the Dervish monasteries in Turkey, and is now a *Museum of Turkish Arts and Crafts*, showing musical instruments, costumes, embroidery, etc. Next door to it is a *mausoleum* with the tombs of sixteen sheiks.

At the end of the street is *Atatürk Square* (*Map* **14**), with its tall, grey, granite pillar brought from Salamis and erected by the Venetians as a mark of their supremacy. Pulled down by the Turks in 1570, it was re-erected in 1915 – though the lion of St Mark which had originally surmounted it was lost.

Walking south again, turn right along Mufti Ziya Eff St to the *Arab Achmed Mosque* (*Map* **13**), built in 1485, where the gravestone of Francesco Cornero may be seen – and, annually displayed to the faithful, a hair from the Prophet's Beard. Farther south yet, at the end of Victoria St and close to the Green Line, is the Armenian *Church of the Blessed Virgin* (*Map of Nicosia Outside the Walls*, p. 89, **2**), which was once a Benedictine convent dedicated to St Mary of Tyre. The Turks, after 1570, used it as a salt store, but then presented it to the Armenians as a reward for services rendered.

Along Paphos St, to the east, is the *Beuyuk Khan* (*Map* **11**), an old Turkish caravanserai or inn which would originally have sheltered both travellers and their animals. Later, under the English, it became a prison; it is now being restored – as is the near-by *Kourmandjilar Khan* (*Map* **21**), where the Turkish Cypriot Antiquities Department has its headquarters.

The *Selimiye Mosque* (*Map* **15**), along Arasta St, was originally the Cathedral of Santa Sophia. A small church was built here in 1193, and was used for the coronation of King Amaury in 1197. Some marble decoration from this first building can still be seen incorporated in the present north doorways. It was in 1209 that the foundations of the cathedral itself were laid, and the building was finally consecrated in 1326. It was a fine design, which made provision for important public figures to sit at the west window, between the twin towers, whence they could watch the processions and comings and goings on great occasions.

When the cathedral became a mosque in the sixteenth century, all sculpted figures were removed (in accordance with the Muslim abhorrence of representations of the human figure), and the high altar, the painted altar-screen, the choir stalls and the paintings in the vault (golden stars set in a dark blue vault) were all ripped out or painted over – though the Turks were not alone responsible, for the building was pillaged by the Genoese and the Mamelukes, and two earthquakes also severely damaged it. The interior, with its enormous cyclindrical pillars, is still impressive – partly because of its empty severity. There were five chapels, and through what was once the northernmost one – where the archbishop passed in procession from his palace – is now the entrance to the women's gallery of the mosque. The chapel next door was once the cathedral's treasury, and the mihrab now occupies what was once the lady chapel. The second chapel from the west end was originally dedicated to St Thomas

Aquinas; in it is a collection of Crusaders' tombstones which once lay on the floor of the cathedral proper.

The onetime *Church of St Nicholas* ('of the English') (*Map* 22) is next to the cathedral. Once associated with the cult of St Thomas à Becket, it became the Greek Orthodox Cathedral during the Venetian occupation, and was later used as a grain store and a textile market or *bedestan* (its present, Turkish name). Byzantine, Gothic and Venetian styles are represented – Venetian coats-of-arms stand above the east door, with a figure of St Nicholas (probably) in the middle. There are some Medieval tombstones to be seen.

North-east of the Selimiye Mosque is the *Musée Lapidaire*, or Jeffery's Museum (*Map* 16), a Venetian house with a small collection of carved stone; across the way is the nineteenth-century *Sultan Mahmoud's Library* (*Map* 17), with rare books in Turkish, Arabic and Persian.

To the north, up Kirizade St, very near the home (at 1 Haidar Pasha St) of Lord Kitchener when he served on the island as a captain is the former St Catherine's Church, now the *Haidar Pasha Mosque* (*Map* 18): a fourteenth-century Gothic building on to which a minaret and pierced windows have been somewhat uncomfortably grafted. There is a strangely shaped space at the north of the apse which may have been made in preparation for a tower which was never raised. The interior is in a very bad state, and most of the carvings were mutilated when the church became a mosque; the Turks particularly hated the Latin rite, and did their best to erase all signs of it. But there are three carvings of a rose with a dragon on each side of it, some wrecked shields above the southern doorway (a nice window over them), and, oddly enough, some carvings of human heads surviving on the corbels north of the apse.

EXCURSIONS FROM NICOSIA
Nicosia to Morphou, Soli and Vouni

As the only access to North Cyprus is through the checkpoint by the Paphos Gate in Nicosia, you would now have to travel to Soli and Vouni either by way of Kyrenia, or via Myrtou and Morphou, a total distance of about 55 km. from Nicosia.

Morphou

In this town is the *Church of the Monastery of St Mamas*, originally a Byzantine building, rebuilt in 1725 after a disastrous fire in the early sixteenth century; the dome dates from this rebuilding. The iconotasis incorporates marble columns with Gothic capitals, and fruit is carved in high-relief on the lower panels – obviously set there by the Venetians in about 1500, for there are Venetian heraldic devices at the corners. The painted pulpit dates from 1761. The monastery itself has not been used for some years, though the Bishop of Kyrenia used to use the modern west wing when he was in residence.

St Mamas is a somewhat obscure saint who, as a stalwart opponent of taxation, perhaps deserves to be better-known to modern Western civilisation. When the soldiery came to arrest him for failing to pay his taxes, he calmly accompanied them towards the capital, but as they were passing through a wood a lion suddenly appeared (rather a surprise, since none had previously been seen on the island). St Mamas held up his hand in the manner of a traffic policeman, whereupon the lion stopped, and wagged its tail. The saint climbed on to the animal's back and rode it unmolested to the palace of the Byzantine king, who rapidly granted him exemption from future taxation. The saint's shrine lies in the north wall of the church, and can be seen from outside as well as inside. It is said to exude a liquid which was useful in stilling tempests.

The road south-west out of Morphou passes through countryside where the earth is as red as that of Devonshire; in 17 km. just west of the ancient port of **Karavostasi** (on the left of the coastal road) is the site of the great city of **Soli.**

Soli

Soli is said to have been founded in 600 BC on a site suggested by Solon, the Athenian politician, where previously had stood one of the ten kingdoms of Cyprus. During the Roman period it was notable for the export of copper (Karavostasi has always been associated with this trade). The first public library on the island is said to have been in Soli, and its theatre was also a notable focus of Roman culture. As has happened at so many sites, neighbouring towns (especially in the eighteenth century) plundered the stone of which Soli was built, and there is consequently little sign of its temples and palaces. There was an extensive archaeological dig in 1930, when the *Theatre* was excavated and the Aphrodite of Soli found, now to be seen in the

Cyprus Museum, where is also one of the friezes (showing the battle between Amazons and Greeks) which originally stood in the Temple of Aphrodite and Isis. The Theatre is the most notable visible monument, restored and sometimes used for performances. A small-ish fifth-century BC *basilica* has since been found, but excavation of the ancient city, which formerly progressed a little each year, has presumably ceased since the invasion.

A further 3 km. to the west along the coastal road a track to the right leads to **Vouni**.

Vouni Palace

This is a somewhat mysterious building, apparently built sometime after 600 BC, of whose history practically nothing is known. Here is a sprawling site on which an evidently wealthy man during a time of peace (for there are no defences) built a home of the greatest luxury, with splendid baths and heating systems and plenty of room for servants and for stores. Decorative carvings were brought from Greece, and there were altars, too – and a little *Temple to Athena* not far away where stood a bronze cow which is in the Cyprus Museum. Two carved reliefs showing lions attacking bulls have been removed, one to Nicosia, the other to a museum in Stockholm. The palace seems to have been burned down in about 380 BC. This is not an easy site to explore without a good and knowledgeable guide, and perhaps indeed it is its position which is the main attraction, for below it lies the Bay of Morphou sweeping from Cape Kormakiti to the north to the little island of **Petra tou Limniti** in the west, where Stone Age artefacts have been found

Nicosia to St Hilarion, Kyrenia and Bellapais Abbey

Leave Nicosia on the direct road to **Kyrenia** which leads through **Geunyeli** at 4 km.), then over the low hills for another 12 km. to the *Castle of St Hilarion* up on the left.

St Hilarion Castle

There may be some difficulty in seeing over this castle, which within the past few years has been a Turkish stronghold, but tourists may find their passports help to effect relatively easy entry.

St Hilarion is certainly one of the most picturesque of all Cypriot strongholds, over 600 metres above sea-level, perched between two rocky outcrops known as the Didymos, or Twins. The castle is allegedly on the site of a hermit's cell – presumably that of a St Hilarion (though not perhaps the celebrated Palestinian saint of that name). A monastic foundation was set up here in his honour, and it was only in the eleventh century that the place was turned to military use.

Kyrenia, Buffavento, Kantara, and St Hilarion constituted a formidable chain of defensive castles – they communicated with one another by the use of bonfires – which under the command of Isaac Comnenus stood out against Richard the Lion Heart in 1191. St Hilarion finally surrendered to Guy de Lusignan only in 1229, and was to remain for some time a fortress against which any adversary of the Establishment had to set his arms. It was here that the boy-king Henri I and his protector Jean d'Ibelin faced the forces of the Emperor Frederick II. During a century of relative peace the castle became an official summer residence of the sovereign and his family, and in particular a refuge when plague struck the island. But in 1373 there was another violent episode, when the regent, John, Prince of Antioch, held out here with his nephew Philip II, guarded against the attacks of the Genoese by his own band of Bulgarian mercenaries. The Bulgarians threatened mutiny, whereupon he had the lot of them thrown out of a window, one by one – a self-defeating process, for he was eventually left entirely without a bodyguard, and was taken. In the interests of economy the castle was 'slighted' – or purposely ruined – in 1489, but what remains is a fascinating wilderness of corridors, staircases, roofless halls and towers.

The castle has three Wards. There is a church in the *Middle Ward*, once domed, and near by is a pleasant vaulted belvedere from which there is a marvellous view; near it are what were once kitchens: aptly, there is a restaurant here in part of a range of royal apartments used in Byzantine times. Grander royal rooms were built later, for the Lusignan family, in the *Upper Ward*, where *Prince John's Tower* hangs above a vertical drop to horrid rocks – the scene, it is alleged, of the free-fall descent of the Bulgarian mercenaries. The Lusignan rooms were on two floors, looking westward to **Lapithos** and Cape Kormakiti in the distance. These rooms have particularly beautiful windows, one of which, with handsome tracery and side-seats, is known as the Queen's Window.

From the castle, the road leads on for 7 km. to **Kyrenia**.

Kyrenia

Kyrenia is a beautiful little town, a *Castle* hanging over it backed by a handsome range of mountains; its waterfront has altered little over the past two or three centuries. Before the occupation it was particularly attractive to the British – during the 1950s there was an extensive colony of expatriates here – and had a lively social life, with a Harbour Club and a Country Club, several excellent hotels (the Dome was in its day perhaps the best hotel on the island), fine restaurants, and in the season some excellent entertainments, including traditional singing and dancing.

The town was probably founded around the tenth century BC (when it was known by its original name of Cerynia) and was one of Cyprus's city-states. Under the Romans it was called Corineum. Kyrenia itself was never of much importance; the castle was another matter. It makes its first appearance in modern history in 1191, when Isaac Comnenus's wife and daughter, sent for safety to the castle during the invasion of Richard the Lion Heart, were captured by Guy de Lusignan. During the following decade there was extensive rebuilding and improvement of its defences; then it became the royal palace of Henri I (or rather of his regent, Jean d'Ibelin). Between then and the late fourteenth century rebuilding and refurbishing continually took place, though the defences were eventually, as it were, turned inside-out, for it became a prison. Among its prisoners was the beautiful Joanna L'Aleman, mistress of Pierre I, shut up here in 1368 by his wife, during Pierre's absence abroad. (He was interested in foreign travel, and once spent some time immured in Kyrenia castle with his brother as a punishment for planning a tourist excursion to Europe.) In 1373 the castle regained its dignity during a determined siege by the Genoese, gallantly resisted by the castellan against the most modern engines of war. Ten years later, as Jacques I, that same castellan understandably made Kyrenia his favourite residence.

The Venetians saw the importance of the castle, and kept it in excellent repair during their occupation, placing two solid towers in the north-west and south-east corners and buttressing the massive walls. The castle nevertheless fell to the Turks in 1570: not, however, because of any weakness in its physical defences, but because of the lack of backbone of its defenders.

The castle became a prison again during the British regime, and was also a training school for the police force. In 1950 it was handed over to the Department of Antiquities, but was taken back again during the EOKA disputes, and once more became a prison. Now it is merely a monument, whose chief interest is perhaps its possession of the '*Kyrenia Ship*', a vessel wrecked off the Cypriot coast in 300 BC and successfully raised by an expedition from the University of Pennsylvania – the oldest vessel ever to be lifted intact from the sea bed, together with its cargo of plates, oil jugs, containers of almonds, amphorae, ship's tackle. It was placed on exhibition in the castle just before the Turkish invasion.

Take the coastal road eastward from Kyrenia; almost immediately turn left through the village of **Bellapais** (where Lawrence Durrell made his home in the 1950s, and wrote his classic account of Cypriot life, *Bitter Lemons*, which remains essential reading for the visitor). The village has great charm, but the reason for visiting it is of course the presence there of *Bellapais*, the great Lusignan abbey.

Bellapais Abbey

The abbey was probably founded by Amaury de Lusignan, crowned King of Cyprus in 1197. During the next 200 years Bellapais was known as 'the White Abbey' in reference to the habits worn by its community – members originally of the Augustinian order to which the abbey lands were granted by Hugues I at the time of the loss of Jerusalem (where the order had originally guarded the Church of the Holy Sepulchre). The Augustinians had adopted the white robes of the canons of the Order of St Norbert, whose rule they now accepted.

Bellapais quickly became wealthy and influential, especially under the patronage of Hugues III (1267–84), who may have been buried here, though if so his tomb has been lost. His successors continued to support the abbey, giving its abbot the privilege of wearing a mitre and carrying a gilded sword and spurs when riding outside the abbey grounds.

The Genoese badly damaged Bellapais when they looted it in 1373, making off (among perhaps richer treasure) with a fragment of the True Cross. The abbey still played a major part in the life of the island during the succeeding Venetian occupation, at least until a delegation of the Venetian Senate compiled a vigorously antagonistic report of activities there, including the fact that many of the monks were supporting wives – in some cases two or three – and were appropriating abbey funds to their own use. Even before the Turkish occupation, which began in 1571, opprobrium had sullied the abbey's reputation, and only a few villagers continued to worship at its church under permission of the Turks. As with so many places, the abbey buildings fell into serious disrepair as a result of their stone being carted off by the local peasantry to build their own houses. Centuries later the British army contributed to the wreckage. The Cypriots themselves showed little interest in preserving such buildings as remained, and the ruins are picturesque but incomplete.

The church, the oldest surviving building – thirteenth- (or probably fourteenth-) century – once had wall-paintings, but there are only vestigial signs of where these once were; the interior was much altered when the Greek Orthodox Church took it over, and the iconostasis severely damages its proportions. However, it remains a graceful building with some pleasant detail – the capitals of the thirteenth-century pillars, for instance. A small spiral staircase leads to the unusual flat roof and the treasury. The cloister is a beautiful and quiet place, with fine tracery under the arcades and some interesting stonework in the corbels and bosses of the rib-vaulting. In the north-west corner of the cloister is a second-century marble sarcophagus, decorated in high relief, in which the monks washed their hands before meals. A stairway from the cloister leads to the dormitory, where – as can be seen in the west wall – each monk had a window by his bed and a wall cupboard for his few belongings. The Refectory has been well preserved, with substantial walls, within one of which a staircase leads to a little platform where stood a brother to read aloud from holy books during meals. The windows in the north wall offer a splendidly distracting view of the sea and, on the clearest of days, of the coast of Asia Minor.

On the way back to Nicosia you could come back via Buffavento Castle and St Chrysostomos Monastery but this would make a very long day trip (see below instead).

Nicosia to St Chrysostomos Monastery and Buffavento Castle

Take the Famagusta road out of Nicosia, and in 3 km. turn left to Mia Milea (which is exactly one traditional Cypriot mile from the city) and then continue north for 8 km. to **Koutsovendis**. Here on the ruined wall of an old church can be seen in remarkably vivid colours a large 800-year-old portrait of Christ and another of St George. This area is at present occupied by the military. Just beyond the village, white-walled and prominent, and with its enormous cypress tree as an additional landmark, stands the *Monastery of St Chrysostomos*.

The Monastery of St Chrysostomos

The monastery belongs to the Orthodox See of Jerusalem rather than the Church of Cyprus. There are two churches, the northern one dedicated to St John Chrysostomos (347–407), an archbishop of Constantinople. In 1963 much work was done to reveal the beauty of the fine eleventh-to-twelfth-century wall-paintings which once covered the whole interior of the churches, among them beautiful heads of the saints. The *twin church to the south* is the older of the two, said to have been built by St Helena after her visit to the Holy Land, but substantially rebuilt in 1891. There is a fine geometrically patterned marble floor, and set in a marble door-frame a remarkable door which, like the architectural bridge at Cambridge, is made of numerous pieces of wood fitted together without the use of nails. The church also possesses, if it is still there, a famous and revered sixteenth-century icon of Chrysostomos.

The monastery buildings are modern, though here and there remnants of earlier buildings have been used; they are now commandeered by the military, though it is believed that there is still public access to the churches, and even an army cannot commandeer the marvellous view over the plain of central Cyprus. Into a spring here the pet dog of a Byzantine princess once fell, to emerge cured of its eczema. Since which time the spring is said to cure leprosy and more minor human skin ailments.

The Castle of Buffavento

Almost seeming to be a part of the yellowish rock from which it springs, is the *Castle of Buffavento*, which lies some 15 km. north of the monastery. From a car park there is a vertiginous hour-long climb through pine trees to the ruins, which stand over 980 metres above the plain. The view is as panoramic as might be expected – over Kyrenia and on to Karpas, with Famagusta to the south, Nicosia and the Troodos mountains to the west.

The castle was originally called the Castle of the Lion, and was later known as 'Spitia tis Regina' after a Cypriot queen who was said to have established here 101 rooms; and yes, of course, whoever finds the 101st will never be seen again. It was the Lusignans who called the place 'Buffavento', in honour of the winds which buffet it still. The

Frankish wards are ruined, and were ruined even in 1570, when the citizens of Nicosia took refuge here during the Ottoman siege. It was at Buffavento that the megalomaniac Pierre I (1359–69) imprisoned his friend Sir John Visconti, whom he suspected of slandering his queen; Sir John died of starvation – a more merciful fate perhaps than that suffered by the political prisoners whose cries were unheard as they were tortured to death. Escape was perhaps just possible: one of two brothers imprisoned here during the reign of Jacques I (1382–98) is said to have managed to climb down the horribly dangerous northern precipice – but only to find his torturers and eventual executioners waiting at the bottom.

Buffavento is really a picturesque castle rather than one where there is anything to be seen other than ruins. The Romantic poets would have loved it.

Nicosia to Kythrea, Sourp Magar and Antiphonitis Monastery

Kythrea
Along the main Nicosia–Famagusta road, *Kythrea*, the site of a settlement which originated in the twelfth century BC, is clearly signposted about 9 km. from the town. One of its claims to fame is as the home of the cauliflower, which was introduced to Europe from here in 1604. Another is the famed depravity of its women centuries ago. They were alleged to be specially beautiful and approachable (due, one visitor conjectured, to the heat and the continual absence of the men at market). A fine bronze statue of Septimus Severus was found near here, and it is to be seen in the Cyprus Museum.

Sourp Magar
Driving from Kythrea and through Halevka to the north-east for about 7 km., one reaches the Armenian monastery of Sourp Magar. The original church is lost – demolished by earthquake – and the present church, built in 1811–14, is dull; however, it is a peaceful and restful spot, and from it the road continues through forested areas towards Mount Pentadactylos: the configuration of five hills is a memory of the hero Dighenis, who placed his hand here to vault over the mountains in pursuit of the Saracens.

Antiphonitis Monastery

This is reached by driving eastward through spectacular mountainous country from Halevka. Now deserted, it was patronised for years by the Lusignans, and a Cypriot bought it from his own purse when, during the earlier Turkish occupation, there was a chance of its being converted to a mosque. There are some frescoes in the church, of no special value but of some physical size. They include a huge head of Christ in the large dome, supported by eight columns.

Nicosia to Lambousa, the Monastery of Akhiropiitos, Cape Kormakiti and Ayia Irini

Take the road northwards to Kyrenia, then at the coast turn left, westwards, past **Ayios Yeoryios** and **Karavas** (a village much concerned with the production of lemons). Just past the latter village, 7 km. from Kyrenia, turn right, and in about a kilometre you are at the ruins of the once great city of *Lambousa*.

Lambousa and the Monastery of Akhiropiitos

The whole area of the ruins at Lambousa has often, during the immediate past, been under military control, and only the Monastery of Akhiropiitos has been open to visitors. It is assumed that this is still the case.

Though it was founded during the eighth century BC, Lambousa was at the height of its magnificence during the Roman and Byzantine periods; sacked and all but destroyed by the Arabs in the seventh century AD, it became important again during the Middle Ages. But much of the stone of the ruins was removed for local building, and little remains.

Situated not far from the ruins of the lighthouse of Byzantine Lambousa, the Monastery of Akhiropiitos was said to have been transported magically, whole and entire, from Asia Minor by the Virgin Mary (to prevent its desecration by the heathen). It was known therefore as the monastery 'built by no hands'. The church is an olla-podrida of styles: a fourteenth-century body (double-domed and cruciform), a fifteenth-century apse (semicircular on the inside but with a seven-sided exterior), a slightly later narthex and exonarthex. 'Improvements' were made at the cost of one Alessandro Flatros, whose gypsum tomb can be seen, with his portrait in court dress. There are (or were) a number of seventeenth-century icons here, the oldest much venerated, within its silver-gilt cover: it shows St Veronica and the Holy Handkerchief. The Handkerchief is supposed to have been the Holy Shroud, kept here before being taken to Turin.

There are two separate churches near by: the first a *Chapel of St Evlambios*, once a mere hole in the rock, but later excavated to stand above ground, its walls still made of the rock from which it was hewn. Here was originally found the 'Lambousa Treasure' – a collection of sixth-century plates showing the life of King David, which was divided between the Cyprus Museum, the British Museum and the Metropolitan Museum, New York. They are among the earliest examples of hallmarked silver. The second church, *St Evlalios*, is sixteenth-century.

Lapithos, Vavilas and Cape Kormakiti
About 5 km. inland from Lambousa, up on a hill away from the main road and among lemon-groves, is the village of **Lapithos**, served by a beautifully clear spring of water emerging from the rock at **Kephalo-vryso** 250 metres above sea level. This spring was probably a good reason why the Greeks founded the village, which was one of the four principal capitals of Roman Cyprus – under the Lusignans it had a population of 10,000. The churches are rather dull, though the modern *Church of St Anastasia* has a sepulchre to one Seleukios with nice vine-leaf carvings.

The fishing village of Vavilas, a few kilometres farther west, is pleasantly unsophisticated. Shortly after this the main road turns inland and there is a climb from the Myrtou bypass for 8 km. up to the village of **Kormakiti**, overlooking Cape Kormakiti, whence it is 66 km. to the coast of Turkey. There is nothing here but a modern lighthouse and a sea view, though just off the coast is said to lie a fourteenth-century Turkish ship laden with treasure.

Ayia Irini
Back at Myrtou, turn right then right again to **Dhiorios**, and in 8 km. is **Ayia Irini**, in the sand-dunes not far from the coast of Morphou Bay. Near here was found, on a site occupied between 1300 BC and the end of the sixth century BC, the collection of terracotta figures now to be seen in the Cyprus Museum.

FAMAGUSTA

HISTORY

Famagusta lies within its bay 58 km. to the east of Nicosia along the 'new' road which was completed in 1962 on the foundation of a railway line disused since 1951. The old town, within its Medieval walls, used to be inhabited almost exclusively by Turkish Cypriots, while the Greek Cypriots tended to live in the modern commercial port (originally called Varosha) to the south, where the main shopping centre and hotels flank the long beach. Now, of course, the town is in the Turkish-occupied sector of the island.

H. V. Morton, the finest of travel writers, might seem to have insulted Famagusta when he called it 'one of the most remarkable ruins in the world' (*In the Steps of St Paul*, 1936); but within the walls the place is almost a ruin – a jumble of tumbledown houses crowded around the cathedral (converted, of course, to a mosque). Over the past century or more the ancient town has been allowed to fall to pieces so that walking or scrambling around it is like moving among the results of an earthquake long past: none of the agony, but all of the muddle and confusion, remains. The modern town is another matter; it has a fine deep-water harbour, and before the invasion was the bustling main port of the island. It was a fine tourist centre, too, with admirable hotels, and there were plans for an ambitious yachting marina.

It was only after the decline of Salamis that Famagusta began its climb to prosperity and success. By the fourteenth century it was already flourishing, with many wealthy merchants among its citizens – and, according to one witness, an admirable selection of beautiful courtesans. It was a handsome town, with fountains of water at every street corner, and many fine buildings.

The famous eight-month siege of Famagusta which took place from September of 1570 subjected the walls to the most severe test. They stood despite the Turkish trenches driven beneath them, and despite the assaults of the most modern instruments of war. The carnage was great – 50,000 Turks and almost 6,000 Greeks and Venetians were slain – and the cruelty savage, culminating in the famous flaying of Bragadino. The devastation of the old town when it finally fell, together with an earthquake and the removal of much building material for the building of – of all things – the Suez Canal, led to the wreckage which still largely remains. By the middle of the eighteenth century European tourists found it a picturesque ruin, wild plants and bushes growing on the battlements and around the useless cannon, the near-by harbour silted up.

The 'new' Famagusta rose in the former suburb of Varosha and thrived until 1974, when the advancing Turkish army seized it, confiscating millions of pounds' worth of goods and looting the town – including its museums, much of whose contents were (apparently with the connivance of the Turkish government) sold to European collectors. The formerly largely Greek new town became Turkish, a ferry started running regularly to the Turkish mainland, and Famagusta's days as the island's chief port were (at least for the time) over.

Places of historical interest in the town

Famagusta's *walls*, outlining the rectangular shape of the town, remain almost entire, averaging fifteen metres in height and in some places almost eight metres thick. The two original gates, the *Sea Gate* and the *Land Gate*, at the east and the south-west, were later supplemented by two more. There are ten bastions, more or less complete, and with Venetian names – *Andruzzi*, *Palacazaro*, *Diocare*, and so on – though the Turkish equivalents are presumably now used. The *Djamboulat* bastion, at the south-east corner of the walls, contains the tomb of the Turkish general of that name who fell near by in 1571 while attacking the arsenal.

The small, square citadel with little round towers at its corners which used to be commonly known as *Othello's Tower* has of course nothing to do with Shakespeare's hero, but has been identified with him for centuries. Interestingly, the lieutenant-general of Cyprus between 1506 and 1508 was called Cristoforo Moro. He was not Moorish – but perhaps Shakespeare somehow or other heard his name, and it rang a faint note which was eventually transmuted into the full orchestral roar of creation. Or it may be that the man of whom the playwright heard was a dark-skinned Italian mercenary, Francesco de Sessa, who fought for the Venetians and was known as 'the Moor'. The citadel itself was built in the fourteenth century, heavily remodelled in 1492 by one Nicolo Foscarini, whose name can be seen above the Venetian winged lion at the main entrance.

The Cathedral of St Nicholas, now known as the *Lala Mustafa Mosque*, was consecrated in 1326, and is pure Gothic without recent additions other than the three side-chapels. Even externally, apart from its minaret, it looks much as it has always looked, despite a certain amount of damage done by war and earthquake. The saints' statues and much of the decoration have, as usual, been removed, the frescoes whitewashed over, the stained glass smashed and taken out and the altars demolished. One or two tombs remain in the north aisle, but those of the last two Lusignan kings, the bastard Jacques II and his son Jacques III, who were buried here, have vanished. The interior, bare and spacious, is nevertheless attractive and impressive. The handsome west door has a balcony above it which until 1372 was used for coronations: upon it, the Lusignan kings of Cyprus appeared to be crowned a second time as kings of Jerusalem (a ceremony with only symbolic significance). It was here, too, that Caterina Cornaro officially abdicated, in 1489. The great rose-window must once have been magnificent.

It was here, in the *Parvis* – a once-spacious square said in its time to be the largest in Europe – that great crowds gathered for a sight of the king. Here, too, between two granite columns, Bragadino was flayed alive (see p. 65). The *loggia* which stands on the south side of the square is said once to have been a grammar school attached to the cathedral; it now has a fountain used for Muslim ablutions. Near by is a little piece of frieze showing animals chasing one another through a spiral of leaves, which may once have been part of a Roman temple. The *Palazzo del Proveditore*, or palace of the Venetian provincial governor, has a façade including granite pillars brought from Salamis.

The Greek Orthodox Cathedral, originally the Church of St George of the Greeks, consists of an original Byzantine cathedral dedicated to St Epiphanios (said to be buried here before removal to Constantinople), with a large Gothic building added to it. Both churches were badly damaged during the siege, and the earlier is ruined. There are several other churches in the town: ten years ago most of them were either ruined or in extremely bad repair, and it is extremely unlikely that their condition has improved during the past decade of Turkish occupation.

In 1966 a huge *underground cave* capable of holding 2,000 people was discovered beneath the two northernmost bastions of the town. Carved out of the rock, it has pillars to support its roof, ventilation shafts and cisterns for water storage. The cave was used as a shelter during the siege, but may well pre-date that event by 1,000 years or more.

EXCURSIONS FROM FAMAGUSTA

Famagusta to Salamis, St Barnabas Monastery and Enkomi/Alasia

Salamis

This site lies 9 km. north of Famagusta, on the east side of the coastal road along the bay to the north of Famagusta. The city was one of the most important in the pre-Christian history of the island. Legend always suggested that it had been founded by Teucer, the son of the king of the Greek mainland Salamis after his return from the Trojan war. During the seventh century BC it was under Assyrian domination – a clay tablet records tribute paid to the great Assyrian king Assurbanipal.

The first-named King of Salamis was the sixth-century Evelthon, mentioned by Herodotus; that royal house reigned until the suicide of Nicrocrean, Ptolemy's appointee, in 295 BC. A quarter of a century later Paphos superseded Salamis as the chief city of Cyprus; later still the former was proclaimed a Roman colony. The Christian community is said to have been founded by SS Paul and Barnabas in AD 45–6, but thirty years later the whole city was devastated by an earthquake. Earthquakes and a tidal wave in 332 and 342 almost totally demolished Salamis for a second time; rebuilt by the Emperor Constantine II, it was renamed Constantia. Constantia became the Metropolis of Cyprus under St Epiphanios, but fell under the hammer of Saracen raids in the seventh century, and after repeated siege, sacking and massacre, more earthquakes and the silting-up of the harbour, the city was finally abandoned and its trade – and many of its ancient palaces and temples, in the shape of building material – moved to Famagusta.

The whole of Salamis is fascinating to the expert, of course; but since the sizable and rambling site cannot now be visited by tourists, and the political situation is unlikely to change in the immediate future, it is fruitless to give too detailed a description of it.

The casual visitor will be impressed, above all, by the *Theatre*, the *Gymnasium* and the *Baths*. The Theatre, largely excavated in 1960, is one of the biggest in the Middle East, holding about 15,000 people in fifty rows of seats. It dates from about the time of the Emperor Augustus Caesar, though there may have been an earlier, Hellenic, theatre on the same site. The present building was enlarged and repaired during the first and second centuries AD, but was largely destroyed during the fourth-century earthquakes. Plans to excavate the actors' dressing-rooms have been abandoned since the invasion.

The Gymnasium and Baths are set around the Forum with its four porticoes, where the naked athletes exercised. An existing dedication to Ptolemy V Ephiphanes (205–180 BC) can be seen between two columns at the entrance to the south portico, and proves the existence of a Hellenic gymnasium on this site. The central forum, or palaestra, was built by Constantine II; its columns were re-erected in the 1950s after lying for centuries where they fell during one of the Salamis earthquakes. Most of the statues found on the site are now in the Cyprus Museum in Nicosia, but a few have collected here in the annexe at the north end of the east portico, including a splendid Persephone carved in dark marble, though her face and hands (which would have been of white marble) are missing. At the south-west corner of the palaestra is a spacious public lavatory with open-plan seating for no less than forty-four people, its drainage and water system providing an excellent example of early sanitary plumbing. Here the citizens would sit on their marble thrones, entirely without embarrassment, exchanging gossip, betting on the athletes, inviting their friends to dinner.

The athletes' Baths were clearly either built or renovated under Roman advice. Some good late Roman mosaics were uncovered here, and in a niche in the South Hall (originally the *Sudatorium*, or hot-steam room) there is a fine representation of the River God Evrotas with Zeus (in the guise of a swan) presiding over a large upturned jar from which fresh water flows. Another niche shows traces of a mosaic of Apollo and Artemis fighting the Niobids.

Other remains near by include those of an *early Christian basilica*, a second much larger basilica thought to have been the metropolitan *Church of St Epiphanios*, the so-called *Stone Forum* or market-place, and a *Temple of Zeus*. There is scarcely a square metre of the site which would not repay archaeological excavation, and it is one of the numerous tragedies of the occupation that serious work has ceased.

The *Royal Tombs* lie to the east of the Famagusta road. The largest of these is that known traditionally as St Catherine's Prison (perhaps because it was once used as a chapel dedicated to her). Excavation, however, uncovered a phenomenon repeated in other tombs in the area – the ceremonial killing and burial of the horses which had drawn the remains of the dead king. The tombs were known to local people for centuries, and nineteenth-century archaeologists had taken it for granted that everything worthwhile must long ago have been looted. But in 1957 serious excavation was started by the Cypriot Department of Antiquities, and soon uncovered fascinating material below ground-level: bronze cauldrons containing human remains, necklaces and sheets of gold which had ornamented the bodies, and the skeletons of the horses. It was clear that these tombs – known but ignored for so long by archaeologists – were in fact the long-lost necropolis of Salamis.

The site was fascinating for all sorts of reasons: first because it actually confirmed the truth of what was previously thought to be a fairy story – that the city had indeed been founded by Teucer on his way home from Troy. There was confirmation too, in St Catherine's Prison (now labelled simply Tomb One) and the others, of the accuracy of Homer's reporting of death ceremonies: the funeral of Patroclos as set out in the *Iliad*, for instance; for here were not only the skeletons of sacrificed horses (some of which had broken from their harness, terrified at the death of their team-mates, and been killed in distant parts of the tombs), but also those of sacrificed slaves and asses. The chariots of the dead kings lay in these tombs, with beautiful ivory furniture, and vessels which had contained honey and other funerary food. The skeletons of the horses still lie where they fell, now under glass; the artefacts have been removed to the Cyprus Museum (though a few bronze horsemen used to be on show in a small museum at the site).

Near these tombs are more plebeian ones – hundreds of them, cut into the rock, and used continually for burial between 700 BC and the end of the fourth century AD.

St Barnabas Monastery

The monastery lies close by – return to the coastal road, turn right and right again, passing the empty tomb where the saint's remains are said to have been miraculously discovered. Barnabas was originally called Joseph, and was a native Cypriot who, having become one of the earliest disciples of Jesus, came home to the island accompanied by St Paul to preach in the synagogues of Salamis. Christian tradition has it that he was killed by Jews at Salamis, and that St Mark hid his body in the rock-tomb where it was rediscovered in 477 (see p. 54).

St Barnabas Monastery is uninteresting except in marking the place's association with the saint; the monks here for many years painted, by a sort of assembly-line method, commemorative icons sold to pilgrims and tourists. The original fifth-century monastery was sacked by the Saracens; the present church is relatively modern (c.1756) but was damaged in an earthquake in the 1940s. There is a holy well near by with the reputation of curing skin diseases.

Enkomi/Alasia

On the way back along the coastal road towards Famagusta, along a turning signposted Nicosia, is a site which was formerly simply called *Enkomi*. It had its second name added after Professor René Dussaud of the Académie des Inscriptions et Belles-Lettres had identified it, in 1952, as the ancient city of *Alasia*, the capital of Cyprus 1,600 years before Christ.

It is fair to say that this has not been established to universal satisfaction; but there is certainly some circumstantial evidence – as that, for instance, Enkomi was certainly for some time a centre of the copper trade, and that tablets at Tell-el-Amarna, in Egypt, refer to the receipt of consignments of copper from Alasia. Archaeological work has gone on here for half a century, at first on the *Necropolis*, which was always known, and later on buildings contemporary to the tombs and obviously part of an important city. In the 1960s the *Sanctuary of the Horned God* – where a remarkable twelfth-century BC statue, now in the Cyprus Museum, was found – and the *House of the Pillar* and *House of the Bronzes* were uncovered. The city which stood on this site was evidently extremely prosperous by 1550 BC, when its population of perhaps 15,000 had a relatively luxurious standard of living. The richest tombs date from the fourteenth and thirteenth centuries BC, just before the area's prosperity began to decline as a result of invasion from Greece and Asia Minor. Much of the city was destroyed by fire in the twelfth century BC, and it seems to have been completely abandoned by the eleventh. It is thought that excavators were, in 1974, on the edge of discovering the remains of the great *Palace of Alasia*, where it might be expected that there would be archival tablets revealing much of the place's (and Cyprus's) ancient history. Work has now ceased, and many artefacts from Alasia have been hijacked to Europe since the occupation and illegally sold to greedy and immoral international collectors.

Famagusta to the north-east peninsula

The north-eastern peninsula of Cyprus, leaning out into the Mediterranean from Famagusta Bay to its attenuated final tip at Cape Andreas, is happily (since it is part of the occupied sector) not of great importance to tourists interested in the history of the island, though its landscape is attractive. The villages sometimes have mildly interesting small churches, and there are pleasant eccentricities (like the two statues carved from limestone 1,600 years ago, and still lying on the ground near **Ayios Thyrsos**), but all in all only **Trikomo**, *Kantara Castle*, *Kanakaria Church* and *Apostolos Andreas Monastery* are at all notable.

Trikomo

Driving north out of Famagusta, in 18 km. bear left to Trikomo, with its little fifteenth-century *Church of St James* in the village square. This is a plain but delightful building whose charm is indefinable but pervasive: Queen Marie of Roumania so fell under its spell that she built a replica of it as a private chapel on the shores of the Black Sea. The village itself is most notable as the birthplace of the EOKA leader, General Grivas (1898–1974).

The road due north from Trikomo leads after 7 km to **Ardhana**, where it begins to climb through the mountains towards *Kantara Castle*.

Kantara Castle

Here is another picturesque storybook castle, approached by a serpentine road and hanging high (600 metres) over eastern Cyprus, looking out over Mesaoria and Famagusta Bays, and over the tail-end of the island straggling off to the north-east.

Kantara is first heard of as the castle where Isaac Comnenus hid after his argument with King Richard, and later as being seriously damaged by catapult attack while under siege by royalist forces in 1228. Never a palace, but merely a watchtower and a conveniently isolated prison for political prisoners, it was also sometimes a place of sanctuary (the Prince of Antioch hid here after escaping from the Genoese in 1373). The castle is ruined, and has been since the Venetians left it as long ago as 1525; only the occasional hermit has lived here since then. It is still possible to identify the guard room, which has an opening through which prisoners could be passed without the main gate being opened. There are military quarters complete with latrines, and various other rooms, including 'the Queen's Room' (though no queen has ever been particularly associated with the place).

Kanakaria Church

Due west from Kantara Castle lies **Kanakaria**, its simple church a tragic monument to the effect of the Turkish invasion on the culture as well as the contemporary life of Cyprus. It was celebrated for centuries for rare mosaic, believed to have been made by the same artist who set out the one at Kiti (see p. 109). It showed the Virgin and Child – Mary seated with the Child on her knee – and some experts dated it as early as the sixth century AD. It can no longer be admired, however, for since the invasion it has been removed, and is now no doubt in some unscrupulous European collector's gallery. It is to be hoped (not, alas, too confidently) that it may eventually be recovered and replaced.

The Karpas peninsula was once dominated by the city of *Karpasia*, which lay near the present town of **Rizokarpaso**. The *Church of Ayios Philon* stands just by what must once have been an extremely impressive earlier basilica, judging by its (much damaged) marble mosaic floor, with a beautiful central pattern in red, yellow, black and white. The ancient city was sacked and burned by the Saracens in AD 802.

Right at the tip of the peninsula, once known as Dineretum, was a *Temple to Aphrodite Areia* – the remains are so vestigial as not to justify (except on grounds of exercise) the 6 km. plod involved in reaching it. Near by is the *site of a Neolithic settlement*, the earliest yet found in Cyprus; it was excavated in 1971–3.

The Monastery of Apostolos Andreas

The main road ends at the Monastery. The building is, in fact, not a monastery at all, but a fifteenth-century Gothic chapel. It was a centre for pilgrims, who tended to meet here chiefly on the feast days of 15 August and 30 November, when there were ceremonies to invoke blessings on the crops and on the sea. The chapel used to contain many wax models of sick people or their afflicted limbs, placed by those hoping for a cure.

SUGGESTED READING

The kind of non-guidebook you will want to read before you go to Cyprus, or to take with you, will depend mainly on your own interests. It is also true, as always in this field, that many of the most interesting books are difficult to find in ordinary bookshops, and sometimes are out of print altogether. The Travel Bookshop, at 13 Blenheim Crescent, London W11, is invariably helpful in dealing with both categories, as is the Hellenic Book Service at 122 Charing Cross Rd, London WC2. Bookshops in Cyprus are of course an excellent source of more specialist books.

As far as general reading is concerned, Sir Harry Luke's *Cyprus: a Portrait and an Appreciation* (Harrap, 1965) and Sir David Hunt's *Footprints in Cyprus* (Trigraph, 1982) are useful, while anyone who does not know Lawrence Durrell's *Bitter Lemons* (Faber, 1957) has missed perhaps the happiest evocation of life in northern Cyprus before the invasion.

The fullest account of the island's past is Sir George Hill's enormous four-volume *History* (Cambridge University Press, republished 1972). A briefer account can be found in Sir Ronald Storr's *A Chronicle of Cyprus* (Nicosia, 1974).

For those visiting Curium and the Temple of Aphrodite, apart from the many other archaeological sites, V. Karageorghis's *The Ancient Civilisation of Cyprus* (Barrie & Cresset, 1969) is useful; so is Rupert Gunnis's *Historic Cyprus* (Methuen, 1947). Those who are interested by the legends of Aphrodite and Adonis and the rest might go to Robert Graves's great *Greek Myths* (Cassell, 1960); accounts of the Aphrodite and Adonis rites are found in James Frazer's *The Golden Bough* (Macmillan, reprinted 1960). The poet and critic Geoffrey Grigson gives a fascinating account of the legend of Aphrodite in *The Goddess of Love* (Constable, 1976).

Among the books which may be bought in Cyprus are Helena Wylde Swing's excellent guide to *The Ancient Kourian Area* (Nicosia, 1982), which you can buy at most archaeological site offices, together with site guides when they exist. Andreas and Judith Stylianou's *The Painted Churches of Cyprus* (Nicosia, 1986) is an excellent guide. Walkers will be specially grateful for Geoff Daniel's *Landscapes of Cyprus* (Nicosia, 1986), a first-rate guide to the countryside.

Finally, the atmosphere of the country is often beautifully presented in memoirs and travel books published many years ago. Of these, *A Lady's Appreciation of Cyprus*, published by a Mrs Lewis (Remington, 1894), is charming, and so is W. H. Mallock's *In an Enchanted Isle* (Bentley, 1889).

METRIC CONVERSIONS

Centi-metres	Inches	Metres	Yards	Kilo-metres	Miles	Litres	Gallons
5	1.9	1	1.09	1	0.6	1	0.23
10	3.9	5	5.40	5	3.1	5	1.10
15	5.8	10	11.90	10	6.2	10	2.20
20	7.8	15	17.30	15	9.3	15	3.30
30	11.8	20	21.80	20	12.4	20	4.40
40	15.7	30	32.80	30	18.6	30	6.60
50	19.6	40	43.70	40	24.9	40	8.80
60	23.6	50	54.60	50	31.1	50	11.00
70	27.5	60	65.60	60	37.3		
80	31.4	70	76.50	70	43.5		
90	35.4	80	87.40	80	49.7		
100	39.3	90	98.40	90	55.9		
		100	109.30	100	62.1		

INDEX

The spelling of Cypriot names is often problematical. Current guide-books will often be found to spell them dissimilarly; so will maps, and even official Cypriot publications. Choices (between, for instance, Kourion and Curium) are often arbitrary, but cross-references should clarify any problems. The figures in **bold type** denote major entries.